COUNTRYSIDE LAW

COUNTRYSIDE LAW

FOURTH EDITION

Brian Jones
Julian Palmer
Angela Sydeham

Shaw & Sons

Shaw's
Since 1750

Published by
Shaw & Sons Limited
Shaway House
21 Bourne Park
Bourne Road
Crayford
Kent DA1 4BZ

© Shaw & Sons Limited 2004

First Edition .... June 1987
Second Edition .... June 1991
Reprinted with Supplement .... January 1993
Third Edition .... March 1997
Fourth Edition .... September 2004

ISBN 0 7219 1063 7

A CIP catalogue record for this book is available from the British Library

Cover photograph and design by
Roy Sands, Bexleyheath, Kent

Printed in Great Britain by
Bell & Bain Limited, Glasgow

CONTENTS

PREFACE

This edition is dedicated to the untiring enthusiasm for its subject of the late Professor Jack Garner. The genesis of the book was the wish on Jack's part to produce a readable and instructive account for non-lawyers of the mass of laws relating the protection and enjoyment of the countryside. Notwithstanding some gradual lengthening of the text, some care has been taken over the past two decades to remain true to that essential aim. From the time of initial writing in 1986 to the preparation of the present edition, the task of working and re-working the text has been one of my happiest, as well as challenging, writing experiences. Jack's presence in the preparation of this edition has been much missed, but his influence has remained. As each new sentence has been written or reviewed I have been ever-mindful of the response from Jack which it would have elicited. Reviewers of previous editions have over the years been very kind in their comments on the balance struck between explanation of points of law and attempts to assess the success with which law and administrative policies have achieved their declared aims. It is my main hope that this new edition will be similarly received.

The preparation of this edition could not have been completed without the valuable assistance received from Angela Sydenham and Julian Palmer. I believe that their contributions have brought a good many new insights to the book, helping it to remain alert to those issues which are of current significance.

As ever, my thanks must go also to Crispin Williams at Shaw & Sons, both for his patience and for the reassuringly watchful eye that he maintains over the text.

Brian Jones
Consultant, Herbert Smith (London)
Honorary Professor, University of Wales (Aberystwyth)
August 2004

Chapter 1

PROTECTION AND ENJOYMENT OF THE COUNTRYSIDE

INTRODUCTION

Scope and Nature of this Book

Although this book is principally about the law it is not directed primarily at lawyers, although it is hoped that it will be of interest to them. Rather, the book has been written for the "lay" reader who is interested generally in the protection and enjoyment of the countryside, and who would like some knowledge of the main areas of the laws of England and Wales which relate to those matters. In so far as the law of England and Wales now contains within itself a body of rules emerging from the legislative processes of the European Union, we shall also be concerned from time to time with the impact of European Community environmental (and to some extent also its agricultural) law and policy. The book does not, however, cover the laws of Scotland and Northern Ireland, which in numerous respects differ from those in England and Wales. Moreover, since devolution of certain responsibilities to the Welsh Assembly, there are a number of matters covered within this book where Welsh law and policy may differ from that in England.

In stating the law we have tried to avoid lawyers' jargon so far as possible; and where this has not proved possible we have sought to explain terms so as to render the text comprehensible. In a book of this size we have, naturally, not been able to give comprehensive accounts of the various branches of law described. We have tried, however, to avoid giving over-simplified summaries of the rules. To have done so would have been to mislead the reader. Moreover, much of the interest of the law lies in its intricacies, so long as the reasons for those intricacies are explained.

In addition to providing an account of legal rules and

1

principles, an attempt has been made briefly to describe and assess the changes which are occurring to, and the threats which face, our countryside; by which term we refer not only to the physical landscape itself and its flora and fauna, but also the various forms of ongoing human activity which are vital to the maintenance of that physical and natural environment. Fuller, more detailed, accounts of these matters may be found elsewhere:[1] our own aim has been simply to provide sufficient information to show the need for the law as an instrument to help protect and promote the countryside, and to help to assess the adequacy of the laws which presently exist. In this last connection it should be noted that, to be effective, laws need to be both appropriate in form and also need to be adequately applied and enforced. For this reason, we shall include discussion of the various legal powers and duties of central and local government, and also those of a number of other specialised agencies with specific legal functions in relation to the countryside. Wherever possible, we shall try to avoid simply providing a bare account of rules of law, and seek to give some idea of the effectiveness of the rules in practice.

In substance this book covers a wide range of matters. We have interpreted our chosen title, *Countryside Law*, as extending beyond simply a discussion of those laws which aim at the protection of scenic amenity, fauna and flora, to including laws which promote access to and enjoyment of the countryside by the now predominantly town-dwelling public. Thus, we include not only rules about habitat and species protection, planning restrictions and pollution controls; we also give accounts of the laws relating to public rights of way, rights of access to open country, and rights in respect of common land.

---

[1]   See, for example, M. Shoard, *The Theft of the Countryside* (1980); and *This Land is Our Land: The Struggle for Britain's Countryside* (1987); R. Mabey, *The Common Ground* (1980); Pye-Smith and Rose, *Crisis and Conservation* (1984); B. Green, *Countryside Conservation* (3rd ed. 1997); Pye-Smith and Hall, *The Countryside We Want: a Manifesto for the Year 2000* (1987).

Conflicts

Of course, these twin aims of "protection" and "promotion of enjoyment" of the countryside both overlap and conflict. They *overlap* in the sense that little enjoyment is likely to be gained by members of the public rambling along a right of way through a landscape denuded of hedgerows, trees, wild flowers and birds, and polluted in its air and water. The aims *conflict* in that certain dangers exist of harm being done to the countryside as it becomes opened up for public enjoyment. Ready access from the cities has necessitated major roads and motorways, and the presence of visitors has tended to mean litter, the picking of wild flowers and the disturbance of animal and bird life; as well as creating a demand for car parks, caravan sites, cafés and hotels. Even visitors who mean well and behave well may do harm unintentionally. In some locations mere pressure of visiting numbers causes problems. As Oscar Wilde wrote in his *Ballad of Reading Gaol:* "... each man kills the thing he loves."

Development of Countryside Law

In one sense "countryside law" may be regarded as a twentieth century phenomenon. Certainly, the first glimmerings were to be seen in legislation relating to commons in the 1860s and 1870s,[2] the creation of the National Trust in 1895[3] and, perhaps, in the publication in 1901 of Ebenezer Howard's *Garden Cities of Tomorrow.*[4] However, little more happened until after the mass trespass on Kinder Scout in Derbyshire by members of the embryonic Ramblers' Association in 1932, which made the Access to Mountains Act of 1939 virtually inevitable. Then, after the war, came the *Hobhouse Report*[5] of 1947 and the important National Parks and Access to the Countryside Act 1949, creating the National Parks Commission and making legal provision for the establishment of National Parks, Areas of Outstanding Natural Beauty, nature reserves

---

2 Metropolitan Commons Act 1866; Commons Act 1876. See further, below, p.204.
3 See below, p.193.
4 See below, p.81.
5 *Footpaths and Access to the Countryside* (Cmd 7207).

and sites of special scientific interest. The Countryside Act of 1968 provided for country parks, but it was not until the conservation and environmental movements of the 1970s, inspired in part by the example of the United States,[6] had awakened public opinion, that the Wildlife and Countryside Act 1981, the foundation of much of the modern law, was passed.

The Common Law and the Countryside

In another sense, however, countryside law is as old as the common law of England. By "common law" is meant the principles of law developed by the judges through their decisions in particular decided cases – a process of legal development which continues to this day: novel points for decision still arising with a surprising frequency, and earlier decisions of the courts sometimes seeming ripe for judicial reconsideration.

From early times, the common law was much concerned with the land itself, and this until comparatively recently meant the open countryside and its agriculture. Many of the intricate rules of land law, the law of estates and tenures, the relations between landlord and tenant, the law of fixtures and the law of waste, developed in and for an agricultural community living and working in the countryside.

However, since the industrial revolution of the eighteenth and nineteenth centuries, and the mechanisation of transport in the twentieth century, conditions in, and the demands made of, the countryside have changed dramatically. Today, while agriculture remains important to the nation's economy, it is responsible for the employment of no more than 5% of people who live outside the cities – some 80% of such people now making their living from manufacturing, distribution, financial or public service employment. At the same time, the countryside has become of considerable importance as the nation's recreation ground. The Peak District, for example, annually provides open air recreation and exercise for some 20 million people

---

[6]   In particular by the National Environmental Policy Act of the US Congress of 1969.

from Manchester, Birmingham and the Black Country, and the East Midlands; while the grasslands and moors of the Lake District are annually being eroded by the boots of thousands of tourists and walkers. The Countryside Commission estimates that each year some 1.1 billion visits are made to the countryside – nearly half involving short trips just a few miles outside city boundaries (emphasising the importance to cities of this urban fringe of countryside). The modern problem is, however, not simply to reconcile the various and often conflicting claims of farmers, recreational visitors and conservationists. Additional pressures result from the movement of people's homes from cities to rural areas – some half a million having made this move over a recent five-year period. A principal means of reconciling, or at least achieving some compromise between, these differing interests is through the machinery of the law, and accordingly the law of the countryside is now more concerned with such matters than with the traditional law of property.

Statutes and Modern Countryside Law

In achieving these various objectives, the judge-made principles of common law are now of rather less importance than the detailed provisions of statutes passed by Parliament, and of regulations made under statutory authority by the central government ministries and certain other bodies. Nevertheless, we shall need to consider certain branches of the judge-made common law at appropriate points. For example, we shall consider the law of nuisance as part of our discussion of pollution control,[7] the laws of trespass and nuisance in our discussion of public rights of way,[8] and the rules as to "rights of common" in our chapter on common land.[9] As regards *statutory* protection of the countryside, we shall be most concerned with the provisions of the National Parks and Access to the Countryside Act 1949, the Wildlife and Countryside Act 1981, the Planning Acts of 1990 (re-enacting

---

7   Chapter 7.
8   Chapter 3.
9   Chapter 5.

earlier legislation dating from 1947 and incorporating amendments since that date), the Planning and Compensation Act 1991, the Environmental Protection Act 1990, the Water Resources Act 1991, the Environment Act 1995, the Countryside and Rights of Way Act 2000 and the Planning and Compulsory Purchase Act 2004.

As we shall see, even in relation to statute law the role of the judges is important. Where provisions are ambiguous or unclear, it will be necessary for a judge to interpret the legislation to decide a case; and that interpretation will establish a precedent settling their meaning.

The International Dimension

In addition to these "domestic" sources of law, there is also a body of countryside law which derives either from international treaties to which the UK is a party, or from the environmental law and policy of the European Community. As regards the former, it is important to note that under the British Constitution (unlike the position in some other countries) treaty obligations do not in themselves give rise to any enforceable rights in our national courts; nor do they confer powers on government to take action which would otherwise be unlawful. The consequence is that when an international obligation is entered into by the UK it is necessary for the government to consider whether the law as it stands is sufficient to achieve "formal" compliance with the new obligations; or whether, as will very commonly be the case, new legislation needs to be passed by Parliament. An example of the former situation is the way in which the UK has protected certain wetland sites of internationally important habitat value for wildfowl by means of agreements entered into with site owners (in some cases bodies such as the RSPB or county conservation trusts), or by means of orders under the pre-existing legislation providing for the creation or designation of nature reserves or sites of special scientific importance (SSSIs). An example where special legislation has been necessary is in relation to our obligations under the Convention on International Trade in Endangered Species (CITES).

The situation is a rather different in relation to European Community obligations. Such obligations may derive directly from the constitutional treaties[10] which underpin the Community (establishing the several Community institutions and detailing their remit); or may derive from the legislative activity of the Community's law-making institutions[11] (acting in combination as prescribed by the treaties). Obligations of the former kind are to be found in the Treaty *articles*; of the latter, in laws called *regulations* and *directives*.

All of these Community rules bind the United Kingdom in its capacity as a Member State of the Community. There is a procedure (Article 226) under which infringement proceedings before the European Court of Justice may be brought by the European Commission against any Member State which it considers to be in breach of its Community obligations.[12] Such proceedings may be based either on the view of the Commission that a State has failed properly to have engrafted Community law requirements into the laws and procedures of its own legal system;[13] or may allege that the State has failed adequately to secure that substantive Community law requirements (*eg* environmental quality standards) are actually being met, or complied with, within its territory.[14] It is quite common for

---

[10] Principally the original Treaty of Rome (1958), as amended by: the Single European Act (1986), the Treaty on European Union (1992), the Treaty of Amsterdam (1997) and the Treaty of Nice (2000).

[11] The European Commission, the Council of Ministers, and the European Parliament.

[12] For an example of a case against the United Kingdom in the environmental law context, see Case C-56/90 *Commission of the EC v United Kingdom* (July 14, 1993): failure to have taken all measures to ensure compliance with bathing water directive quality standards.

[13] For example, infringement proceedings were commenced (but subsequently discontinued) against the United Kingdom in respect of what the Commission perceived to be a failure to have imposed environmental assessment obligations on projects which were "in the pipeline" as regards approval procedures at the date when the Environmental Assessment Directive's provisions came into operation.

[14] For example, Case C-337/89 *Commission of the EC v United Kingdom* (November 24, 1992): failure to have complied with maximum admissible concentrations of lead and nitrate in drinking water under the drinking water Directive.

such proceedings under Article 226 to constitute the Commission's response to a complaint originally sent to it by an individual, or an interest group (*eg* Friends of the Earth), from within the Member State under scrutiny: the Commission having relatively scant resources to undertake its own routine monitoring of compliance with obligations.

The procedure under Article 226 by which the European Commission brings proceedings against recalcitrant Member States provides some stimulus towards compliance with Community obligations. However, the procedure is not noted for the speed with which matters arrive before the Court of Justice. Nor, beyond the fact of an adverse judgment were there, until relatively recently, enforcement mechanisms analogous to those which exist within national judicial systems. Ultimately much depends, at inter-State level, on the good faith (motivated by longer term self-interest) of Member States in taking appropriate action following any findings that they are in breach of obligations. In general, Member States seem to have been willing to accept and act upon adverse judgments from the Court of Justice, in this as in other contexts of EU law and policy. Nevertheless, following any such adverse judgment from the Court of Justice, a further period of time will necessarily elapse before steps taken by the Member State may be regarded as demonstrating full compliance.[15]

For quite rare cases when the Commission may regard a Member State as having failed properly to have responded to an adverse judgment of the Court of Justice, a procedure now exists under which the Commission may refer the case back to the Court with a request that the Court should impose a daily fine, payable until such time as the offending State may have taken all necessary steps to secure compliance with EU laws. An early example of this sanction being applied was in relation to Greece and its failure properly to have regulated a problematic

---

[15] Following the drinking water and bathing water judgments against the UK, substantial investment programmes to secure eventual compliance were commenced.

landfill site. A fine of 20,000 Euros per day was imposed in July 2000. By the time of Greek compliance, this fine had accumulated to several million Euros.

It is not, however, only before the *European Court of Justice* that arguments in court may be founded upon provisions of Community law. It was from an early time in the Community's history made clear by the Court of Justice that a certain part of Community law should be regarded by *national* courts as being a part of the law which they should apply in cases which come before them.[16] Such Community law is what is termed "directly applicable" or "directly effective". Moreover, the Court of Justice went further. In the event that such a provision of Community law should differ from a rule of national law, there exists an obligation on the national court to apply the Community rule: what is called the doctrine of the primacy of Community law.[17] In addition, a procedure exists under the treaties which ensures that issues which arise in national courts as to the meaning and applicability of EU laws are to be referred to the Court of Justice for interpretative rulings, rather than left for possibly more restrictive (and non-uniform) interpretation and application by the numerous national courts.[18]

It will be evident that such integration of EU and national law, together with the notion of the primacy of EU law, makes discussion of those aspects of Community law which relate to the environment (and agriculture) of particular, and growing, significance for this book.

Two further questions therefore need to be addressed. First, which rules of Community law have this quality of being directly applicable or directly effective; and how are these rules to be distinguished from other rules, in respect of which

---

[16] See *eg Van Gend en Loos v Nederlandse Administratie der Belastingen* (Case-26/62) [1963] ECR 1.

[17] See *eg Administrazione delle Finanze dello Stato v Simmenthal SpA* (Case-106/77) [1978] ECR 629.

[18] Article 234.

the Article 234 procedure (complaint to the Commission in the hope of proceedings being commenced before the Court of Justice) must suffice? The second question will be to ask what content is to be found in Community laws relevant to the protection of the countryside. This will raise the issue of why the Community has sought to involve itself in such matters, apparently rather outside or beyond its principal raison d'être: the establishment and development of a single market for goods, labour and capital.

To take the first question first. The Treaty itself provides some guidance. Article 249 provides that Community laws in the form of "regulations" shall be directly applicable in Member States. At first sight this might seem to suggest that other forms of Community law should operate only at the level of the Court of Justice and need not trouble the judges of national courts. Such a conclusion was, however, from early times unattractive to the Court of Justice and in a line of decisions that court has developed a set of guiding principles by which to distinguish those *articles* and *directives* which have direct effect from those which do not. The tests can be elaborated at some length. However, ultimately what they provide is that the particular provision of the article or directive must be examined to discover whether it lays down rules which are sufficiently precise and clear and unequivocal to be capable of founding rights, or of imposing duties, such as are properly definable and enforceable through national courts. This test reflects the different kinds of provision to be found in articles of the Treaty and directives, as compared with regulations. The latter are used for detailed and precise legal prescription. Articles and directives, however, tend to lay down objectives of a more general nature. However, such a general statement serves only to disguise the fact that some articles of the treaties do have more precise content,[19] as do some provisions of some directives. Where this is the case, the provisions in question will have direct effect and may, in certain circumstances, form the basis of a successful argument in a national court.

---

[19] For example, Article 141 (equality between the sexes).

However, two immediate words of warning are necessary. First, a substantial proportion of the provisions contained in the Treaty itself and in directives on environmental matters do not have the necessary quality to be directly effective.[20] Second, a significant limit to the utility of the direct effect doctrine must be noted.

This limit is that, as regards directives, the notion of direct effect operates only in so far as a provision of Community law may be used to counter an argument presented to a national court by a "State" body based upon a national law which is not in conformity with Community law. In other words, the basis of the idea of direct effect of directives is to prevent a Member State which has failed properly to have given local legal effect to Community obligations from succeeding in cases in its local courts on the basis of local laws which are, through its own default, not in conformity with Community rules. This idea of the applicability of such Community rules in cases in local courts involving "State" bodies is called the doctrine of "vertical direct" effect. In contrast, in cases not involving a "State" body, there is no parallel doctrine of "horizontal" direct effect, at any rate in relation to directives.[21] In this connection it is, however, significant to note that the idea of "emanation of the State" has been given quite wide interpretation, embracing, for example, privatised utility companies.[22]

Although in a "directive" case not involving a State entity the doctrine of direct effect will not provide assistance, this does not mean that the content of Community obligations will be of no relevance. Although the national court will regard its task as being limited to the application of the rules of English law to the facts of the case, it may be influenced in its interpretation of those rules of "English" law by what is sometimes called the

---

20 See eg *Comitato di Coordinamento per la Difesa della Cava v Regione Lombardia* (Case-236/92) (1994).
21 In contrast, the provisions of the Treaty articles may, in appropriate circumstances, have both "horizontal" and "vertical" direct effect. In other words, they may apply in cases involving private individuals on both sides.
22 See eg *Griffin v South West Water Services Ltd.* [1995] IRLR 15.

doctrine of "sympathetic interpretation". This doctrine, which involves the duty of national courts as state agencies to play their part in securing national compliance with Community law, calls upon judges to interpret local laws so as to be consistent with Community law rather than not in conformity or compliance.[23] This obligation is not limited to cases in which an emanation of the State is involved as a party. For this reason the idea has sometimes been described as introducing the concept of horizontal (as well as vertical) "indirect" effect. The leeway available to national court judges to interpret laws so as to achieve compliance is substantial, but should not be exaggerated. It is one thing to resolve clear *ambiguity* in a way which fits with Community rules rather than as running counter to those rules. It is to expect something rather more of a national court that it should interpret a local law contrary to its clear meaning simply because a non-directly applicable and non-directly effective Community rule might otherwise be infringed. Nevertheless, the doctrine of sympathetic interpretation (indirect effect) is a significant development. It adds to the legal armoury of those who may seek to use the provisions of Community law to found, or to bolster, arguments in local courts.

This outline of the linkage which exists between the legal system of the Community and those of Member States has been reasonably fully described because the influence of Community measures on the laws we describe as countryside law has been quite substantial. So, for example, in the chapter on planning controls we shall describe the requirements of the existing Environmental Assessment Directive and also the imminent *Strategic* Environmental Assessment Directive. And in the chapter on specially protected areas we shall see how the idea of Environmentally Sensitive Areas (along with other environmentally-orientated agricultural support measures) derive from Community agricultural law and policy. We shall see also how some of our home-grown designations (*eg* statutory

---

[23] See *eg Marleasing SA v La Comercial Internacional se Alimentacion SA* (Case C-106/89) [1990] ECR I-4135.

nature reserves and sites of special scientific importance) have been utilised in order to comply with Community obligations as regards the protection of wild birds, plants and animals; as well as natural habitats more generally.

Some brief explanation of the legal justification for European Community involvement in this subject area is perhaps called for. It is not, at first sight, any part of the Community's essential business to prescribe rules for the protection of the environment. Indeed, a scrutiny of the original treaty – the Treaty of Rome 1958 – reveals that the "founding fathers" included no reference to the task of environmental protection as a Community function. During the early years, a few pieces of Community legislation were enacted which we now consider to form part of its corpus of environmental laws. But at the time of enactment their principal motivation was, rather, to secure harmonised rules (on product standards, *eg* sulphur content of fuels) in order to further the Community's chief ambition, the establishment of a single market.

Explicit recognition of the need for a discrete environmental policy did not occur until 1972. In that year, following the impetus created by a United Nations Conference on the Human Environment in Stockholm,[24] the Heads of State and Government of the Community called upon the Commission to formulate an action programme in relation to the environment. This request was accompanied by a declaration stressing that the economic development objectives of the Community should not be regarded as embracing merely the "material" well-being of its inhabitants. Their well-being should be judged by reference also to non-material "quality of life" considerations also.

In response, the Commission produced its first Environmental Action Programme: a document outlining the principles and objectives of Community environmental policy, and indicating the progress intended as regards development of Community legislation over the following five years. This policy of producing

---

[24] The precursor of the *Rio* conference two decades later.

a strategic document in which the Commission indicates its principal aims, and these being agreed in principle by other Community institutions, has continued to this day.[25] The Commission is presently engaged in seeking to implement the strategies of its Sixth Action Programme (extending to 2012).

Under this initial impetus, during the 1970s and into the 1980s, a substantial number and broad range of environmental measures were adopted by the legislative organs of the Community; and this notwithstanding that the treaty under which they derived their legislative powers contained no explicit reference to "environment" as a subject upon which laws might be passed.

The legal bases upon which "early" laws were founded were, either or both of, the then Articles 100 and 235. The former provided an appropriate legal foundation for legislation in any context where harmonisation of law was felt necessary in order that distortion of the single competitive market be eliminated. This provided a legitimate foundation for harmonising laws in relation, for example, to product standards (*eg* exhaust emissions of vehicles) and industrial emissions to air and discharges to water. The existence of differing national rules on these matters was considered likely to hinder free trade in goods within the Community, and artificially to distort operating costs of industry as between the different States. Of course, the need for harmonised or uniform rules across the Community did not, of itself, require that those laws be drafted so as to impose *onerous* environmental requirements. However, the political commitment at this time to "the environment" sufficed to ensure that harmonisation tended to be at the level of the more environmentally enlightened of the Community Member States.

The other provision by reference to which some environmental legislation was at this time adopted was Article 235. This provides a reserve power, authorising legislation on any matter

---

25 Indeed, Action Programmes now come under the co-decision procedure. As such the European Parliament may veto a proposed plan.

within the stated objectives of the Community, in the absence of any more specific article in the Treaty upon which the measure could be based. Once it became accepted that environmental quality was a component of economic development, it became possible for Article 235 to provide a legal base. This was significant for measures which could not readily be justified by reference to single market considerations.[26]

Matters were put on to a more regular footing when the treaties were revised in the Single European Act of 1986. Three new Articles were introduced – Articles 130 R, S, and T – conferring on the Community for the first time clear and defined environmental competence. And matters were subsequently taken a step further by the Maastricht revisions. Since 1993, the Treaty has included as one of the principal stated objectives of the Community "a policy in the sphere of the environment" (Article 3b). Moreover, the objective in Article 2 to "promote ... sustainable and non-inflationary growth" is to be pursued in a way which recognises the obligation, also there stated, of "respecting the environment".

This discussion will have made apparent the explicit authority of the Community to develop and implement an environmental policy. Moreover, its competence in this area has become explicit at a time when the general breadth of the Community's legislative competence has been a matter of concern on the part of, at least, certain Member States. There was, indeed, some concern, following the Edinburgh Summit of 1992, that environmental policy might suffer a set-back in the subsequent review of Community laws in the light of the then emergent principle of "subsidiarity". This not very meaningful label is given to a principle to be found in the Community treaties which provides that the Community shall take action "only if and in so far as the objectives of the proposed action cannot be sufficiently achieved by the Member States and can, therefore, by reason of the scale or effects of the proposed action, be

---

26   For example, the Wild Birds Directive of 1979.

better achieved by the Community." Given that environmental problems have a tendency towards cross-border effects requiring concerted action by States, it has not proven difficult to demonstrate the consistency of the bulk of Community environmental measures with the principle of subsidiarity.

Nevertheless, some constraint upon Community policy in this area may be discerned. This is a reflection of Article 3(b)(iii): "any action by the Community shall not go beyond what is necessary to achieve the objectives of the Treaty." The Commission was advised by Member States at the European Council in Edinburgh that its measures should be such as to leave as much freedom of response as possible to individual Member States; and that, where objectives may seem so to be achievable, use should be made of non-binding recommendations and voluntary codes (as distinct from more formal, legally-binding and rigidly prescriptive, legal measures).

Over and beyond the discrete environmental policy pursued within the Commission by the Environment Directorate, some reference should be made here to provisions of the Treaty which require that environmental considerations be taken into account in the development of other areas of Community policy. Such objectives were introduced by the Single European Act and strengthened at Maastricht. That "environmental protection" should be integrated into the definition and implementation of other Community policies represents recognition of the important fact that it is not sufficient that one directorate of the European Commission (or one ministry of a national government) should seek to implement environmental protection measures. In accordance with the "preventive" principle of environmental policy, it is much more likely that broad environmental objectives will be achieved if the other important and powerful directorates are mindful of environmental considerations in their own formulation of policies. At Community level this has involved directorates whose principal focus of attention has been on such matters as agriculture, energy, transport and industry being required to integrate into their policy formulation factors which derive from their own obligations to further the Community's objective of respect for the environment. An important example of this, from our point of view, has been what has been referred to as the "greening" of the Common Agricultural Policy, dating from 1992 and given much further impetus in changes agreed in 2003.

ADMINISTRATION

To administer and enforce this mass of legislation, it has been necessary to establish certain specialised agencies as well as conferring powers and duties on the ordinary, pre-existing, agencies of central and local government. However, it is the latter which we shall consider first.

Central Government

Central government is responsible for drafting new domestic legislation and steering such measures through Parliament; and for making such regulations and other forms of subordinate legislation as may be needed to implement provisions contained in statutes which have previously been passed by Parliament. The central government departments have numerous important powers in relation to the matters we shall discuss. These include powers to license otherwise prohibited activities (such as those, described in Chapter 6, on the protection of birds, animals and plants); to decide appeals from decisions of local authorities or other bodies (for example, appeals against refusals of planning permission); to confirm or reject orders which such bodies seek to make (such as compulsory purchase orders, or footpath closure or diversion orders); and to make grants or loans from the central exchequer for statutorily authorised purposes. The most important ministry in relation to conservation of the countryside is the Department for the Environment, Food and Rural Affairs (DEFRA) – established in June 2001 by the merger of certain functions of the former Department of the Environment with those of the former Ministry of Agriculture, Fisheries and Food. The aim of this rearrangement was to secure better integrated policy administration across the spectrum of environment, food and rural affairs; a need brought to light during the Foot and Mouth Disease outbreak of early 2001.

Local Authorities

Legislation which we shall need to consider has also conferred a large number of important functions on the numerous multi-purpose **local authorities.** Such authorities, outside London, have traditionally been of three kinds: parish councils (of which there are several thousand), district councils and county councils. In addition there is a growing number of "unitary" councils. Here a single authority possesses all the former "county" and "district" council functions within the unitary authority's geographical area. This is the position throughout Wales, in the City of London, in the Metropolitan Districts which were established following local government reform in 1974 (*eg* Greater Manchester) and, following more piecemeal changes in the 1990s, in a number of other urban parts of England. The discussion below concentrates, however, on the division of responsibilities where county and district councils share functions within an area.

Most of the local government functions with which we shall be concerned are the responsibility of the **district councils.** It is they, for example, who are the planning authorities responsible for most development control matters (although it has been the county councils which have been responsible for the preparation of "structure" – as distinct from "local" – development plans,[27] and are responsible for decisions in respect of "minerals": mining, quarrying, sand and gravel extraction). The main functions of the **county councils,** from our point of view, are as highway authorities and in relation to the registration of commons. As regards the **parish councils,** which exist in all rural areas, we would suggest that although their formal legal powers are of a rather limited nature they do represent the organ of local government most minutely

---

27 But note the changes introduced by the Planning and Compulsory Purchase Act 2004, below at p.69.

concerned with the countryside. They constitute the most localised form of decision-making, and may help foster local pride and civic responsibility in relation to their areas. The powers of these councils include the installation of bus shelters and seats in public places;[28] they may accept responsibility for the control of litter;[29] they may acquire unenclosed or waste land and make it available for public use as an open space;[30] and they may take steps to safeguard public rights of way.[31] A further function of parish councils is to respond to the district council's notification to them of planning applications in their areas. Such notification is obligatory where the parish council has informed the district council that it wishes to be so notified; though the parish council may choose to confine the notification requirement to particular kinds of planning application only. The district council is not obliged to accept the views of the parish council in relation to applications, but this arrangement can produce an enhanced degree of public participation in planning decisions and may be of value in ensuring that more fully informed decisions are taken.[32]

Each parish council must, at least once a year, hold a parish meeting, attendance at which is open to all local government electors in the parish.[33] Parishes having less than 200 inhabitants do not have to have a parish council. There must, nevertheless, still be a parish meeting. The expenses of parish councils are met by demands (called "precepts") which they serve on their district councils; this money is then collected by district councils as part of the Council Tax.

In Wales the parish councils are known as **community councils** but the difference is one of name only; they have the same

---

28 Local Government (Miscellaneous Provisions) Act 1953 s.4; Parish Councils Act 1957 s.1.
29 Litter Act 1983 ss.5, 6.
30 Open Spaces Act 1906 ss.9, 10.
31 Highways Act 1980 s.130.
32 See Town and Country Planning Act 1990 (TCPA 1990) Sched. 1 para 8 and Town and Country Planning (General Development Procedure) Order 1995 (TCP (GDP) Order 1995) Article 13.
33 Local Government Act 1972 ss.9-16.

powers as their English counterparts. Similarly, in some small towns in England, parish councils may exist under the name of "town" council; again their powers are not different, though the council's chairman and vice-chairman become known as "town mayor" and "deputy town mayor" respectively!

Water Authorities

There were, for a period up until 1989, ten regional water authorities in England and Wales, each covering one or more river basins. Their boundaries were different from those of local authorities, being drawn so that the newly-formulated objective of "integrated river basin management" could be sought. Put simply, the boundaries of the regional water authorities were defined in terms of physical watersheds, rather than the historical administrative borders represented by counties.

Regulated by the Water Resources Act 1963, and the Water Acts of 1973 and 1983, the regional water authorities were statutory corporations whose members were appointed by the Secretary of State. The authorities levied their own rates and were responsible for the collection and conservation of water, for its supply to domestic, commercial and industrial users, for the collection, treatment and discharge of sewage, and for the prevention of pollution of inland, estuarine and coastal waters.

Important, and controversial, changes to the structure of the water industry were made in the Water Act 1989.[34] This "privatisation" Act provided for the assets and functions of the water authorities to be divided between:

(i) successor, privatised, water supply companies and sewerage companies. These have inherited the *utility* (water supply and sewerage) functions of the former water authorities, and perform these functions under the superintendence now of a Director General of Water Services and the Water Services Office;

---

[34] Later consolidated, with other water legislation, in the Water Resources Act 1991 and the Water Industry Act 1991.

(ii) a new national public body, the National Rivers Authority (since 1995, the Environment Agency), which inherited functions related to river and coastal pollution control, land drainage and flood defence, water resource management (*eg* abstraction from rivers, drought orders), fisheries and navigation.

This separation of functions between the new commercially-orientated water supply and sewerage companies and a new national regulatory and enforcement agency marked a considerable improvement on earlier government proposals under which all the functions, except for land drainage, were to have been conferred on the privatised companies. The likelihood of privately owned companies performing adequately the sort of functions now conferred on the Environment Agency (including monitoring their own activities and taking action where necessary) was generally felt to be slim. The revised scheme separating commercial activities from those of a regulatory/enforcement nature was a welcome development from an environmental point of view.

Although this separation of functions received general support, the privatisation legislation did in various other respects give rise to much concern amongst environmental and amenity groups. In particular, fears were voiced that access by members of the public to reservoirs and surrounding catchment land might be curtailed by the new water utility companies. Over the years the former water authorities had somewhat moderated their earlier more restrictive attitude that such public access was a threat to water purity, and many such areas had become of considerable recreational value. A high proportion of reservoirs had been made open for fishing, sailing, sail-boarding and canoeing; the surrounding land commonly being open to access for walking, horse-riding or bird-watching. The significance of this land for these purposes is shown by the fact that, of some 440,000 acres owned by the former water authorities, some 180,000 fell within national parks, areas of outstanding natural beauty or sites of special scientific interest. Amenity groups feared that such public use of this prime scenic and recreational land would be restricted as the new commercially-oriented water companies might seek to generate income by selling off any such land as might be surplus to wants; and perhaps, it was feared, even by charging for access to other remaining land.

This controversy resulted in the inclusion in the Water Act, as eventually enacted, of a number of provisions designed to impose environmental obligations on the new privatised companies. For example, it is provided that ministers and the companies should in the exercise of their functions *take into account* the effects of their actions on the beauty or amenity of any rural or urban area (and its flora, fauna, features and buildings), *have regard to* the desirability of protecting and conserving buildings, sites and objects of archaeological, architectural or historic interest, and *exercise their powers* so as to further the conservation and enhancement of natural beauty and the conservation of flora, fauna and geological or physiological features of special interest.[35] More specifically, the legislation goes on to impose duties to:

(a) have regard to the desirability of preserving for the public any freedom of access to areas of woodland, mountains, moor, heath, down, cliff, or foreshore and other places of natural beauty;

(b) have regard to the desirability of maintaining the availability to the public of any facility for visiting or inspecting any building, site or object of archaeological, architectural or historic interest; and

(c) take into account any effect which any proposals would have on any such freedom of access or on the availability of any such facility.

The value of such very general duties as these in legislation has, in some quarters, been doubted. The duties are rarely absolute; they are commonly subject to compatibility with other, more

---

35 See now, Water Industry Act 1991 s.3.

fundamental, objectives or duties contained in the Act. They are usually couched in rather limited terms – "to have regard to", "to take into account", "so far as it considers desirable". Moreover, it is often not clear what follows from failure to comply with such duties.

In this particular context, these problems have been addressed in two ways. The Act makes provision for its terms to be "fleshed out", so as to provide more precise guidance as to obligations imposed, by the promulgation of Codes of Practice. Such Codes are intended to give "practical guidance" as to "desirable practice". Contravention of such a Code does not of itself constitute a contravention of the Act's obligations, nor will it, of itself, give rise to any criminal or civil liability. Nevertheless, Ministers are under a duty to consider such breaches (or their likelihood) in determining whether and how to exercise their various statutory regulatory powers over the water supply and sewerage companies.[36] A Code on Conservation, Access and Recreation was issued in 1989 (S.I. 1989/1152). More recently, the matter of public rights of access to land such as this has been dealt with by the Countryside and Rights of Way Act 2000 (CROWA), considered more fully below in Chapter 3.

As regards enforcement of the more general statements of environmental obligation, the legislation includes these obligations amongst a list of duties which are enforceable by way of a special procedure. Under section 18 of the Water Industry Act 1991, the Secretary of State can make enforcement orders against water companies not complying with certain of the obligations imposed under the Act. It will therefore be appropriate for those aggrieved to draw the attention of the Secretary of State to any failures to comply with the various environmental duties described above. The Secretary has a duty to serve an enforcement order on any company in contravention of its obligations. This *duty* does not apply, however, to cases of trivial contravention, to cases where an

---

[36] See Water Industry Act 1991 s.5(2).

"undertaking" had been given by the company that it was going to comply with obligations, and to cases where the duties were not complied with because of the primacy of other more fundamental duties in the Act. In these three situations, the Secretary of State retains a *power* to invoke the enforcement order mechanism but is not under a duty to do so.[37]

The enforcement order served on the water company will state what is required to comply with its terms. Failing such compliance, the Secretary of State may go to court to obtain an injunction to reinforce his order; in an extreme case a special administration order can be sought under which the court will appoint an administrator to take over the running of the company.

Even apart from these specific provisions, it may be argued that such quite broad statements in legislation are of importance. They demonstrate the significance attached by the legislature to environmental matters, they constitute a range of items to be borne in mind as a matter of routine, and provide a very clear foundation for environmental "objectors" or campaigning groups to expect to have their views heard and taken into account.

Whatever may be the value of the provisions described above, they proved inadequate to assuage the fears, expressed above, about loss of amenity land as a result of sales by the new companies. The Water Industry Act 1991 has, therefore, sought to deal with this problem by providing specifically (section 156) that sales of land by the new companies shall require ministerial consent. In determining applications for consent, the Secretary of State is, at least in relation to land in national parks, areas of outstanding natural beauty, the Broads and sites of special scientific importance, obliged to comply with the general environmental duties described above. Consent may be given conditionally. Such conditions may include an

---

[37] Water Industry Act 1991 s.19. For an interesting case challenging the Secretary of State's decision to seek *undertakings* from water companies that they improve drinking water quality to meet EC standards (rather than to take other, immediate, enforcement action), see *R. v S.S.E. ex p Friends of the Earth, The Times*, June 8, 1995 (CA).

obligation first to offer the land (or an interest or right over the land) on stated terms to a specified person or body (*eg* a conservation body) at market price; and where the land falls within an area such as that just described (*ie* national park, etc.) the consent may contain a condition of having to consult with the Countryside Agency or English Nature (Countryside Council for Wales) (as appropriate) and to enter into such management agreements with those bodies as the Secretary of State may require. The Act further empowers companies intending to sell land to enter into a covenant with the Secretary of State accepting obligations with respect to public freedom of access to the land or to the use or management of the land. Any such agreement or covenant will then be binding on any purchasers of the land and their successors in title. Where the land falls within a national park, the Broads, an area of outstanding natural beauty or a site of special scientific importance, the Secretary of State may *require* that the company, on disposing of land, enter into such a covenant.

Forestry Commission

Another public body with functions which are of considerable significance to the countryside is the Forestry Commission. This body was established, by statute, in 1919 to ensure that an adequate supply of timber would be available for national needs; the long period of time between planting and felling making this an unsuitable matter to entrust entirely, or even substantially, to free enterprise response to supply and demand.

The Commission is the largest landowner in the United Kingdom, and has powers of compulsory acquisition for forestry purposes. Its own holdings amounted, until quite recently, to nearly 1.1 million hectares. Fuller information about the activities and environmental responsibilities of the Forestry Commission may be found, below, in Chapter 4. At this stage, however, we may note that in 1982 the Conservative government extended its "privatisation" policy to forestry. This was partly an application of principle: the view that forestry need not be a government or public sector activity; and partly an attempt to secure a limitation on general public expenditure, the Forestry Commission traditionally being a loss-making concern. Accordingly, the Commission embarked upon a policy of selling woodland plantations, with instruction that it should dispose of some 250,000 hectares of land by the end of the century. Following the 1997 General Election, this policy was changed and the Commission retains ownership of more than a million hectares of land (of which some 350,000 hectares are in England and Wales).

These twin objectives of government policy were reflected also in institutional division within the Forestry Commission. Since 1992 the Commission has consisted of the *Department of Forestry* (itself comprising a "Policy and Resources Group" which advises ministers and develops policy objectives, and a "Forestry Authority" which implements forestry policy in its role as the forestry grant-provision and regulatory agency) and *Forest Enterprise* (the body responsible for managing the Commission's own forests). This institutional reform has been aimed at securing a separation of function between the regulatory and executive functions of the Commission (to seek to separate the "poacher" from the "gamekeeper") and to provide a more suitable framework within which to set clear financial targets (with an aim at financial self-sufficiency) for the "enterprise" side of the Commission's operations. More recently still, following Scottish and Welsh devolution, "forestry" has become a devolved matter. Under the umbrella of Forestry Commission GB, there exist separate Commissions for England, Scotland and Wales; and Forest Enterprise now exists as three country-based agencies.

Conservation and amenity groups during the 1990s expressed much concern both at the very fact of the sale of Commission land, and also at some of the particular sales which have taken place. Indeed, on a number of occasions voluntary organisations made "rescue" purchases of tracts of woodland which they considered to be of important wildlife habitat value. Since such purchases were often made with the assistance of government grants (through, for example, the National Heritage Memorial

Fund or English Nature) there was criticism that such sales simply constituted the recycling of public money.

Even where the woodland transferred to private ownership was not itself perceived to be under threat, problems existed where the new private owner was thought likely to be less willing to permit public access than had formerly been the case when the woodland was owned by the Forestry Commission.

The Commission's own willingness to permit public access dates back at least to 1935 when its first Forest Park was established.[38] More recently, it has established numerous Woodland Parks which are managed with recreational use specifically in mind. In addition, Forest Enterprise runs information centres, camping and caravaning sites, and cabin sites within its forests. The general policy is one of freedom to roam except where forest management, conservation or safety requirements (or lease arrangements under which the Commission may hold the land) prevent this. It has been estimated that each year there are some 350 million visits to Forest Enterprise land, as compared with some 170 million visits to the coast.

SPECIALISED AGENCIES

In addition to the conferment of statutory functions of environmental significance on the institutions described above, there have also been created a number of specialised agencies whose responsibilities have been focused exclusively on the protection of, or promotion of enjoyment of, the countryside.

A little history may be helpful here, as the bodies with which we shall be concerned have moved through a number of changes of name, and focus of activities, over the last half century. Very broadly, we may say that the "countryside" agencies with which we are dealing are those which have been concerned to do one or more of three principal things: to

---

[38] In England and Wales, Forest Parks amounted in 1996 to some 160,000 hectares.

enhance rural economies, to protect countryside which has been afforded some special status in terms of landscape or similar value, or to protect some natural feature for its own particular scientific (rather than amenity) value.

In terms of agencies set up to secure these various aims and objectives, the first of note was the Rural Development Commission, set up by Lloyd-George's government in 1909 to try to counter certain aspects of rural decline. Throughout its existence, the Rural Development Commission was a somewhat "low key" (and low-funded) body. With the establishment in the 1940s of agencies with specific landscape amenity and scientific nature protection functions, the social and economic aspects of countryside protection seemed to take something of a back seat.

The two bodies set up during the 1940s were the Nature Conservancy and the National Parks Commission. The former was established by Royal Charter in 1946. It became a statutory body and changed its name to the Nature Conservancy Council in 1973; two decades later it divided into (for England) English Nature and (for Wales) the Countryside Council for Wales. The National Parks Commission was established by the National Parks and Access to the Countryside Act 1949. It was reconstituted by the Countryside Act 1968 as the Countryside Commission.

The principal focus of each of these two bodies was rather different. The National Parks Commission/Countryside Commission had, as we shall discuss more fully when we consider the National Parks, a mission to "manage" those Parks so as to maximise their long-term value to the public. It was clear from the start that this involved both protecting and also exploiting the recreational and similar potential of those areas, and that, where there might be a conflict between these things, the need to preserve the Parks as long-term assets meant that the protection function should "trump" more short-term public benefits. Nevertheless, in a real sense, the Commission worked on the basis that the value of the Parks was to be found in their ongoing benefit to the general public. In contrast, the

Nature Conservation Council/English Nature operated from a more "scientific" perspective: exercising a range of statutory functions whose basic premise was that certain species and certain habitats warranted protection for their own sake, rather than as simply an aspect of securing more direct public benefit.

The difference in approach between the two agencies is apparent from a short statement of their principal functions. The Countryside Commission's functions were broadly to seek the preservation and enhancement of the National Parks and other areas of countryside (eg Areas of Outstanding Natural Beauty) and to encourage the development and improvement of facilities for informal recreation in such places and access to the countryside by members of the public. To these ends the Commission possessed few executive powers and was not a rural land-owning body. It sought to achieve its objectives by a combination of advice to, and lobbying of, organs of central and local government on countryside matters, and advice to farmers (bolstered often by grant payments being conditional on taking that advice). In terms of formal statutory powers, the most noteworthy has been that of developing over the several decades the network which now exists of National Parks, AONBs and Long Distance Trails. In contrast, the Nature Conservation Council/English Nature has a focus on the establishment and management of National Nature Reserves, Marine Nature Reserves and Sites of Special Scientific Interest; together with a range of functions relating to the species and habitat sites to be protected under the EU Directives on Wild Birds (1979) and Habitats (1992).

These two broad approaches – "countryside for the public" and "nature for its own sake" – have characterised the work of these two principal agencies. However, this is not to suggest that the two agencies have been in conflict with each other in the performance of their functions. Although they have viewed matters from differing perspectives, this has not generally led each to develop policies or programmes which are contrary to the objectives of the other.

An institutional change was made in 1999 when the Countryside Commission and the Rural Development Commission were merged into a single new body: the Countryside Agency. Straight away this body made it evident that its "countryside" concerns were to be of a broader nature than had been those of the Countryside Commission. Although it remained an adviser rather than a policy-maker or a direct deliverer of services, it regarded itself as having an important role in terms of what it called the "rural-proofing" of the policies and proposals of the various central ministries: meaning that it would be watchful to see that the impact of such policies on rural communities should be properly assessed and understood.

The focus of the Countryside Agency not just on landscape and access but also on "communities" is evident from its tripartite statement of aims:

(i) to conserve and enhance England's countryside;

(ii) to spread social and economic opportunity to people wherever they live;

(iii) to help everyone, wherever they live and whatever their background, to enjoy the countryside.

The Countryside Agency's focuses were also apparent from its initial listing of priorities. These were to:

(a) show how to tackle rural disadvantage;

(b) improve transport in rural areas while taming the impact of traffic growth;

(c) demonstrate a more sustainable approach to agriculture;

(d) increase the amount and quality of access to the countryside.

This in turn led the Agency to develop six priority areas for its work:

(i) Vital Villages: empowered, active and inclusive communities;

(ii) Essential Services: high standards of rural services;

(iii) New Enterprises: vibrant local economies;

(iv) Living Landscapes: all countryside managed sustainably;

(v) Wider Welcome: recreation opportunities for all;

(vi) Countryside for Towns: realising the potential of the urban fringe.

The effect of the institutional change in 1999 has aptly been described in the following words:

> "The CA brings together all the different countryside dimensions – economic, environmental, community and enjoyment – into a single national body."

There is one further element to this brief history. In March 2004, DEFRA announced that there would be a merger of English Nature and the Countryside Agency, to form a truly "integrated" countryside body. This would seem, in principle, to make good sense; just as did, as we saw a little earlier, the bringing together into DEFRA of functions related to environment, agriculture and food. Suspicions have been voiced, however, that there may be a hidden agenda within this ostensibly sensible move: that of "clipping the wings" of English Nature, a body which has perhaps more often in the past come into opposition with government plans than has the Countryside Commission or Agency.

THE COUNTRYSIDE TODAY: MYTH AND REALITY

The Countryside Agency recently produced a Report on the *State of the Countryside*. For present purposes the two main features of the Report which stand out are, first, that according to a poll more than 90% of people (whether living in town or country) want to keep the countryside "as it is now"; and secondly, that the Report contains a wealth of information which collectively may be said to build up a picture of the countryside which is rather different from what most people would imagine to be case. In consequence, we may have to face a reality in which most people want the countryside to be something it no longer is (and maybe never was). The "ideal" of the majority of people may well be a "myth" they would wish to be strived for, rather than the continuation of what presently is, or recently was. A few basic facts presented by the Agency may help to demonstrate these points.

We focus much in this book on the impact of farming, forestry and tourism on the landscape, on habitats and on species. It is certainly true that agriculture and forestry are the land-uses which affect over 80% of the land area of England. However, at the same time, less than 5% of people who live in the countryside work in farming, with over 80% working in manufacturing, distribution and financial and public services. In terms of what measures may best produce a vibrant rural economy, these figures may be significant.

The Report notes that there is an ongoing movement of people from cities to the country or to market towns, some 750,000 making this move annually. Yet there are evident socio-economic problems for those who live in rural areas, at any rate for those without private transport. Almost three-quarters of England's villages have no shop and over a half have no pub or youth club. Moreover, and perhaps as a consequence of the movement of people from the cities, in recent years property prices in rural areas have increased by an even higher percentage than those in towns.

The area of land devoted to woodland grew during the twentieth century. Admittedly, at the start of that century it was an all-time low: only some 5% of Britain being so covered. A hundred years later this figure was 12% (and rising). Wood supplied from English forests has doubled in volume over the past thirty years and is set to double again in the next twenty. In similar vein, the area designated as green belt land for planning permission purposes has grown over the past few years.

A picture seems to emerge which is not perhaps quite that which is commonly in the mind of the ordinary person polled about his or her attitude to the countryside. Moreover, it is interesting to juxtapose a further opinion poll finding. It seems that 90% of people want the countryside kept as it is; but only 65% admitted to having visited the countryside during the previous year. We seem to find a substantial proportion of people expressing opinions about somewhere they do not choose to visit; as well, one suspects, as a substantial number of people visiting the countryside and finding that its basic social and economic fabric is not quite what they had understood.

At one and the same time the Countryside Agency is seeking that rural policies should be based upon fact rather than myth or nostalgia, yet a good many individuals may find that it is that myth or nostalgia to which their minds are rooted when considering countryside issues.

THE OUTLOOK

In the chapters which follow much will be said of the very great changes which have taken place in our countryside during the post-war period. The loss of hedgerows and broadleaved woodlands, the drainage of wetlands for arable cultivation, the ploughing of moorland and heath for coniferous afforestation and cultivation, and the shift in many other areas from pasture to cereal production has much altered the visual appearance of many areas of our countryside, and has proved harmful to many plants and animals by the destruction of their habitats. It has been estimated that over the past half-century Britain has lost around 125,000 miles of hedgerows, nearly all its flower-filled hay meadows, and over half its heathland, marsh, downland and natural woodland. In Thomas Hardy's day the heathland of Dorset covered some 100,000 acres. Today only about a sixth of this remains. In addition to all this, some 50,000 acres of countryside are lost each year for residential, commercial and other development.

However, although complacency is not appropriate, some hopeful signs for the future may be detected. The over-production of cereals has now been recognised and, since the late 1980s, financial support for agriculture has concentrated on *extensification* of production (*eg* set-aside arrangements), and attention has been paid to incorporating environmental and amenity requirements as conditions of such support. The reform of the EC Common Agricultural Policy – involving the "Greening of the CAP" – dating from 1992 and culminating in a new system of farm grants as of 2005, is significant in this respect. The new system will involve a "decoupling" of the link between support payments and production.

In terms of the quality of the environmental media, there can be seen a gradual but consistent improvement in surface water quality. As the EU Water Framework Directive is implemented over the next decade, we should see a move towards that directive's target that all surface water and groundwater shall be of "good" quality by 2015. Moreover, that same directive is requiring that more attention be paid to water *quantity*, and this has required amendments within the Water Act 2003 to allow the Environment Agency more powers of control over the abstraction and impoundment of water.

Air quality within the United Kingdom is generally improving, but curiously it is the urban areas which appear to be making the greatest progress. In part this is because the localised air pollution problems were more marked there and easier to address. A problem presenting much more difficulty is that of low-level ozone and, paradoxically, this is an air quality problem which manifests itself more in the country than in towns.

A question mark appears to exist regarding soil. There is, it seems, a lack of both raw data and assessment criteria in terms of this environmental medium. Neither in terms of soil quality nor in terms of soil structure can firm conclusions be drawn.

A good deal of work is going on in the area of landscape protection. Two new National Parks are imminent in the more heavily populated south of England and there is a move towards more integrated coastal zone management as a means of preserving the coastal landscape. In recent times, that "Cinderella" landscape designation – Area of Outstanding Natural Beauty – has received a double "boost": the enhancement of management arrangements for such areas and firm official recognition that these landscapes are as valuable and should be as strongly protected in "bias against development" terms as National Parks.

Add to this the "open land" countryside access rights which will be introduced between the summer of 2004 and the end of 2005, together with the establishment of new National Trails beside Hadrian's Wall (2003), in the Cotswolds (2005), and as a bridleway along the Pennines (2006), and there may be said to be a positive picture to set alongside the more popular headlines relating to pollution and environmental degradation. This is not, of course, any plea for complacency; merely a call for balanced assessment of the positive against the negative.

The final word in this short section on "outlook" may be afforded to the Countryside Agency, which has opined that:

"... in future less land is likely to be needed for food production. More land is likely to be used for crops for industry and energy. More is likely to be managed for conservation, recreation or community benefits. And there will be more woodland."

And in terms of achievement of objectives for the countryside, a key point stressed by the Agency, and a recurring theme of this book, is that:

"... the countryside is largely the product of past economic activity – our farmed landscapes, open country, villages, market towns and fine country houses. Economic activity will be central to conserving and enhancing the countryside in the future."

Chapter 2

PLANNING

INTRODUCTION

In this chapter we shall examine some aspects of the law and practice relating to land-use planning. Broadly speaking, the capacity of local planning authorities, the district and to a lesser extent the county councils, to protect and promote the countryside through the exercise of their planning powers arises in two ways.

On the one hand they have been required to produce "development plans". This has required them to survey and assess the present and future needs of their areas and to decide how best to accommodate competing demands for residential, industrial and commercial development, for mineral extraction, and for recreation and leisure; whilst at the same time not being wasteful of agricultural land and seeking to preserve and promote the visual amenity of the urban and rural landscape. Much effort has gone into the production of these "development plan" documents. However, the realisation of these "blueprints" is not an easy matter: productions and forecasts may prove to have been faulty or may be falsified by subsequent events, and in a relatively free rather than authoritarian society there are few positive powers of compulsion of individuals and businesses in order to achieve the future as planned. Nevertheless, such "forward" or "strategic" planning is essential, not only to provide a background against which the merits of individual applications for planning permission may be assessed, but also in order that local government (and central government) can anticipate likely needs for the various kinds of public services – roads, schools and so on. This is obvious enough in the urban context; but the same is true also in respect of the countryside. In particular, the very great increase since the 1950s in the ability, because of increased leisure-time and mobility, of the residents of towns to visit and enjoy the countryside has required central and local government to plan carefully how to accommodate such recreational use.

The other means by which local authorities may through their planning powers protect and preserve the countryside is by the way in which they exercise their powers of development control; in other words, through their decisions, case by case, in relation to applications received for planning permission.

The plan of this chapter will be to begin by outlining the main features of the **development control** system (*ie* the need for, and decision-making in respect of, planning permission) and thereafter to consider the law relating to the preparation of **development plans.**

DEVELOPMENT CONTROL

Origins

The modern system of land use planning in England and Wales can be traced back at least to an Act of Parliament of 1909;[1] though there were earlier non-statutory powers of control over land use available in the controls that could be exercised by landlords over their tenants through covenants in leases, and also by the insertion of restrictive covenants on the outright sale of land. Thus, a landowner leasing land to a developer might impose covenants in the long-term building lease, and these covenants would bind the sub-lessees to whom the developer let the buildings. The famous Royal Crescent in Bath, the Bedford Estate in Bloomsbury, and parts of the Calthorp Estate in Edgbaston, Birmingham were effected and regulated by this means. It was only, however, in the middle of the nineteenth century that the law came to recognise the power of a vendor on the outright sale of land (sale of the freehold) to impose restrictive covenants as to the use which might be made of the land sold, for the benefit of retained adjoining land. Such restrictive covenants were enforceable by and against successors in title to both the land affected (the "servient tenement") and the land benefited (the "dominant tenement"). And early this century this principle was extended to the concept of the "building scheme", whereby a builder of

---

[1] Housing, Town Planning etc. Act 1909.

a new development might impose identical conditions on each purchaser of a plot, and on completion of the development these restrictions would be mutually enforceable by each of the plot owners.

Such control over land use by restrictive covenants was, however, wholly dependent on private initiative and was inevitably very much localised in operation. For comprehensive control over the use of land it was necessary for governmental statutory powers to be established. Although a start was made by the 1909 Act, referred to above, the first application of statutory controls to the *countryside* came in 1932,[2] and the system which remains the basis of the present law was introduced by the Town and Country Planning Act 1947. This Act, together with later legislation, was first consolidated in the Town and Country Planning Act 1971; subsequently a second, more recent, consolidation has produced the present principal statutes: the Town and Country Planning Act 1990, the Planning (Listed Buildings and Conservation Areas) Act 1990 and the Planning (Hazardous Substances) Act 1990. However, here as elsewhere, the law does not stand still. We shall need to take note of some significant changes introduced since 1990; most notably by the Planning and Compensation Act 1991 and the Planning and Compulsory Purchase Act 2004.

Need for Planning Permission

The most outstanding feature of the system dating from 1947 was, and remains, the "nationalisation" of the right to "develop" land.[3] Since that time no owner or occupier has been able lawfully to "develop" his land unless either he has obtained planning permission from his local district council, or the proposed development falls within one of a number of exemptions contained in the statute[4] or in regulations made

---

[2] Town and Country Planning Act 1932.
[3] For the meaning of "development" see below, p.40.
[4] Numerous exemptions are set out in s.55(2) of the Town and Country Planning Act 1990.

under the statute. The meaning of the term "development" will be considered in some detail below. As regards the exemptions, the most important provisions are to be found in the Town and Country Planning (Use Classes) Order 1987,[5] which excludes certain defined changes of use of land from the need for planning permission; and in the Town and Country Planning (General Permitted Development) Order 1995, which lists certain operations on land as being ones in respect of which planning permission may be deemed to have been obtained.

Meaning of "Development"

It is clearly of fundamental importance to know what is meant by the term "development". The legislation defines this concept in some detail, but the point to note initially is that there are essentially two broad limbs to the definition: two fundamentally different species of "development".

Development may take place either by "the carrying out of building, engineering, mining or other operations in, on, over or under land", or by the "making of any material change of use of any buildings or other land". The distinction between the two kinds of development can, perhaps, best be explained in the words of Lord Denning MR:

> " 'operations' comprises activities which result in some form of physical alteration to the land which has some degree of permanence to the land itself, whereas ... 'use' comprises activities which are done in, alongside or on the land but do not interfere with the actual physical characteristics of the land."[6]

"Operational Development"

The meaning of certain of the activities which comprise operational development is further elaborated in the legislation. Thus, for example, it is provided that "building operations" includes:

---

5   S.I. 1987/764.
6   *Parkes v S.S.E.* [1978] 1 WLR 1308.

(a) demolition of buildings;

(b) rebuilding;

(c) structural alterations of or additions to buildings; and

(d) other operations normally undertaken by a person carrying on business as a builder. (1990 Act section 55(1A).)

Moreover, the definition section of the Act (section 336) defines "building" broadly as including "any structure or erection".

In interpreting these provisions, the courts have offered some helpful guidance on whether operations have resulted in "development". In one case, for example, it was argued by counsel that, since a mobile tower crane, which rested upon tracks laid on the ground, was not fixed to the land and did not change the physical character of the land, its construction on a site did not amount to development. Dismissing this argument, the court held that the crane could be considered to be a "structure or erection". Accordingly, it was a "building" within section 336 and its erection constituted a "building operation".[7]

The court in the crane case attached much weight to an earlier judgment in which Jenkins J had indicated that, although each case might turn on its own particular facts, there are three factors which are likely to influence the final decision as to whether what has occurred constitutes development of this kind: *(i)* size; *(ii)* permanence; and *(iii)* physical attachment. In particular, as a general rule, this category comprises things constructed on-site (being too unwieldy to be brought to the site ready-built and in final form) and which will need to be dismantled eventually (rather than just taken away).[8]

Nevertheless, none of these factors is in itself necessarily determinative. Thus, the placement upon a site of a mobile

---

[7] *Barvis Ltd. v S.S.E.* (1971) 22 P&CR 710.
[8] *Cardiff Rating Authority v Guest Keen Baldwin's Iron and Steel Co.* [1949] 1 All ER 27.

home has been held to be operational development.[9] In contrast, the erection of fairground swing-boats (capable of dismantlement within one hour and being carried away complete by six men),[10] and the installation of a wheeled coal hopper and conveyor (16-20 feet in height)[11] have been regarded as not amounting to development. In a celebrated case in 1992, a householder in Oxford who surprised his neighbours by incorporating a fibre-glass shark into the ridge-structure of the roof of his house was regarded as having engaged in operational development. In due course, planning permission was granted for this relatively harmless instance of eccentricity.[12]

The provisions of section 55(1A) make quite clear that rebuilding is included in the concept of "building operations". Thus to rebuild a structure which has collapsed, perhaps following years of neglect, requires planning permission. A distinction must, however, be noted between "rebuilding" and "works for the maintenance, improvement or other alteration of any building ... which ... do not materially affect the external appearance of the building".[13] Such works do *not* constitute development. The word "materially" is significant: adding a window to a wall will involve development; in contrast, replacing one style of door with another will not.[14]

Perhaps surprisingly, it is only quite recently that there has been any certainty in the law as regards when acts of *demolition* may amount to development.[15] It has for long been understood that demolition requires consent in relation to properties

---

[9]　[1978] JPL 571. Where a structure is only transportable to a site by means of large vehicles and heavy-lifting machinery, its delivery (and site preparation) may itself be regarded as an "engineering" operation. Contrast the bringing onto land of towable caravans: not operational development (but may involve "change of use"; see below).

[10]　*James v Brecon* C.C. (1963) 15 P&CR 20.

[11]　*Cheshire* C.C. *v Woodward* (1962) 2 QB 126.

[12]　(1992) 7 PAD 481.

[13]　s.55(2)(a).

[14]　See (1977) 35 P&CR 387 and [1969] JPL 151.

[15]　Witness the differences at first instance and on appeal in *Cambridgeshire City Council v S.S.E.* [1991] JPL 428; *The Times*, February 12, 1992.

within conservation areas, and also as regards listed buildings.[16] It has also been accepted that *partial* demolition involves the structural alteration of a building and, as such, amounts to development.

Doubt existed, however, as regards *total* demolition; in one view, apparently shared by the DOE, this did not meet an essential requirement of a "building operation" – that it should involve some *constructional* activity.

Following a court decision in 1991 doubting the correctness of this view, the whole matter was clarified, albeit in somewhat complex legal form, in 1992. We deal with this matter in some detail because the legal forms chosen to secure the intended result are instructive.

First, the Planning and Compensation Act 1991 amended the definition of "building operations" to include a clear reference to "demolition of buildings". This broadened definition within the principal statute is, however, narrowed by provisions in regulations excluding the demolition of *certain categories* of building from the concept of "development"; see now, the Town and Country Planning (Demolition – Description of Buildings) Direction 1995. The result is that planning permission is *not* required in relation to the demolition of:

(i) listed buildings, scheduled monuments and buildings in conservation areas;

(ii) buildings with a volume of less than 50 cubic metres; or

(iii) buildings other than dwelling-houses or buildings adjoining dwelling-houses.

This needs a little explanation. It suggests that planning permission is only necessary for the demolition of buildings which are dwelling-houses; and even in respect of such buildings, it is not necessary to obtain planning permission where the building is listed or is sited in a conservation area. This is true,

---

[16] For these, see below, pp.77 and 80.

but is somewhat misleading. We need to explain the position a little more fully.

With regard to listed buildings and buildings in conservation areas, the reason why demolition is excluded from the definition of development is that in both such cases the pre-existing obligation to obtain consent under those more specific legal regimes has been continued. In other words, it is not necessary to obtain planning permission, but it is necessary to obtain *other* consent to demolition.[17]

As regards *buildings which are not dwellings* (*eg* shops, offices), it is not necessary to obtain permission to demolish except in the situation where the activity is of such technical complexity that it may fall within the category "engineering operation" and so amount in that way to development. In any event, it should be noted that subsequent site engineering work may similarly involve "engineering" operations and so require planning permission.

What, however, of the demolition of dwelling-houses of over 50 cubic metres volume (*ie* all but the very tiniest)? Notwithstanding that the Act and Direction state such demolition to involve development, the reality is that even here it is not necessary, instance by instance, to seek planning permission. This is because of a provision of the Town and Country Planning (General Permitted Development) Order 1995. This Order, as will be explained more fully later in this chapter, lists a substantial number of categories of operational development in respect of which planning permission is by that Order deemed to have been granted; it therefore not being necessary in each individual case to seek express approval from the local planning authority.

It is a feature of the TCP(GPD) Order scheme that for development to benefit from such *deemed* permission it must comply precisely with any requirements specified within the Order. Moreover, it is open to any local authority, by means of

---

17   See below, pp.77-80.

what is called an "Article 4 Direction", to exclude or limit the operation of provisions of the Order in its own area (either generally or in relation to a specific development).

It is through the combination of these two principles that the potential for local authority control over the demolition of dwelling-houses exists. The Order requires that to take the benefit of "permitted development" the developer must comply with a "prior notice" and "approval" procedure laid down in the Order. In this way the local planning authority will become aware of the developer's intentions and have a period of 28 days in which to consider the matter before demolition may lawfully take place. During this period the authority may impose requirements as regards the demolition in order, for example, to seek to minimise the local impact of the operations or to require certain site reinstatement measures to be undertaken. An appeal to the Minister against the imposition of such requirements is provided. Demolition which complies with such prior approval is lawful, having the benefit of planning permission under the TCP(GPD) Order. Demolition not in such compliance involves a breach of planning control.[18]

This rather complex web requires one further piece of disentanglement. It might be expected that such a prior approval procedure would involve, within itself, a power in the planning authority to withhold permission for demolition *altogether*. Not so. The procedure relates only to the method of demolition and the nature of site restoration. If the planning authority wishes to *prohibit* demolition, it must act by means of an Article 4 Direction, withdrawing permitted development rights in respect of the building (or perhaps, in relation to buildings more generally within its area). If such a Direction is made and demolition proceeds without an express grant of planning permission having been obtained, there will have occurred a breach of planning control.

This discussion of planning controls over demolition provides a valuable example of a familiar technique of planning law: to

---

[18]   For the implications of this, see below, p.69.

describe quite broadly the range of matters for which permission is required, but then to detract from the burden which such extensive control would impose (on developers and on planning authorities) by means of general conferment of "deemed" permission for particular defined species of development. It provides an important warning to look both at the Act and at the TCP(GPD) Order before coming to any conclusion about the need to apply for planning permission. We shall note a similar technique (under the Use Classes Order) in the next section, when we consider whether an application for planning permission is necessary for a change of use of land.[19]

"Material Change of Use"
The question whether a particular alteration of activity in relation to a site requires an application for planning permission is a matter of some complexity. We shall begin with the statutory elaboration of the concept, and then proceed to the guidance that has been offered by the judges.

The 1990 Act lists a number of changes of use which are specifically *not* to be regarded as a material change of use of land. These comprise:

(i) the use of buildings or other land within the curtilage[20] of a dwelling-house for any purpose incidental to the enjoyment of the dwelling-house as such (section 55(2)(d));

(ii) the use of any land for the purposes of agriculture or forestry and the use for any of those purposes of any building occupied together with land so used (section 55(2)(e)). (The wide exemption afforded from planning control to farmers and foresters is discussed further later in this chapter);

(iii) changes between uses falling within the same Class of the Use Classes Order (section 55(2)(f)).[21] (This is also explained further, below.)

---

[19] See below, p.48.
[20] A term with not much clearer meaning for lawyers than to others!
[21] Town and Country Planning (Use Classes) Order 1987 (S.I. 1987/764).

In reverse direction, the Act also provides that certain changes *are* to be regarded as involving material changes of use. These are:

(i) the use of a previously single dwelling-house as two or more separate dwelling-houses (section 55(3)(a));

(ii) the deposit of refuse or waste materials on land (section 55(3)(b));

(iii) the use of external parts of a building not normally so used for the display of advertisements (section 55(5)).

Some of these provisions merit further comment or explanation.

We may begin with the exclusion from development of uses of buildings or other land within the curtilage of a dwelling-house for purposes of enjoyment of the dwelling-house. An important issue here relates to the operation of this provision in relation to the siting of caravans. On the assumption that bringing a caravan onto land does not involve "operational" development, the question arises whether any subsequent use of the caravan may amount to a change of use of the land. In principle, in a case where a caravan is used for temporary or permanent residential purposes, this will be the case. It may, however, be argued that, where a caravan is sited in the vicinity of a dwelling-house, benefit may be taken of the statutory exclusionary provision referred to above. In fact this will, probably, only be the case in quite limited circumstances. For one thing there must be some clear connection between the users of the caravan and the dwelling-house; the residential use of the caravan must be "incidental to the enjoyment of the dwelling-house". This means that commercial letting (*eg* to holidaymakers) will be unlikely to come within the provision. Even where there is a clear connection between the residents of the caravan and the dwelling-house, the provisions in the statute may not necessarily be satisfied. Much will depend upon whether the caravan is genuinely used as overspill accommodation for the dwellers of the house; or whether it is essentially an independent unit of accommodation, albeit used by individuals with a close family or other connection. Has the home been expanded into the caravan; or has a caravan brought with it relations or friends to be no more than "near neighbours"? That the latter situation should not be exempt from planning controls may be regarded as a corollary of the statutory provision, already referred to, that the use of a single dwelling-house as two or more separate dwelling-houses does require planning permission.

Some discussion is also necessary to explain the non-applicability of planning controls to changes of use within the same Use Class within the Use Classes Order. This important document may be regarded as very broadly the equivalent, in relation to "material change of use", to the TCP(GPD) Order in relation to operational development. However, the two sets of provisions do not operate entirely separately from each other. It is not quite true to say that the General Permitted Development Order is only concerned with operational development. Thus, for example, the GPDO contains important provisions conferring permitted development status upon certain changes of use *from certain Use Classes to certain others*.[22] It will be apparent that a close awareness of the categories to be found within the Use Classes Order is essential to any detailed appreciation of the meaning of "development".

We may now move from the explicit statutory provisions about the scope of "material change of use" to a consideration of the assistance which the judges have afforded as to the meaning of this concept.

To begin with it should be stressed that the courts have made clear that the term "material" means material in the planning sense,[23] so that it is the likely effects of a change of use on local amenity which determine its materiality, and have stressed that whether or not a change is material in any particular case

---

[22] There is a technical significance to the distinction between not needing to apply for planning permission because of deemed permission and not needing to apply because the matter does not involve "development" at all. This is, however, beyond the scope of this discussion.

[23] See, *eg Marshall v Nottingham Corporation* [1960] 1 WLR 707.

is essentially a matter of "fact and degree" rather than a matter of "law", thereby restricting the scope of review by the courts in determining planning appeals.[24] This is not, however, to suggest that if a use remains the same, but that same use begins to have a more pronounced impact on local amenity, there can be said to have been a change of use. An example would be a change from a "local" to a "fun" pub. The latter may have a substantially more significant external impact (music, lights, more customers coming and going) than the former. However, as both are "pub" uses it would seem wrong to regard the altered impact as resulting from any change of use.[25]

However, a contrast needs to be drawn between the approach of the courts described immediately above, and their approach where the *intensification* of a use may be regarded as changing the very nature of that use. The distinction which the courts seem willing to draw appears to be between the *mere* intensification of an existing use, which will not amount to a "change of use", and intensification which is such as to render appropriate a quite different description of the use to which the land is being put.[26] The difference necessary is, perhaps, that of a "private residence which is let occasionally" becoming a "holiday home"; or a "field with a caravan in it" becoming a "caravan site"; or a "field with a rusty car in it" becoming a "scrap-heap".

It is clear from the cases that the courts have been anxious to avoid intensification *per se* being regarded as "development", even in spite of such intensification's enlarged effect on surrounding amenity. This may appear curious from a planning control point of view. However, to take the alternative approach would involve the danger, in the commercial context at least, that it would require planning permission (in relation to certain uses) to continue to make a success of one's business![27]

---

[24] See further, below, p.83.
[25] See [1984] JPL 122. See further, below, at p.258 on the relationship between planning permission and actionable nuisance.
[26] *Royal London Borough of Kensington and Chelsea v S.S.E.* [1981] JPL 50.
[27] See *Lilo Blum v S.S.E.* [1987] JPL 278.

The courts have also held that a use may be *abandoned*, with the consequence that resumption of that former use may amount to a change of use requiring planning permission.[28] However, clear evidence is necessary to show that a use has indeed been abandoned rather than simply having ceased with some intention to recommence; and this is particularly the case where the use in question is one which is by its nature intermittent or seasonal. Evidence may, however, be direct or indirect. Thus, for example, the period of time during which there has been non-use may, in an appropriate case, lead to an inference of abandonment. It should be noted, however, that *mere* cessation or abandonment of a use (without any subsequent resumption) does not amount to a change of use. Otherwise, by refusing planning permission for abandonment, a local planning authority could compel continuation of a use![29]

In recent years the case law has been much concerned with the question of the determination of the "planning unit" within which to assess whether there has been a material change of use. To take a simple example – is there a change of use when a use which was formerly carried on in one part of a person's land is transferred to another part? If the land is regarded as a single unit, the answer will be "no". If, however, the land is regarded as separate adjoining units, albeit in common ownership, the answer may be the opposite.

The approach of the courts has, broadly, been as follows. The starting-point has been to assume that the *unit of occupation as a whole* is the appropriate planning unit unless or until it appears that some smaller unit is appropriate. Where the land occupied is used for a single main "use" together with other incidental or ancillary uses, the fact that these other uses take place at particular defined locations (*eg* certain buildings or fields) does not by itself warrant division of the area into

---

28 *Hartley v Minister of Housing and Local Government* [1970] 1 QB 413.
29 Equally, where there have existed dual uses (neither ancillary to the other) and one use is abandoned, the fact that the other use becomes the single use of the land does not amount to development: *Philglow v S.S.E.* (1984) 51 P&CR 1.

separate planning units. Equally, it is still generally appropriate to consider the land as a single unit, where there are several activities carried on without any being merely incidental or ancillary to the others, in situations where the different activities are not confined rigidly to distinct areas of the land. However, where several unrelated activities are carried on in clearly distinct areas, it may be appropriate to regard each as a separate planning unit,[30] notwithstanding that the whole site may in terms of legal title (freehold or tenancy) be in single occupancy.

The statements in the last paragraph about identification of the appropriate planning unit in order properly to formulate questions about material change of use refer to the concept of uses which may be "ancillary" to, or "incidental" to, the main use of a site. This involves oblique reference to a doctrine under which the courts have accepted as lawful the engagement (without planning permission) in uses which may be regarded as ancillary/incidental to the (lawful) main or dominant use. To take an agricultural example, the use of land for agricultural purposes will permit the use of such land for the repair and maintenance of farm vehicles and equipment.[31] However, the use in question must be genuinely ancillary to the main use. Planning permission may be needed as and when the ancillary use acquires a "life of its own". To continue the example just given, the "ancillary" use may have acquired a life of its own where a farmer begins to repair other farmers' vehicles, or perhaps allows them to use his workshop facilities. Returning to the *bête-noire* of "caravans" and the like (*ie* movable structures of visually intrusive appearance), we may note that planning controls may not be applicable where the use to which such a "mobile" structure is put can be regarded as ancillary to the main use of the site in question.

Before completing our discussion of "material change of use", we should note that the TCP(GPD) Order permits "temporary use" of land without need for express application for planning

---

[30] *Burdle v S.S.E.* [1972] 1 WLR 1207.
[31] [1972] JPL 388.

permission. Such temporary use may be of any kind except use as a caravan site. The temporary use provisions do not apply, however, within buildings (*ie* we are concerned here with outdoor uses only); nor, in relation to areas which are sites of special scientific interest, do they permit motor sports (including practising), clay pigeon shooting or war games.

The temporary use provisions, where applicable, permit the use in question to occur for not more than 28 days in any calendar year (only 14 days where the use in question is the holding of a market, or motor sports). It is an as yet unresolved question whether a use which is periodic and apparently ongoing (*eg* on a regular monthly or fortnightly basis) can properly be regarded as a "temporary" use so as to fall within this provision. The better view is probably that use on such a regular and intendedly continuing basis requires planning permission. It is an *intermittent* use rather than a temporary one.

Agriculture and Forestry

As explained earlier, it is not *all* proposed development, as defined above, which requires planning permission. A number of important exceptions to this obligation exist. From our point of view the most significant of these exemptions are those which relate to agriculture and forestry. The legislation provides that the change of use of land from an existing use to use for the purpose of agriculture or forestry (including afforestation) (and also the use for such purposes of any building occupied together with[32] land so used) does not amount to development;[33] nor does any change from one kind of agriculture or forestry use to a different kind.[34] The very wide scope of this exemption from planning control is emphasised by the Act's definition of agriculture as including:

---

[32] For the breadth of meaning of this expression, see *N. Warwickshire B.C. v S.S.E. and Amrik Singh Gill* (1983) 50 P&CR 47.

[33] Town and Country Planning Act 1990 s.55(2)(e), as interpreted in *McKellen v Minister of Housing and Local Government* (1966) 188 E.G. 683.

[34] *Crowborough Parish Council v S.S.E.* [1981] JPL 281.

"horticulture, fruit growing, seed growing, dairy farming, the breeding and keeping of livestock (including any creature kept for the production of food, wool, skins or fur, or for the purpose of its use in the farming of land), the use of land as grazing land, meadow land, osier land, market gardens and nursery grounds and the use of land for woodlands where that use is ancillary to the farming of the land for other agricultural purposes."

It therefore follows that changes in the course of husbandry between pasture and arable, woodland and open meadow, and many other changes of use concerned with agriculture, are all outside the system of planning control.

In the days of traditional forms of agricultural activity, this approach may have seemed unexceptionable. However, in modern times, with farmers seeking new activities, or new techniques of agricultural production, both the policy of exemption from control and also the very scope of the concept of "agriculture" have become matters of debate. As regards the latter issue, the courts have been willing to accept that the concept covers intensive fox-breeding, notwithstanding that in the words of the planning inspector such activity "involved a form of animal husbandry which is [not] dependent upon the land for its subsistence ... The animals are permanently confined to specially constructed cages standing on previously open land, they are not reliant upon the surrounding land for exercise or for physical well-being, their food is not produced from the surrounding land but is imported in its entirety." The court was satisfied, nonetheless, that the use of the "buildings" should be regarded as agricultural. It was not necessary for the land *around* the cages to be used in support of that agricultural activity.[35] It should not, however, be thought that the concept of agricultural use can be stretched indefinitely. It has, for example, been held, perhaps inconsistently with the fox-breeding decision, that use for fish-farming may fall within the change of use exception where the fish are reared for food, but

---

[35] N. *Warwickshire B.C. v S.S.E. and Amrik Singh Gill* (1983) 50 P&CR 47.

not where their destiny is ornamental ponds or where they are reared to provide sport for anglers.[36]

Arguments have arisen in some instances as regards the circumstances in which the keeping of horses on land falls within the concept of agricultural use. It appears that to do so the horses must be kept on the land in order that they may "graze" there. If grazing is not a prime reason for the horses being present (eg their fodder is brought to the land), or if they only graze incidentally (the land principally providing recreational space), the use will not be agricultural. This distinction may be of significance where horses are stabled on land of insufficient size to produce adequate grazing. In such a case, the use not being agricultural, there may also be no permitted development rights in relation to the use of associated buildings as stables.

Retail sales of farm produce direct to the public would seem to come within the idea of "agricultural" use or, at least, it may be a legitimate use ancillary to agriculture. However, a distinction needs to be drawn here between the sale of raw produce of the particular farm in question, and retail sale of general farm produce cultivated across a variety of agricultural units. In the latter situation, the activity may well be regarded as a commercial activity in its own right and no longer a use ancillary to the agricultural use of the land.[37]

Further difficulties have surrounded the activities of farmers who have sought to *process* their own-grown produce on site, or who have provided storage facilities on a commercial basis for produce from other farms. In each such situation the courts have been prepared to regard the use as having extended beyond agricultural use of the planning unit in question.[38]

---

[36] [1980] JPL 480. Note that the *construction* of fish-farming facilities will normally amount to operational development. But note TCP(GPD) Order 1995 Part 5A.

[37] See further, [1992] JPL 366.

[38] See eg *Salvatore Cumbo v S.S.E.* [1992] JPL 740; *Warnock v S.S.E. and Dover D.C.* [1980] JPL 590.

The general policy of exclusion of agricultural matters from planning control is further evidenced by the fact that many building and other operations concerned with agriculture are covered by the General Permitted Development Order (Part 6) and, as such, their construction does not require express planning permission. This exemption applies only to agricultural land of more than 0.4 hectares (1 acre). For agricultural units of more than 5 hectares the permitted development is as set out under Class A; for units of between 0.4 and 5 hectares, Class B applies. Class C confers permitted development rights as regards the winning and working of minerals reasonably necessary for agricultural purposes within the same agricultural unit. The exemptions in Classes A and B apply to building or other operations which are "requisite for the use of that land for the purposes of agriculture". Class A permitted development may, subject to conditions and limitations, involve the *erection* of buildings; Class B development extends only to the *extension* or *alteration* of buildings. The building or alteration of *dwellings* is expressly excluded from the Order, but the provisions would cover a wide range of other matters such as barns, glass-houses and other agricultural buildings, the erection of fences, the removal of hedges, the filling in of dips in land to ease ploughing and cropping, and the filling in of ponds. Permitted development rights impose limitations as regards floor area, height, proximity to roads and other matters. Furthermore, local authorities may impose requirements as regards matters of siting, design and external appearance. The General Permitted Development Order contains parallel provisions conferring permitted development rights in relation to *forestry* buildings and operations (Part 7).

The policy of excluding agriculture and forestry from planning control has become increasingly controversial in recent years. The alteration of the agricultural landscape to secure greater efficiency in farming, most marked in eastern England, has had important consequences both for the visual appearance of the landscape, and also in terms of habitat protection for flora and fauna. The drainage of wetlands, the removal of hedgerows and copses to maximise field areas and facilitate use of modern machinery, the change in husbandry between arable and pasture as and when subsidy changes have altered their relative attractiveness, the block-planting of conifers in ways which mask the contours of valleys and hills, and other such matters have all given rise to much concern. Pleas that the agriculture and forestry exemptions be removed, or be made more limited, have been voiced on many occasions; but governments have resisted such demands, preferring to seek to protect the environment from agricultural and forestry damage in other ways than by giving a licensing power to planning authorities. Many of the alternative safeguards will be considered later in this book: see, for example, the discussion of Sites of Special Scientific Interest, Nature Reserves, Environmentally Sensitive Areas, management agreements entered into between landowners and public authorities such as the Countryside Agency or local authorities, environmental obligations attached to government grants (*eg* the Countryside Stewardship Scheme), duties in relation to the environment imposed by statute on the Forestry Commission and other public bodies, Tree Preservation Orders and Conservation Areas. Such methods of protection are of undeniable value, but are considered by some to be inadequate or ill-suited to protection of the ordinary, as distinct from the more especially valuable or beautiful, countryside. Moreover, some government policies on agriculture have, even in the relatively recent past, seemed to be in conflict with conservation objectives. The spectre of grant-aided removal of hedgerows and woodlands and drainage of wetlands attracted much criticism from conservationists, including publicly-funded bodies such as the Countryside Commission and the Nature Conservancy Council. The outlook appears, however, to be more promising. The trust in farmers to preserve and protect the landscape and countryside may in the first three post-war decades have been misplaced; but environmental knowledge and consciousness seems to be growing, and not least amongst the farming community. This, allied with problems of overproduction and the consequent need to encourage the "set aside" of land and the "extensification" of production gives cause for some optimism. Moreover, much progress is being made in terms of decoupling the link between agricultural grants and production levels, and integrating "environmental" conditions into grant schemes.

To the above statements about the exemption of changes in the agricultural use of land from any requirement to obtain official permission, there has recently (2002) been introduced one significant exception, albeit within a consent regime different from that of the planning system. This exception arises out of implementation in the United Kingdom of an EU law requirement that, prior to permission being afforded to certain activities, there must be conducted an investigation of the environmental impact of those proposed actions. In order to comply with this EU obligation, it has been necessary within the UK to subject certain agricultural operations to a system of official permitting and then to engraft the impact assessment obligations on to that permitting system.

The requirements in question do not apply to all changes in agricultural land use. They apply only where changes are proposed in respect of land which is presently uncultivated or which is in a "semi-natural" condition. Explaining the importance of the new controls, DEFRA has stated that they are designed to protect natural resources and promote sustainable agriculture by helping to stop any further loss of environmentally valuable uncultivated land and semi-natural areas in England – natural resources that have been in sharp decline since World War II. For example, there was a 97% loss of lowland unimproved grassland in England and Wales between 1930 and 1984, and an 84% loss of heathland between 1800 and the late 1980s.

The new controls apply to land within the following three main categories:

(i) *unimproved grassland, heath and moorland* (such as meadows and grazing pastures; downland or open or enclosed upland grassland; grassland with tree cover, such as orchards, parkland and wood pasture; lowland and coastal heathland; and moorland and upland rough grazing);

(ii) *scrubland* (where such land is cleared or managed so that it can be converted to arable or stock farming);

(iii) wetlands (such as marshes, fens, open water, watercourses, saltmarshes, ditches and ponds).

In relation to such lands, in some cases farmers now need to conduct an environmental impact assessment and seek DEFRA approval before undertaking any projects of the following kinds:

— cultivation;

— spreading soil or other material (including fertiliser or lime) in excess of existing routine application rates;

— drainage works;

— land reclamation;

— modifications to watercourses;

— flood defences;

— infilling ditches, ponds, pits, marshes or historic earthwork features;

— clearing vegetation in preparation for cultivation;

— introducing livestock (including poultry) at intensive stocking rates, or increasing stocking rates to intensive levels.

Where a farmer wishes to undertake any such project on the kinds of land listed above, the procedure is to seek a decision from DEFRA as to whether it appears that that project will give rise to "significant environment effects". Before forming a view on this DEFRA will consult with local authorities and a variety of interested statutory bodies.

If DEFRA takes the view that the project will not give rise to significant environmental effects the farmer may proceed. If DEFRA forms the opposite preliminary view the farmer is required to conduct an investigation of the likely environmental impacts and produce a public document – an Environmental Statement. It is on the basis of that investigation of the likely impacts of the proposed land use changes that DEFRA will make a final decision to allow (or otherwise) the project to proceed.

Procedures

So far in this chapter we have considered the circumstances in which planning permission is or is not needed. Assuming that a formal application for planning permission *is* required for an owner or occupier's proposed actions, the procedure is that he or she must make out a written application supported by plans of the site and send it, with the prescribed fee, to the local district council. The application will be acknowledged and a decision be given within two months, unless the applicant agrees to an extension of that time.

Significance of the Development Plan

Although all "development" has since the 1947 Act required local governmental planning permission, the approach which planning authorities were required by the Department of the Environment to adopt through most of this period was that a presumption should exist in favour of the grant of permission. This presumption should only be displaced where the proposed development would cause "demonstrable harm to interests of acknowledged importance".[39]

An amendment to the 1990 Act, made by the Planning and Compensation Act 1991, requires some restatement of this fundamental position. The new section 54A of the 1990 Act provides:

> "Where, in making any determination under the Planning Acts, regard is to be had to the development plan, the determination shall be made in accordance with the plan unless material considerations indicate otherwise."

Given that the development plan is, by virtue of section 70(2), a consideration to which planning authorities must have regard

---

[39] See *eg* White Paper – *Lifting the Burden* (1985).

in reaching their planning permission decisions, this new section now provides, in the language of revised *Planning Policy Guidance 1*:

> "a presumption in favour of development proposals which are in accordance with the development plan."

The document continues:

> "An applicant who proposes a development which is clearly in conflict with the development plan [will] need to produce convincing reasons to demonstrate why the plan should not prevail."

The effect of section 54A is to enhance the status of the development plan in guiding planning authorities as to their decisions. Its intention was to bolster the planning legislation's original scheme of being a "plan led" system of discretionary political decision-making. The legislative change has made it all the more important for a broad variety of persons to monitor proposed amendments to structure and, more particularly, local plans. The "new" presumption in favour of the development plan applies, of course, in both directions. Applications in conformity should carry high expectation of approval; applications in conflict will need to be accompanied by much persuasive argument.

We noted earlier that planning authorities have since 1947 been required to have regard to the development plan in coming to development control decisions. They have also been required to have regard to all "other material considerations". This phrase has bred a substantial case-law. Through a long succession of cases the inspectors, Ministers and the courts have been called upon to decide rather difficult questions as regards what are, and what are not, considerations relevant or material to the proper exercise of planning decision-making functions. Whatever uncertainty may, nevertheless, exist in relation to certain factors, it is reasonably clear that many environmental considerations will be regarded as relevant to the operation of planning controls. Matters such as visual amenity, traffic congestion, noise and odours have for long been considerations high on the agenda of planning authority concerns. This is not to say, however, that planning authorities should seek by their decisions to supplant the regulatory functions of the specific environmental pollution regulatory bodies. Indeed, recent case-law[40] and a planning guidance document (PPG 23) have affirmed the view that planning authorities should decide applications on an assumption of adequate ongoing regulation, inspection and enforcement by the environmental agencies.

A quite recent modification to national planning policy should here be noted. In March 2001, the central planning ministry made clear to local planning authorities that they should take a *positive* approach to well-conceived farm diversification proposals for business purposes which are consistent in their scale with the rural location; and that farm diversification proposals should not be rejected when they will give rise to only modest additional traffic and will not have significant impact on minor roads.

Environmental Impact Assessment (EIA)

In this way it has been possible to argue that, at least in relation to matters requiring application for planning permission, this country has for half a century possessed arrangements for the environmental impact assessment of development proposals. However, in modern usage the phrase "environmental impact assessment" refers to something rather more thorough and systematic that the arrangements just described. When the EC agreed the terms of its Environmental Assessment Directive in 1985[41] (effective from 1988), it required of the United Kingdom that a more elaborate system be engrafted upon the basic structure of planning decision-making.

The 1985 Directive was revised, and its ambit quite significantly extended, in 1997.[42] The essential aim of environmental impact assessment remains, however. It is a means of drawing

---

[40] *Gateshead M.B.C. v S.S.E.* [1995] JPL 432.
[41] EC Directive 85/337.
[42] EC Directive 97/11.

together in a systematic way a project's likely significant environmental effects, and to put this information into the public domain prior to any official consent being afforded. It involves processes which may bring to light, at a relatively early stage of project design, alternative forms of development which may have a lesser environmental impact.

The Directive does not apply to all species of development. Rather, it lists a range of kinds of development project which fall within the scope of its provisions. The list is in two parts. Those in Annex I comprise projects in respect of which environmental assessment is mandatory in all cases.[43] Those in Annex II come within the Directive's requirements only in cases where the local planning authority considers that such assessment is required because of the likelihood that the project in question will give rise to significant effects on the environment by virtue of factors such as its nature, size or location.[44]

The lists within the Annexes are quite long (particularly Annex II). The transposition of the Directive into English law has been principally by means of the Town and Country Planning (Assessment of Environmental Effects) Regulations 1999. A procedure exists whereby a developer may seek an early decision from the local authority about whether what is proposed falls within Schedule I or Schedule II to the Regulations (equivalent to the Annexes referred to above); and if within Schedule II, whether the authority considers EIA to be necessary. There is also a procedure by which a developer may obtain a "scoping" opinion from the local planning authority, indicating its views on the matters upon which the Environment Statement should focus, and the matters which are likely not to be of importance.

A matter in respect of which some concern has been expressed is the possibility of a developer dividing a project into a number of ostensibly separate developments for the purpose of obtaining planning permission. Is it possible in this way to avoid EIA

---

[43] *eg* intensive rearing of poultry or pigs beyond a certain threshold.
[44] *eg* changes to uncultivated land and to "semi-natural" areas.

requirements, on the assumption that whatever might be the impact of the project considered as a whole, the likely impact of each component may be acknowledged to be relatively slight. The answer is that such evasion may be prevented by local planning authorities. It seems that, in reaching their decisions about whether each such Schedule II project should be subject to EIA, they may take into account not just the likely impact of that particular project but also of the more substantial development of which it is in reality an integral part.[45]

In cases where EIA is required, what obligations are imposed? The first point to make is that where EIA applies the developer is required to submit to the planning authority what is called an Environmental Statement. This comprises a document, or series of documents, providing specified information. The development proposed must be described, along with a description of its likely effects (direct and indirect) on the environment. The effects must be explained by reference to the possible impact on the following matters:

— human beings, fauna and flora;

— soil, water, air, climate and landscape;

— the inter-action between the factors listed above;

— material assets and the cultural heritage.

In any case where significant adverse effects are identified in relation to any of these matters, the statement must describe the measures envisaged in order to avoid, reduce or remedy those effects.

The information in the Environmental Statement is designed to promote informed decision-making. Its preparation typically requires the expertise of technically qualified environmental consultants. The danger that such persons might produce a report of bewildering scientific complexity and hence of little value to "lay" decision-makers was appreciated by the legislators.

---

[45] *R. v Swale B.C. and Medway Ports Authority ex p RSPB* [1991] JPL 32.

Hence the requirement that, within the Environmental Statement, a non-technical summary must be provided.

The Environmental Statement is not a document intended for the eyes of the planning authority alone. It is intended not just to assist that body in its eventual decision, but also as a document to be available to the public and other interested bodies (*eg* a range of statutory consultees with interests and responsibilities for a variety of facets of the environment) in order to provide a solid foundation for informed debate. The statement is therefore a vehicle to assist and raise the quality of objectors' contributions to the process leading up to the planning authority's decision. For this reason, the regulations contain requirements as regards site display, press notices and public deposit of the statement.

Before we leave the matter of environmental assessment, we should note that, although most of the obligations under the EC Directive have proven capable of being transposed into English law within the context of planning consent procedures, this has not been the case in respect of certain categories of project. The reason is two-fold. On the one hand, certain of the kinds of project listed in the Directive do not fall within the realm of United Kingdom planning control (*eg* afforestation). Second, certain projects there listed were found to fall within planning permission but within the categories covered by permitted development rights. In order that the United Kingdom should comply with its obligations there has been required, first, a substantial number of specific measures to incorporate assessment into such decision-making procedures as exist in respect of such projects (and in some cases to introduce new permission requirements, *eg* in the context of forestry);[46] and, secondly, to withdraw permitted development rights in order to bring any such environmentally impacting projects into the development consent procedures.[47]

---

[46] Environmental Impact Assessment (Forestry) (England and Wales) Regulations 1999 (S.I. 1999/2228).

[47] TCP (Environmental Assessment and Permitted Development) Regulations 1995 (S.I. 1995/1199).

Planning Conditions

A planning authority granting planning permission may do so either unconditionally or "subject to such conditions as they think fit".[48] The courts have, however, imposed certain limits on this ostensibly unlimited power to attach conditions. In particular, a condition must have been imposed for a planning purpose and not for an ulterior purpose; and the condition must fairly and reasonably relate to the development permitted by the planning permission. It must also be reasonably precise in its terms (an aspect of elementary administrative fairness: and also relevant to its enforceability), and it must not be unreasonable in its terms.[49] Accordingly, a condition in a planning permission for a caravan site which required the implementation of a rent control scheme was held invalid as not relating to amenity and so not being for a planning purpose.[50]

Appeals and Third Party Interests

Any refusal of permission, or attachment of conditions to permission, must be accompanied by reasons. If an application is refused, or if the applicant regards conditions that may have been attached to a grant of planning permission as unacceptable, (s)he has the right to appeal to the Secretary of State.[51]

Such appeals are in most cases determined by inspectors, appointed by the Secretary of State, who reach their decisions, in simple cases, after consideration of the papers and an informal visit to the site; and, in more important cases, following the holding of a local public inquiry. Since the early 1980s the policy has been to restrict cases where the decision is taken by the Secretary of State, rather than by an inspector, to cases involving clear issues of regional or national, and not just local, policy. Examples of the former have included the application by the National Coal Board to mine the Vale of Belvoir, and the application by the British Airports Authority

---

[48] TCPA 1990 s.70(1).
[49] *Newbury District Council v S.S.E.* [1981] AC 578.
[50] *Mixnam's Properties Ltd. v Chertsey U.D.C.* [1965] AC 735.
[51] TCPA 1990 s.78(1).

to develop Stansted. Inspectors are members of the Planning Inspectorate, an executive agency with a degree of independence from the central planning ministry, the office of the Deputy Prime Minister. Inspectors are independent and impartial as between the local authority and the appellant.

If the appellant is unsuccessful in this appeal, he may exercise a further right of appeal to the High Court. However, a significant limitation to this appellate function of the courts must be stressed. In hearing such appeals the court is confined to determining whether the planning authority or the Minister has erred *in law* (or as to a matter of procedure); the court is not concerned with issues of fact or planning merits. In other words, the courts take the view that, provided the decision-maker has understood correctly the legal and planning policy principles applicable, his actual decision, reached in applying those principles to the facts, is not challengeable by appeal to the courts. The court will not interfere simply on the grounds that it might itself have come to a different conclusion. The application of a legal rule to facts is in such cases labelled a "matter of fact and degree" rather than a matter of "law". The role of the courts is therefore a limited one, confined to situations where reasons for a decision disclose a clear misunderstanding or misinterpretation of the applicable legal principles; and also to cases where although no such *express* mis-statement is apparent, nevertheless the decision reached on the evidence is so unreasonable as to permit an *inference* that the law applicable has been misunderstood.[52] The significance of this is that it makes the Ministry and not the courts the final arbiter of issues of planning merits; and an understanding of Ministry policy on particular planning issues is essential to an informed knowledge of planning law. To this end, the Office of the Deputy Prime Minister's Planning Policy Guidance notes (PPG),[53] its circulars giving guidance to planning

---

[52] See, for example, *Bendles Motors Ltd. v Bristol Corporation* [1963] 1 WLR 247.

[53] Gradually being superseded by shorter, and more focused, Planning Policy Statements (PPSs).

authorities, and summaries of decisions[54] reached on planning appeals are of considerable importance.

A further point to note in connection with planning appeals is that, where planning permission has been *refused* by the planning authority, and the would-be developer appeals against that refusal, there will be an opportunity for local objectors to state their views to the inspector before the appeal is decided. In contrast, local objectors may have less opportunity to make known their views in cases where the local planning authority are minded to *grant* planning permission. No neighbour, or other affected person, has any right of appeal against a *grant* of planning permission. Accordingly, residents and amenity groups need to be vigilant as to planning applications (*eg* by keeping watch over the public register of applications), so as to be able to make known their views to the local planning authority *before* it reaches its decision. Some enhancement of arrangements for giving publicity to applications has occurred following the Planning and Compensation Act 1991 and regulations are now to be found in the General Permitted Development Order 1995 (variously, site, neighbour and/or newspaper notification depending on the nature of the development). Further, it should be noted that in this connection an alert parish council may exert a valuable influence. Such councils, which exist in all rural areas, have a right to be informed about proposals for development within their areas,[55] thus ensuring for themselves opportunity to make their objections known to the district council before any decision is taken.

In this context, a procedure whereby the Secretary of State may "call-in" a planning application is significant.[56] Where this procedure is brought into operation, the local planning authority reaches no decision on the application. If objections are lodged

---

[54] To be found in, for example, the *Journal of Planning and Environmental Law*, the *Estates Gazette*, and *Planning Appeals*. PPGs and Circulars are included in the *Encyclopaedia of Planning Law* (Sweet and Maxwell).
[55] Local Government Act 1972 Sched. 16, para 20.
[56] TCPA 1990 s.77.

with the Secretary of State, following the call-in, the matter will go to public local inquiry. It will be appreciated that this procedure can give opportunities for objectors to present their cases in contexts where, were the local authority minded to have *granted* permission, their views would not have received such formal attention; nor would objectors have had such opportunity to test by cross-examination the arguments alleged to favour the development in question.

An important question for objectors is, therefore, how willing will the Secretary of State be to call-in planning applications under this procedure. The basic approach to the exercise of this discretion has been clearly stated. The Secretary of State's view has for long been that he should be "very reluctant, except in cases raising important issues of broader than just local significance, to interfere with the ordinary process where initial decisions are taken by locally accountable bodies".

DEVELOPMENT PLANS

In order to assist planning authorities in their many decisions as to planning permission, and also to try to secure some degree of consistency and predictability in relation to those planning decisions, the planning legislation provides for such decisions to be taken against the back-drop of a development plan for the area. Such plans have been drawn up (and revised) by a process involving survey of existing land use, forecast of future needs, production of draft proposals as to optimum future land use, consultation, and public inquiry into objections, prior to eventual approval.

At present, outside London, the metropolitan urban areas, Wales and the new unitary authorities, a development plan consists of two documents: a structure plan and a number of local plans. The former is essentially a written statement supported by diagrams, outlining the county planning authority's general policies in respect of future development in the area, including measures for the improvement of the physical environment and the management of traffic. It contains no maps. Local plans, the responsibility of district councils, supplement the structure plan. They consist of maps with accompanying text, giving relatively detailed information as to planning policy in relation to particular geographical areas. In the metropolitan areas and the unitary districts, where there is single-tier local government, there will be a single plan, but that plan will be divided into two distinct parts, replicating the distinction described above.

This system has not worked entirely satisfactorily. Much of the problem has been that plan-making procedures have been complex (involving rights to lodge objections, public inquiries, etc.) and so, all too frequently, an up-to-date structure and local plan for any particular area has not existed. There has also been felt to be too little input in terms of "regional planning": consideration of spatial planning needs from a perspective broader than even the present "county" viewpoint.

In this latter context it should be noted that as from late 2004 the Planning and Compulsory Purchase Act 2004 will introduce Regional Spatial Strategies (to which development plans must conform) and move the focus of development plan revision down to district council level (rather than being shared between counties and district).

ENFORCEMENT

The preparation of development plans and the requirement of obtaining planning permission would be meaningless in the absence of adequate means of *enforcement* of planning controls. Consequently, the legislation provides that the planning authority may take certain steps in any case of breach of planning control. By "breach of planning control" is meant the carrying out of development without planning permission where such permission is required by law; or the failure to have observed conditions imposed on the grant of permission.

In order to assist planning authorities to obtain information about suspected breaches of control, and also to acquire information necessary for proper initiation of other enforcement procedures, the 1991 Act has introduced a procedure involving service of a "planning contravention notice". Such a notice may require the recipient (owner, occupier or person carrying out operations or using the land) to give such information as may be specified about, amongst other things, any operation carried out on the land, any use of the land, and any matter relating to any conditions subject to which planning permission in respect of the land has been granted. The notice may also, amongst other things, require the recipient to state whether or not the land is being used for a specified purpose, or whether any operations specified are or have been carried on on the land, or state when any such use or operations began. Failure to provide such requested information is an offence.

Armed with the necessary information, the planning authority may proceed by way of enforcement notice procedure. A copy of an enforcement notice must be served on every owner or occupier of the land in question. The notice will require cessation of the offending operations or change of use, as the case may be; and probably require the return or reversion to the *status quo ante*. In the case of breach of planning control by failure to comply with a planning condition, the notice will require compliance with that condition. If the enforcement notice which has been served is not complied with within the time stated in the notice, any person failing to have complied with its terms may be prosecuted for an offence before the local magistrates. It is the failure to comply with the enforcement notice which constitutes the offence; it is not, in general, an offence simply to act in breach of planning control. In the case of breach of control by unauthorised building operations, a failure to comply with an enforcement notice may be followed by the local planning authority exercising its powers to enter onto the land in question and pull down the offending building, and the planning authority may recover its reasonable expenses in so acting from the person in default, suing that person in the courts if necessary.

The legislation does, however, impose a time limit within which planning authorities must act if they wish to issue enforcement notices. This time limit obliges authorities to issue such notices not more than four years after the substantial completion of the breach of planning control which is complained of. However, this time limit only applies in relation to "operations" type development and not to unauthorised changes of use. An unauthorised change of use may be the subject of an enforcement notice except where the offending use commenced more than ten years prior to enforcement action. However, where the change of use is of a building to a single dwelling-house, a four year limitation period applies.

Instead of waiting to be prosecuted, a person served with a copy of an enforcement notice may prefer to try to protect his position by appealing against its terms to the Secretary of State. On such an appeal the appellant may argue that what he has done, or is doing, does not amount to development, or that he does not need planning permission for the development because of the General Permitted Development Order or the Use Classes Order. It is also possible on an appeal against an enforcement notice to argue that, although planning permission was necessary, had it been applied for it ought to have been granted, and accordingly that it is not appropriate for the planning authority to have issued an enforcement notice. Similarly, where an enforcement notice relates to an alleged breach of a condition attached to a planning permission, it is possible on an appeal to the Secretary of State to argue that such a planning condition should not have been imposed in the first place.

Any such appeal to the Secretary of State will be dealt with in a manner similar to that on an appeal against a *refusal* of planning permission: that is, by an inspector, appointed by the Secretary of State, and the inspector will usually take the decision himself. There is a further right of appeal on a point of law (and *not* on an issue of planning merits) from the decision of the Secretary of State (or more usually his inspector) to the High Court.

During the period in which an appeal against an enforcement notice is being dealt with, the "development" which is the subject-matter of the notice may, quite lawfully, continue. No offence is committed, and no enforcement action may take place, until after the appeal has been finally determined. There is, however, a power to issue a "stop notice". Such a notice will bring into play criminal penalties if development continues pending the appeal being heard. Local authorities must, however, act with some circumspection in issuing stop notices. If the appeal against the enforcement notice proves successful, the planning authority will be liable to give compensation for any losses suffered in complying with the stop notice.

The enforcement notice procedure provides exemplary fairness to owners and occupiers of land as regards the hurdles which a planning authority must satisfactorily surmount prior to successful enforcement action (involving perhaps a requirement to demolish a building, or to cease an offending "commercial livelihood" use).

This is perfectly proper. Nevertheless, it was apparent that the procedures were inappropriate in respect of enforcement action in relation to the generally quite minor matter of breaches of planning conditions. Therefore, the 1991 Act introduced a new procedure for the summary enforcement of breaches of planning conditions. There is now an alternative, in this context, to procedure by way of enforcement notice. It involves service of a "breach of condition" notice. No route of appeal to the Secretary of State is provided. Instead, in any case where the breach of condition continues, a prosecution will lie before the Magistrates' Court. At this point a defence may be raised that the defendant had taken all reasonable steps to comply with the terms of the notice.

RURAL PLANNING ISSUES

Urban Sprawl

A major concern during the post-war period has been to preserve the rural landscape from urban sprawl. The uncontrolled suburban development which was such a marked feature of the inter-war period became, after the war, subject to a degree of planning constraint, the new emphasis being placed on the development of New Towns rather than the enlargement of existing urban areas. The "green belts" policy will be considered later but, quite apart from this specific device, in the post-war years there has been a very deliberate policy of trying to contain development within the perimeters of cities and towns, with restriction of new building to "infill" sites: "brown" field rather than "green" field sites. In the immediate post-war period this policy was not of great hardship to developers owing to the need to reconstruct areas of towns destroyed by war-time blitz and the consequent ready availability of sites. In more recent decades the relative attractions to developers of the two kinds of sites have changed. Remaining inner-city sites may be costly to develop owing to land contamination which may need remediation. Public access to "out of town" sites has become very much greater, as traffic congestion within cities has increased. Moreover, people have chosen to seek to live on the edges or outside cities rather than to live in the hearts of, even regenerated, metropolises. This has placed strains on planning policies. These pressures seem set to continue. In spite of population stability, the trend towards smaller family groups and persons living alone is producing a substantial housing need, particularly in the already more congested south-east of England. The Office of the Deputy Prime Minister believes England may need some four million new homes over the next 20 years.

As well as trying to contain urban sprawl in the general sense, there has also long been a policy against ribbon development,[57] with its particular evil of securing the coalescence of formerly separate and distinct towns.

Although not all would agree, these policies have been pursued with some measure of success. The extent of loss of agricultural land to industrial and residential development has been less than would otherwise have been the case; and there have been preserved, within a few miles of even the grimiest and drabbest of our cities, areas of easily accessible and relatively unspoilt countryside. There are, as always, contrary arguments. Some,

---

[57]   Restriction of Ribbon Development Act 1935.

for instance, would point to the high price of, consequentially scarce, development land and also to the resulting high density of communal city living. It is, however, a salutary experience from time to time to fly over the congested south-east of England and to note how little building is visible in comparison with the acres of fields, forest and so on.

As applied to specifically *rural* areas, these general policies have sought to restrict sporadic development to that which is necessary to sustain agriculture. Even development for such purposes (*ie* new farm dwellings) is restricted whenever possible to existing towns and villages. Moreover, geographical expansion of villages to satisfy commuter demand has been a matter that has generally been closely watched. In some cases planning permission for dwellings has been granted subject to the condition that the building be for agricultural workers exclusively, though such conditions are notoriously difficult to enforce. When granting permission for a new agricultural dwelling subject to such an occupancy condition, local planning authorities may also attach similar conditions to existing buildings on the holding, which are under the control of the applicant, do not already have occupancy conditions and are needed in connection with the farm. Where building within or immediately around villages is acceptable, there is a need to ensure that the design of such buildings, and the materials used, are appropriate. The Countryside Agency has piloted a scheme whereby villages produce "village design statements" indicating the main features of local vernacular building. These statements should then feed into local development control policies and counter the growing trend towards national standardisation in the design and appearance of new houses.

In addition to, and supporting, these general policies of containment there has been an especially strong policy of development restraint in relation to a number of particularly highly valued parts of the countryside. These areas include the National Parks, Areas of Outstanding Natural Beauty, Green-Belts, Sites of Special Scientific Interest and what are called, informally, Areas of High Landscape Value. Such areas, along with uplands little suited to development projects, extend to well over half of the total area of England and Wales. The onus on the developer, which may be difficult in any rural area, becomes still greater in such areas.

Industry and Employment

Although these policies are to be welcomed, and many conservationists would call for them to be applied more strongly, there are associated difficulties and dangers. What policy should be adopted, for example, as regards the establishment of businesses and industrial operations in rural areas? It is too easy to suggest blanket exclusion. Ultimately, we may need to accept that if commercial development brings employment, and if employment sustains the population and economy of the countryside's villages, then some degree of landscape harm may be a price worth paying. Much, of course, will depend on the nature of the development in question; and in this connection the Department of the Environment issued a circular as long ago as 1980 reminding us that much industry today is not smoky and noisy as of old, but clean and "hi-tech". Accordingly, it was likely that there would be no serious planning objections to the establishment of such industrial or commercial concerns in residential areas or rural areas. The circular specifically mentioned the suitability of disused agricultural buildings for fledgling small businesses.

Recreation and Leisure

This leads us to a similar issue: to what extent are we willing to sacrifice features of the landscape in order that people may visit and enjoy the countryside? Where is the balance to be drawn between fast access roads to the most scenic areas, and the preservation of the landscape, together with its flora and fauna, in the areas which may be spoiled in constructing those roads. When visitors arrive in the countryside, they wish to be able to park their cars. Car parks are therefore needed. Visitors wish to be able to stay overnight, or for a holiday. Provision is therefore needed for hotels, caravan sites and camping sites. Policies of total exclusion of things such as these may be appropriate for certain prime landscape areas, but generally the task set for planners and developers is one of skilfully siting and landscaping such development so that it is as unobtrusive as is possible. A caravan site on a coastal promontory is an eyesore; if sited in an incline and masked by trees it may offend relatively few and provide moderately priced accommodation for many.

The issue of caravan sites has in fact been a matter in respect of which additional legislative controls have been provided by Parliament. Problems arose during the 1950s from the proliferation of sites, in many cases unauthorised, both for residential and holiday caravaning. Concern focused not only on the despoilment of the landscape which was resulting from inappropriately prominent sites, but also on the lack of proper services and equipment at many sites. The latter public health problem was in large part a result of the common practice of planning authorities granting planning permission for such use on a seasonal basis only.

In 1960, therefore, caravan sites became subject to legislative requirements which operate alongside, and in additional to, ordinary planning controls. The Caravan Sites and Control of Development Act 1960 provides that caravan sites, whether residential or for holiday use, must be licensed by the local authority. A local authority may restrict use of a site to holiday rather than residential caravaning by the use of appropriate planning conditions: for example, a condition limiting use of the site to the summer season, and perhaps also requiring removal of the caravans at the end of each season.[58]

SPECIAL CONTROLS

Advertisements

The legislation also provides a number of *special* controls in relation to certain matters. Thus, there are provisions which

---

[58] For limits to such power see *eg Babbage v N. Norfolk D.C.* [1990] JPL 411.

subject the display of outdoor advertisements (a term which is widely defined[59]) to local authority consent. Application for consent is necessary except in relation to a limited category of exempted classes of advertisement and a category of advertisements in respect of which consent is *deemed* to have been obtained, but in respect of which the local planning authority may order discontinuance. The planning authority's decision, if it be to refuse consent, must be taken on grounds of amenity or public safety. Against refusal of consent, or a discontinuance order, appeal lies to the Secretary of State. A person who displays an advertisement without consent (where this is required) or in defiance of a discontinuance order commits a criminal offence.

Such controls are valuable in allowing local authorities to prevent despoliation of the countryside and architecturally attractive buildings by large numbers of, often gigantic, hoardings as is characteristic of many other countries. Moreover, it helps secure road safety by permitting the prevention of a multitude of commercial signs at cross-roads and roundabouts. Control over advertisements may be made even greater if a district planning authority, with ministerial consent, declares an area to be one of special control. In such event, most of the normal exemptions from control, referred to above, cease to apply. Nearly half of England and Wales is now in this special control category, including nearly all areas of open countryside.[60]

Listed Buildings

Also subject to special controls under the planning legislation are buildings of "special architectural or historic" interest. Insofar as the attractiveness of our countryside is enhanced by certain of the individual buildings to be found within it, it is

---

[59] "... any word, letter, model, sign, placard, board, notice, awning, blind, device or representation ... in the nature of, and employed wholly or partly for the purposes of advertisement, announcement or direction ..." Town and Country Planning (Control of Advertisements) Regulations 1992 r.(1); TCPA 1990 s.336.

[60] A consultation paper issued by the DOE in 1996 has suggested that the "special area" arrangement is unnecessary and should be discontinued.

appropriate for special restrictions to apply to them. The Planning (Listed Buildings and Conservation Areas) Act 1990 provides for the listing, by the Secretary of State, of buildings which are to be subject to this special control. As the system has been in operation for some years, the significance now lies in the *addition* of buildings to the lists. Such addition may result from periodic systematic survey work in relation to buildings in particular areas or of particular types. Alternatively, it may follow from lobbying by a local authority or amenity society. The decision to list a building may have very significant implications (financial and also more simply in terms of his or her freedom to alter the property) for owners of buildings. Yet there is no obligation to notify such persons of impending listing (lest damage immediately be done); nor is there any right to appeal against listing. Nevertheless, opportunities are offered *after* listing for owners and occupiers to make representations informally to the Office of the Deputy Prime Minister. Such representations may prompt a review of the listing.

The listing process has now brought some half a million individual buildings within this scheme of control. A non-statutory grading scheme is used to indicate the relative merit of buildings: Grade I, Grade II* and Grade II. All but about six per cent of buildings fall within the lowest of these categories. Even in respect of these, however, "every effort" should be made as regards their preservation. The criteria for listing have recently been simplified and are now set out in PPG 15 (1994). The principal factors are stated to comprise: architectural interest (design, decoration, craftsmanship, building type, techniques); historic interest (important aspects of the nation's social, economic, cultural or military history); historical associations (close association with nationally important persons, allied to some quality in the fabric of the building itself); group value (where several buildings provide important examples of architectural unity). In addition, the age of a building is likely to be significant. Although some quite modern buildings are listed, the intention is to include a small number only of examples of modern building types.

Where a building is listed it becomes an offence for any person to demolish it; or to alter or extend the building so as to affect its character as a building of special architectural or historic interest, unless in either case listed building consent has been first obtained from the district planning authority.[61]

Applications for listed building consent must be advertised and expressly brought to the notice of certain amenity groups and public bodies. Against a refusal of listed building consent appeal lies to the Secretary of State.

There also exists a procedure by which a local planning authority can serve a building preservation order in respect of a building threatened with demolition which it may consider should be listed. This provides a breathing space of six months. Compensation is, however, payable if, within that period of time, the building is not listed.

The position of owners of listed buildings is safeguarded to some extent by provisions of the legislation. If listed building consent is refused and the owner is unable to make reasonably beneficial use of the building, he may serve a listed building purchase notice on the local authority. On the other hand, owners who fail to take appropriate care of listed buildings may find themselves served with a "repairs notice" requiring specified works to be done to ensure proper preservation of the building. If such steps are not taken in accordance with the notice served, there exists a power by which the local authority may compulsorily purchase the building, subject to payment of compensation at site value only. A palliative exists in that a local authority may, under the Local Authorities (Historic Buildings) Act 1962, make grants towards the preservation and maintenance by private owners of historic buildings. Owners may also seek assistance from the National Heritage Memorial Fund, administered by English Heritage under the National Heritage Act 1983.

---

[61] For details of what is regarded as affecting the character of such buildings, see PPG 15 Annex C.

Conservation Areas

A local authority power with a similar objective to that of control over individual listed buildings is the power to declare an area a "conservation area".[62] This is valuable where a group or cluster of buildings warrants preservation or enhancement on architectural or historic grounds even though individually none may merit listing as a historic building. More than 8000 conservation areas have been created.

The effect of creating a conservation area is to subject applications for planning permission to greater scrutiny. Development plans are likely to contain policies which constrain development in such areas. Moreover, the legislation specially provides that attention be paid to the "desirability of preserving or enhancing the character or appearance of the area": a formula which imposes clear planning restraint upon any positively unsympathetic development.[63]

Permitted development rights are more restricted in conservation areas than generally otherwise. Nevertheless, a report in 1992 by the English Towns Forum has drawn attention to the harm being done to the visual appearance of historic towns even *within* the scope of such narrowed permitted development rights (*eg* changes to traditional windows, doors, railings, roof materials). Further, the *demolition* of buildings comes clearly within local authority control requiring conservation area consent (except as regards categories of building excluded by regulations).[64] Although it is fair to regard conservation areas as primarily a matter of urban planning control, the powers may be valuable also in rural areas, protecting, for example, buildings clustered around a village green or, in some cases, an entire village.

Trees

Provisions of the legislation also provide special protection for individual trees, groups of trees and woodlands by the Tree

---

[62] The power dates from the Civic Amenities Act 1967.
[63] See *S. Lakeland D.C. v S.S.E.* [1992] 1 All ER 573.
[64] See above, p.42 for the position under the ordinary planning legislation.

Preservation Order procedure. This will be considered more fully below in Chapter 4.

RUS IN URBE

In 1902 Ebenezer Howard wrote his influential book *Garden Cities of Tomorrow*, in which he proposed the construction of new towns to relieve the stresses of overcrowded urban life. His objective was an urban environment in which every householder would be able to glimpse at least green fields, while still enjoying the advantages of city life. This notion of *Rus in Urbe* was soon realised in some measure by the development, by private enterprise, of Welwyn Garden City and Letchworth before the First World War.

After World War II the "new town" idea was adopted energetically by the central government. Under the New Towns Act 1946 and its successors some twenty-six new towns have been built in Great Britain in order to help relieve congestion in overcrowded cities, and to ease housing shortages that had been made acute by the devastations of enemy action. Few of these towns may resemble Howard's ideal garden cities but they have certainly gone some way to the achievement of his principal objectives. Howard's ideas can be seen also influencing recent pressures for a "greening" of cities which may improve the look of town centres generally in the future.

No further new towns are at present planned under the machinery of the New Towns Acts, but in recent years private enterprise has been pressing for planning permission to develop considerable areas of open countryside in the South-East of England as modern-day equivalents of the statutory "new towns".

The *Rus in Urbe* concept may also be seen behind the idea of the "green-belt". This is really nothing more than an area of land encircling a large city or urbanised area which is marked out on plans and maps as intended to be kept free from substantial development, thus restricting the creeping enlargement of the urban area, and in some instances preventing the coalescence of adjacent urban areas. The concept was given statutory effect in the case of London by the Metropolitan Green Belt Act 1938 (pre-dating the general comprehensive controls of the Town and Country Planning Act 1947), but elsewhere the observance and continued existence of a green-belt depends entirely on the administration by the local planning authority of the ordinary controls over development under the planning Acts. The total area of land designated as green-belt is increasing: it doubled in area between 1979 and 1989. Nevertheless, in recent years green-belts have been under increasing threat; there were indications from central government in the early 1980s that land in a green-belt could perhaps be released for housing development where suitable building land was in acutely short supply. However, a strong green-belt policy has more recently been reasserted. For example, PPG 6 states categorically that major out-of-town shopping developments have no place in the green-belt nor, generally, in the open countryside. This has been bolstered by the terms of the revised PPG 2 on Green Belts (1995). Nevertheless, as with other planning restraint policies, it cannot be said that green-belts are complete "no go" areas for development. Notwithstanding a strong presumption against many forms of development, the matter ultimately depends on an overall assessment of planning merits. It may be that "very special circumstances" may warrant departure from the normal embargo on development.[65] Ordinarily, however, development on Green Belts is restricted to agriculture, forestry, outdoor sport and outdoor recreation and other uses which preserve the openness of the land.

---

[65]   See, for example, the *British Airways* planning application: [1993] NPC 85; and the *Boss Trucks* application: [1992] JPL 1157.

APPEALS AND INQUIRIES

Procedure

In many of the situations discussed in various parts of this book there is a statutory right to appeal against a decision taken, or order made, by some organ of the executive (very commonly a local authority) to a Minister of the Crown, usually the Secretary of State for the Environment. The commonest example of such a right is the right of appeal against a refusal of planning permission, or against the terms of an enforcement notice; but such rights of appeal "to the Minister" are a common feature of British public administration and apply also, to take examples relevant to later chapters, to the service of notices in relation to Sites of Special Scientific Interest[66] and orders diverting or closing public footpaths.[67] Similar procedures, involving public inquiries, also apply in situations where legislation requires ministerial confirmation of an act or order of a local authority or other body: for example, a compulsory purchase order.

In matters of detail, the procedure regulating such appeals will vary slightly from one context to another; but the basic pattern is reasonably uniform, and can be outlined in general terms.

On receipt of the notice, order or decision against which it is desired to appeal, notice of the appeal must be lodged with the Secretary of State within a specified period of time. The Secretary of State will then refer the case to a "person appointed by him" (commonly called an "inspector", although this term does not appear in the legislation). The inspector will arrange for a local inquiry to be convened, unless, in the case of the less important planning appeals (of which there are a very

---

66 Wildlife and Countryside Act 1981 s.29 as amended by Wildlife and Countryside (Amendment) Act 1985. See further, Chapter 4, below.
67 Highways Act 1980 ss.118, 119 and Sched. 6. See further, Chapter 3, below.

large number), it is decided, with the appellant's agreement, to determine the case on the papers by "written representations".

Where there is to be a local inquiry, advance notice must be given of the time and place at which it is to be held. Inquiries will normally be in the locality of the site in question and are often held at the town hall.

Prior to the hearing, the appellant will be invited to state the grounds of his appeal, and the administrative body against whose action or decision the appeal is being brought may be required to disclose matters upon which it proposes to rely at the hearing. The idea is that advance disclosure aids preparation for the hearing, and assists the orderly presentation of fact and argument at that hearing.

The hearing itself will normally take place in public. The appellant will open his case and call his witnesses in support. He may be represented by a solicitor or barrister, or he may choose to argue his own case. Both he and his witnesses will be subject to cross-examination by the opposing local authority or other body. Then the public authority will be entitled to make their own submissions and call their own witnesses, subject of course to cross-examination on the part of the appellant. Both the appellant and the public authority are entitled, immediately after any of their witnesses have been cross-examined, to re-examine the witnesses to clear up any ambiguities or difficulties revealed in the cross-examination; but not at that stage to try to introduce any fresh evidence. Matters of procedure will be under the control of the inspector, who will normally not insist on any high degree of formality. However, he will be anxious to ensure that all evidence is relevant to the subject-matter of the inquiry. The inspector must, however, ensure that he gives the appellant a fair opportunity of calling any evidence he may genuinely require. Failure to afford an appellant a proper opportunity to present his case may give rise to a successful court challenge on grounds of breach of "natural justice".[68] Other points of note are that witnesses are not required to give

---

[68]   *Nicholson v S.S.E.* (1977) 76 LGR 693.

evidence on oath, and civil servants, when called, are not expected to give evidence to *justify*, as distinct from explaining, a government policy.

At the end of the proceedings the appellant will normally, either himself or through his advocate, make a final speech. Following this, the inspector will commonly arrange to visit the site, which he will do in the presence of all the parties. At such a visit fresh argument will not be allowed, but the parties may be permitted to point out salient features which have been referred to during the oral hearing.

After the close of the inquiry the inspector will either give his determination on behalf of the Secretary of State, or he will prepare a report with recommendations to enable the Secretary of State to make the final decision. In either case the decision will be notified by letter to the appellant. Decision letters include a summary of the evidence heard, the inspector's findings of fact, and his conclusions, leading to his determination or recommendation. The appellant will then normally have a right of appeal to the High Court exercisable within six weeks from the date of the decision letter. On such an appeal the appellant is confined to allegations that there has been some error of procedure or that the decision or order is not within the powers of the Act in question. In other words, while the "merits" of a decision may dominate argument at the initial stages and also before the Minister, argument before the courts is confined to questions of compliance with legal rules and procedures. From the High Court a further right of appeal lies to the Court of Appeal and eventually to the House of Lords.

The procedure outlined above will be followed even in relation to the most major issues, such as controversial development within a National Park, or the proposed construction of a new oil terminal or nuclear power station. However, in such cases, where many persons and much evidence will be heard, it is now customary for the inspector to convene a pre-inquiry hearing at which all the parties likely to be involved at the "inquiry proper" endeavour to settle the order in which the various issues are to be discussed and the order of the speeches of those taking part.

Funding of Objectors?

A matter of some current concern in connection with inquiries is that of the funding of objectors. The issue is whether those who object at inquiries should be entitled to assistance from central government funds towards their legal costs and other expenses? Such objectors might be, for example, a local group of residents objecting to the proposed route for a village or town bypass; or, perhaps, an amenity society such as the Council for the Protection of Rural England, objecting to a public body's proposals for development within a National Park or Area of Outstanding Natural Beauty. In cases like these there is a danger that the "contest" at a public inquiry may seem a rather unequal fight; the objectors, with such funds as they can scrape together, taking on the local planning or highway authority, a public corporation or a large public company (*eg* one of the multi-national mining and quarrying companies). If the inspector is to be sure of being fully informed on all relevant issues, perhaps it is necessary that public funds be available to assist objectors. The principal difficulty with any such proposal is in determining the criteria by which such financial assistance should be awarded. Clearly all objectors cannot be given an entitlement to whatever sums they feel they need. Objectors, for example, who object simply to protect the value of their properties may seem less deserving than those who wish to object on landscape or other environmental grounds. Likewise, some amenity groups may seem to possess resources which may make them less strong contenders for public funding: compare the "group of local residents", referred to above, with the National Trust. These issues are clearly difficult ones, quite apart from the further problems of sourcing such funding at a time of severe restraint in public expenditure.

Chapter 3

ACCESS TO THE COUNTRYSIDE

In this chapter our primary concern will be to describe the law relating to footpaths and other public rights of way, and the new rights of public access on foot for open air recreation to mapped open country and registered common land. These various laws give to members of the public certain rights, by virtue of which they may explore and enjoy the countryside; and the exercise of these rights is not dependent or conditional upon the consent or approval of the owner or occupier of the land in question.[1]

Such access "as of right" in accordance with the principles of law to be considered does not, of course, constitute the only means by which the public may visit and make recreational use of the countryside. In addition should be stressed the very considerable extent to which the public are permitted, by the consent of the owners of the land, to visit prime scenic locations, though sometimes only on payment of entrance fees. One thinks here of the extensive land-holdings of the National Trust,[2] the Forestry Commission,[3] the water companies, the proliferation of the Country Parks,[4] and also the more commercially orientated enterprises of owners of financially burdensome landed estates. In such ways there has been opened up a multitude of opportunities for the moderately enterprising town dweller to enjoy, with the owner's agreement (indeed often exhortation), many facets of the countryside.

PUBLIC RIGHTS OF WAY

Introduction

The existence in England and Wales of a dense labyrinth of footpaths, bridleways, tracks and roads which are open to

---

[1] For the "Countryside Code", which should of course be complied with in the exercise of these rights, see below p.303.
[2] See below at p.193.
[3] See below at p.185.
[4] See below at p.151.

87

general public use as of right is invaluable in terms of the recreational amenity of the countryside.

Public rights of way need to be distinguished from **private** rights of way (called easements). The former benefit the public as a whole: the latter simply allow a particular property owner rights of over his or her neighbour's land.

It has been estimated that public footpaths and bridleways alone total some 140,000 miles (of which the bridleways amount to some 28,000 miles); an average of roughly two miles for every square mile of land, though this average belies substantial regional differences – thus Herefordshire and Worcestershire have a footpath and bridleway density over four times that of Lincolnshire.

The bulk of the network of public rights of way has existed for generations, in many cases for centuries; and came into being for reasons quite different from that which constitutes its main present value, that of accommodating the leisure needs of visitors to the countryside. Many paths still existing today were worn originally by people walking to and from their work, going with animals to market (droveways) or to church (churchways), or simply travelling from village to village, or from town to town. This historical aspect to public rights of way can add a dimension to the pleasure obtained by the modern user. Whether or not the correct answer be known, it may at least be of interest to consider, when walking a path, whether its origin was Neolithic feet, the military might of the Romans, the medieval pilgrimages to Glastonbury, Canterbury or Bury St. Edmunds, the miners and packhorses trudging to and from the lead and tin mines, the geometrical creations of the parliamentary enclosure surveyors of the late eighteenth and early nineteenth centuries, or a public path creation order made only last year by the local county or district council.[5]

Although the law of public rights of way originated as part of the common law, it has been much modified by statutes over

---

[5]   Note also G. K. Chesterton's speculation: "Before the Roman came to Rye or out to Severn strode, The rolling English drunkard made the rolling English road."

the last century. This has, perhaps inevitably, resulted in considerable complexity in the law. The statutory developments have, however, gone some way to bringing the law into line with modern needs; securing a reasonably fair balance between the respective rights and interests of farmers and other land-owners, on the one hand, and the general public on the other.

The Countryside and Rights of Way Act 2000 provides that every local highway authority, other than an Inner London authority, is required to prepare and publish a rights of way improvement plan.[6] The plan must contain the authority's assessment of *(a)* the extent to which the local rights of way meet the present and likely future needs of the public; *(b)* the opportunities which local rights of way provide for exercise and other forms of open air recreation and enjoyment of the authority's area; *(c)* the accessibility of local rights of way for the blind or partially sighted and others with mobility problems; and *(d)* such other matters relating to local rights of way as the Secretary of State or the National Assembly may direct.

The plan must also contain a statement of action which the authority proposes to take for the management of local rights of way and for seeking an improved local network, taking into account the matters dealt with in the assessment.

An authority must make, within 10 years of the publication of the initial plan and subsequently at intervals of not more than 10 years, a new assessment of local needs, review the plan and decide whether or not to amend it. If they decide to amend the plan they must publish it in its amended form. If they decide not to amend it, they must publish a report of their decisions, with reasons.

Public Rights

To Pass and Repass
Public rights of way recognised by the modern law are, broadly, of three kinds: carriageways, bridleways and footpaths. These

---

[6]   s.60.

may be referred to compendiously as "highways". What rights do members of the public have in respect of such rights of way?

The basic principle is that the law confers on members of the public generally the right to "pass and repass" along rights of way "on their lawful occasions". In so doing they do not commit trespass against the owner of the land over which they pass. In addition to such journeying, members of the public may also do things which may be regarded as "reasonably incidental" to passage; stock illustrations being to pause in order to rest, or in order to admire a view. But persons using a right of way must not use it for purposes other than those described above; and if they do so they become trespassers on the land in question. Thus, in 1893, a court held that a man who went onto a public right of way, crossing a grouse moor belonging to the Duke of Rutland, not for the purpose of passage but in order to interfere with the grouse-shooting of the Duke and his friends, was liable to the use of reasonable force to remove him as a trespasser.[7] Likewise, in 1900, a sporting journalist was held to have been trespassing when he walked up and down a right of way over Newmarket Heath, not to get from one place to another but simply in order to note the form of racehorses as they were being exercised.[8]

It is evident, therefore, that those who wander off the route of a right of way, or who use a right of way for an improper purpose, thereby become trespassers. What, however, is the consequence of this? Trespass is, generally speaking, a civil wrong but not a criminal offence. The aim of any court proceedings will be to *compensate* the landowner rather than to *punish* the trespasser; and proceedings will be in the civil courts (county court or High Court) rather than the criminal courts (the Magistrates' Courts or the Crown Court). Quite apart from taking court proceedings to obtain damages, the law gives the landowner the right to use reasonable force to "eject" the trespasser; and also, if repetition is expected, to seek an

---

[7]   *Harrison v Duke of Rutland* [1893] 1 QB 142.
[8]   *Hickman v Maisey* [1900] 1 QB 752. See also *R. v Pratt* (1855) 4 El & Bl 860; *Randell v Tarrant* [1955] 1 All ER 600.

injunction (a court order forbidding or requiring a particular course of action) against the wrongdoer. If, however, *more* than what a court would regard as reasonable force is used to remove a trespasser, the person so ejecting the trespasser will himself commit both a civil wrong and a criminal offence. Ejectors, accordingly, should act with restraint. Where damages are sought against a trespasser, these are assessed so as to compensate for any damage done by the trespasser: if no substantial damage was done in trespassing, the damages will be nominal (*ie* a token amount). If an injunction has been obtained, any person to whom it is addressed who fails to comply with its terms is guilty of contempt of court, the penalty for which can be a fine or a term of imprisonment or both. However, in the the usual situation, where no injunction has previously been obtained against the trespasser, the trespasser will not be liable to criminal penalties unless his actions whilst trespassing involve the commission of some criminal offence. Such would be the case if he has committed acts of criminal damage; for example, by deliberately or recklessly breaking down a fence. Except in circumstances such as these, the warning commonly seen that "Trespassers will be Prosecuted" may be considered to have been correctly described as a "wooden lie".

To these general statements about trespass to land not, of itself, giving rise to criminal liability, certain exceptions exist. Thus, in respect of some ownerships or uses of land, bye-laws may have been made rendering trespass a criminal offence. This will commonly be the case in relation to land owned, for example, by the Ministry of Defence or by Network Rail. Similarly, as we shall see, bye-laws have sometimes been made to exclude the public from nature reserves where their presence, either throughout the year or just at particular times, might be harmful to flora or fauna, or habitat more generally.

Another instance where legislation has imposed criminal sanctions for trespass is in connection with "squatting" in residential houses (Criminal Law Act 1977); and such criminal sanctions in relation to squatters were extended by the Public Order Act 1986 to deal with what was becoming a much publicised problem of "hippy" convoys parking their caravans, and settling, on agricultural land. The 1986 Act introduced provisions enhancing the capacity of landowners, via the police, to secure the removal of non-peaceable trespassers on land, and of even quite exemplarily behaved trespassers where substantial numbers of vehicles were involved. The provisions of the 1986 Act have now, however, been superseded by more stringent rules under the Criminal Justice and Public Order Act 1994.

Section 61 of this Act provides a power for the senior police officer present to require persons and vehicles to leave land in circumstances where the officer reasonably believes:

(i)   that two or more persons are trespassing on land and are present there with a common purpose of residing there for any period; and

(ii) reasonable steps have been taken by or on behalf of the occupier to ask them to leave; and

(iii) that either *(a)* any of those persons has caused damage to the land or to property on the land or used threatening, abusive or insulting words or behaviour towards the occupier, a member of his family or an employee or agent of his; or *(b)* that those persons between them have six or more vehicles on the land.

Failure to comply with a direction made in such circumstances involves the commission of a criminal offence and brings into operation a power of arrest without warrant.

In this context we may also note the provisions of sections 68 and 69 of the 1994 Act. The former creates the offence of "aggravated trespass". A person commits this offence if he trespasses on land in the open air and, in relation to any lawful activity which persons are engaging in or are about to engage in, does there anything which is intended by him to have the effect: *(a)* of intimidating those persons or any of them so as to deter them or any of them from engaging in that activity; *(b)* of obstructing that activity; or *(c)* of disrupting that activity.

Section 69 provides powers for police officers to remove persons committing or participating in aggravated trespasses. The applicability of these sections in relation to "hunt saboteurs" will be evident.

It may be mentioned that each of the provisions of the 1994 Act described here is inapplicable to actions which take place on a highway (except where the highway is in the form of a footpath or bridleway).

Kinds of Traffic
Having considered the purposes for which the public may use public rights of way, we come now to the forms of "traffic" which may use such ways: and here lies the difference between the three kinds of highway – footpaths, bridleways and carriageways. The public have the right to use a footpath on foot only, though it has been held[9] that this does not prevent passage with the "usual accompaniment" of a walker. It was, therefore, held to be permissible to push a perambulator along a footpath, and the rule would probably cover taking a dog.

In the case of bridleways, the public may pass on foot or on horseback or may lead a horse on foot. In addition to horses the rights extend to use with ponies, asses or mules. Also, some bridleways may be driftways and here the rights extend to the driving of cattle. Since 1968, the riding of pedal cycles has been allowed on bridleways provided that cyclists give precedence to pedestrians and persons on horseback.[10] This right may, however, be restricted by orders or bye-laws made by a local authority; and since the highway authorities' maintenance obligations only relate to suitability for use on foot or by horse, the surface may not be such as to be conducive to easy cycling: something which may well enhance the attractiveness of the route for certain users.

The use made of bridleways for cycling has increased very considerably in the last few years with the advent and great

---

[9] *R. v Mathias* (1861) 2 F & F 570.
[10] Countryside Act 1968 s.30.

popularity of all-terrain mountain bikes. In some areas the activities of such cyclists have given rise to concern. This concern has focused both on the inconvenience which may be caused to other users of bridleways, and also on damage which may be caused to the surface of the path and to the landscape in general. For example, the attractions of the slopes of Box Hill in Surrey for stunt-riding have given cause for concern as regards damage to the faces of the hill's chalk slopes. A Code of Conduct on Mountain Bike riding has been produced by the Countryside Agency. This stresses the important fact that riding other than on carriageways and bridleways will usually require the consent of the landowner.

Carriageways afford the most extensive rights of use: they may be used on foot, on or leading a horse, or by any kind of vehicle. The Countryside and Rights of Way Act 2000 has introduced, for the purposes of the definitive map, a new category of right of way, namely the restricted byway. On a restricted byway, the public may walk, ride and lead a horse and drive a vehicle other than a mechanically propelled vehicle.[11]

These various rules relate to the form of traffic for which the right of way was dedicated or was created. Although use other than by the appropriate means may amount to a trespass, such use will not necessarily involve the commission of a criminal offence. However, an offence *will* be committed in any case where a motor vehicle is driven along a footpath or bridleway.[12] Moreover, where appropriate bye-laws or orders have been made by district[13] or county councils[14] in respect of particular footpaths, it may be an offence to cycle or ride a horse on those paths.[15] In relation to cycling, the Cycle Tracks Act 1984

---

[11] s.48.

[12] Road Traffic Act 1988 s.34. The section prohibits such driving "without lawful authority". Such authority may appear in statute (*eg* the Chronically Sick and Disabled Persons Act 1970 s.20) or may arise by consent of the owner of land.

[13] Local Government Act 1972 s.235 (bye-laws).

[14] Road Traffic Regulation Act 1984 ss.1 and 14.

[15] It is also an offence generally to cycle or ride a horse on a *footway*: Highways Act 1980.

should also be noted. This authorises county councils to designate particular footpaths as "cycle tracks", thus giving rights to cyclists which would otherwise not exist.

Dogs

Some further mention should be made of the matter of dogs and public rights of way. Although there is no general obligation to keep a dog on a lead on a right of way, orders may be made by county councils imposing such an obligation in respect of specified ways.[16] Moreover, under the Dogs (Protection of Livestock) Act 1953, a criminal offence is committed by the owner or person in charge of any dog which, on any agricultural land, "worries livestock".[17] When the dog is in the charge of a person other than the owner, the owner is nevertheless liable to prosecution in addition to the person in charge unless he can prove that he reasonably believed the person in charge to be a fit and proper person to be in charge. The expression "worries livestock" is defined in wide terms; it includes not only attacking and chasing cattle, sheep, goats, swine, horses or poultry, but in the case of sheep there is extra protection by virtue of the provision, added by the Wildlife and Countryside Act 1981, that worrying includes "being at large (that is to say not on a lead or otherwise under close control) in a field or enclosure in which there are sheep." The reference to "field or enclosure" would seem, however, to exclude the operation of this provision to open upland. The 1953 Act does not apply to police dogs, guide dogs, trained sheep dogs, working gun dogs or packs of hounds. In addition to the 1953 Act, a self-help remedy is afforded to a farmer whose livestock are being chased or attacked by a dog: he may shoot the dog without any obligation to compensate its owner.[18]

As regards civil liability to pay compensation for harm done by a dog, the position may be summarised as follows. Under the Animals Act 1971, the keeper of a dog is generally liable in

---

[16] Road Traffic Act 1972 s.31.
[17] 1953 Act s.1(1).
[18] Animals Act 1971 s.9.

damages only where the dangerous characteristics of the particular animal were already known to him when the incident in question occurred. In other words, as the saying goes, "each dog is allowed its first bite". If such characteristics are known to the keeper (or his employee or his family), the keeper is liable even though he may, in fact, have taken reasonable steps to try to keep the dog under control. There is, however, one situation where a stricter rule than this operates. Where a dog does damage by killing or injuring livestock (including poultry) the keeper of the dog is liable to pay for the damage even though the dog has no known prior history of such behaviour, and even though the keeper may have taken reasonable trouble to try to keep the dog under control.

Creation of Public Rights of Way

Public rights of way may in law come into existence in either of two ways: by the traditional common law method of "dedication and acceptance", or by the operation of statutory powers. We shall consider each of these methods in turn.

Common Law

Dedication and acceptance involves the dedication by the owner of the land, to the public generally, of certain rights over that land and the acceptance of those rights by the public. Dedication to a section of the public only (*eg* to local residents) is not sufficient to create a public right of way.[19] In some cases it may be possible to point to positive acts of dedication by the owner of the land, but more usually dedication is *presumed* from long user.

The common law rules about dedication have, in practical terms, been superseded by statutory provisions providing for dedication to be presumed if certain conditions are fulfilled. The modern law is to be found in the Highways Act 1980.[20] This states that "when a way has been actually enjoyed by the public as of right and without interruption for a full period of

---

[19] See *Poole v Huskinson* (1843) 11 M&W 827.
[20] Highways Act 1980 s.30.

20 years, the way is to be deemed to have been dedicated as a highway unless there is sufficient evidence that there was no intention during that period to dedicate it." An important point to note about this provision is that it does not provide that *any* twenty year period of uninterrupted user as of right gives rise to the presumption. The twenty year period during which such user must be shown is the one calculated back from the date at which the right of the public to use the way is called into question. This is quite a significant limitation. A case in 1953 illustrates the operation of the principles.[21] Members of the public had used a path across a piece of land between 1914 and 1940. Between 1940 and 1947 the land had been requisitioned and public use of the path discontinued. In 1948 the owner locked a gate and posted notices forbidding public use of the path. It was held by the court that no statutory presumption of dedication arose, because the twenty year period during which uninterrupted user had to be shown was the period dating back from 1948 (when the right of the public to use the way was brought into question) and that public use had not been continuous during that period because of the requisitioning between 1940 and 1948. The period of over twenty years of use prior to 1940 was not of relevance because, although the requisitioning in 1940 led to the use stopping, there was no "calling into question" of the right to use the path at this time. It should be noted, however, that this rule that public user must take place without interruption over the twenty years prior to challenge relates only to the *creation* of rights of way. Once created a right of way remains such even if not used for any length of time. Hence the maxim: "Once a highway, always a highway."

For the statutory presumption of dedication to operate, the user must not only have spanned twenty years without interruption by the owner, but also the user must have been enjoyed[22] "as of right". This means that the use must be without force, secrecy or permission. However there is no

---

[21] *de Rothschild v Buckinghamshire* C.C. (1957) 55 LGR 595.
[22] See *Jaques v S.S.E.* [1995] JPL 1031.

requirement that the users should believe that they have a legal right to use the route.[23]

Owners of land over which members of the public are asserting, in fact non-existent, rights of way must therefore take some care that by their inaction they do not unintentionally allow such rights to become established. It is, however, possible for an owner to prevent this by only a small amount of effort. In the first place he may show that he is not acquiescing in the establishment of a new right of way by periodically interrupting the public's use. Interruption requires something physical, such as blocking the way or personal challenge.[24] A common practice of owners is to close routes used across their property for one day each year. Often Christmas Day or Good Friday are dates chosen, though these dates have no legal significance in this connection.

Another way in which an owner may prevent a right of way becoming established is, even where he allows uninterrupted user to establish the statutory presumption of dedication, to do certain things which the statute provides will rebut (*ie* counter) that presumption. Thus, it is provided that where a notice has been erected and maintained by a landowner, and the notice is visible to users of the "way" and is in terms inconsistent with an intention to dedicate a right of way, the notice shall suffice to rebut the presumption of dedication.[25] It is also provided that in the event of such a notice being torn down or defaced the owner may, rather than re-erecting and continuing to maintain it, instead inform the local county council that no right of way is dedicated, and to the same legal effect.[26] Another course of action available is for the owner of land periodically to submit maps and statements to the county council, together with sworn declarations stating that the rights of way shown are the only ones dedicated. This will rebut

---

[23] *R. v Oxfordshire County Council ex p Sunningwell Parish Council* [2000] 1 AC 335.

[24] *Merstham Manor Ltd. v Coulsdon and Purley U.D.C.* [1937] 2 KB 77.

[25] Highways Act 1980 s.31(3).

[26] Highways Act 1980 s.31(5)

the statutory presumption of dedication of any additional rights of way based on future user.[27]

Statutory Powers
Quite apart from this traditional method of establishment of public rights of way by actual or presumed dedication and acceptance, there are various procedures for creation of such ways by the exercise by public bodies of statutory powers.

Historically, an important example of this were the powers contained in the numerous Inclosure Acts, which authorised commissioners to enclose open land and to create public rights of way in order to allow villagers access to the new enclosed fields.

In modern times the more important provisions have been those conferring on county and district councils powers to create footpaths and bridleways, either compulsorily or by agreement with landowners.[28] Such agreements with landowners may also be made by parish (or, in Wales, community) councils.[29] However, in such cases no payments may be made to the landowners, as is permitted by district and county councils; and nor are parish or community councils under the duty that applies to districts and counties[30] to carry out such work as is necessary to bring such paths into a fit condition for use by the public.

The power to make a compulsory "public path creation order" exists where a county or district council considers there to be a need for such a path in its area and that it is expedient for the path to be created having regard to:

(a) the extent to which the path would add to the convenience or enjoyment of a substantial section of the public, or to the convenience of persons resident in the area, and

---

27 Highways Act 1980 s.31(6).
28 Highways Act 1980 ss.25-29.
29 Highways Act 1980 s.30.
30 Highways Act 1980 s.27.

(b) the effect which the creation of the path would have on the rights of persons interested in the land (account being taken of their rights to compensation).[31]

Procedure is governed by Schedule 6 to the Highways Act 1980. If the order is unopposed it is confirmed by the local authority itself. If opposed, the order is submitted to the Secretary of State who will appoint an inspector to hold a local inquiry[32] or, at least, afford objectors an opportunity of being heard. The Secretary of State will, in the light of the inspector's report and recommendations, decide whether or not to confirm the order (with or without modification).

In fact, this statutory power to create public footpaths and bridleways is not commonly used. In particular, its use to create a new path has been rare except in relation to long-distance routes.[33] The powers are, however, sometimes used alongside diversion and extinguishment orders[34] to secure local rationalisation of paths.

Definitive Maps

Procedure
Although a footpath or bridleway, once created by any of the methods described above, does not in law cease to be such because it is not used or may have become obstructed or overgrown, or simply forgotten, there was clearly a danger that, as use of paths became less a benefit to local people and more a rural amenity for visiting town residents, the number of usable footpaths might diminish, and doubt would set in as to the rights of the public to use particular paths. The best safeguard, recommended by the Hobhouse Committee in its Report on Footpaths and Access to the Countryside and put into legislative effect in 1949,[35] was to impose a duty on local

---

31 Highways Act 1980 s.26(1). Compensation is governed by s.28.
32 For this procedure, see above, pp.83-85.
33 See below, p.116.
34 See below, p.113.
35 National Parks and Access to the Countryside Act 1949.

authorities to survey their areas and to produce definitive maps and written statements of all footpaths and bridleways.

The National Parks and Access to the Countryside Act 1949 introduced a system for registering public footpaths and bridleways on county definitive maps made and maintained by the county councils. The Act provided for surveys of paths after consultations with parish and district councils. The surveys were followed by the preparation of draft maps to which objections could be made. After objections and appeals had been settled, provisional maps had to be published. Owners, occupiers and lessees could challenge these maps by an application to the court. Once the challenges had been determined, the definitive maps and statements were published.

Under the 1949 Act, the duty to prepare definitive maps was imposed on county councils only. This ensured coverage of most of the countryside and all county councils had completed their definitive maps by mid-1982. The urban areas of the larger cities, having former county borough status, and the inner London area were, however, not subject to surveying obligations under the original legislation; and although legislation has now extended obligations to the cities generally, the inner London area remains exempt. The procedures, outlined above, for making the maps and statements have also been streamlined to some extent by provisions of the Wildlife and Countryside Act 1981.

Legal Effect

What then, is the legal significance of the definitive map? The legislation provides[36] that the map and statement are conclusive evidence as to the existence, at the date to which the map applies, of any public rights of way shown and described. It is thus conclusive that a public right of way of the particular nature shown exists (*eg* footpath or bridleway) and that the way is of the width described, and in the position described, in the written statement.

---

[36] Wildlife and Countryside Act 1981 s.56.

It is important to note, however, that the *absence* of an indication of a public right of way is not conclusive evidence that no public right of way exists; nor does the fact that a way is shown as a footpath or a bridleway rule out the existence of *more extensive* public rights to use the way, for example to use a "footpath" on horse or to use either by vehicle.[37] Definitive maps and statements thus certainly "enshrine" those rights which they show, but in so doing they do not preclude persons from establishing the existence of omitted rights of way by the traditional methods of proof of actual or presumed dedication and acceptance.

However, a word of caution is necessary here. These, apparently "enshrined", rights are more precarious than might perhaps have been expected under the legislation. As we shall shortly see, if a right of way has been mistakenly entered on the map (or included as a bridleway instead of as only a footpath) the map is liable to modification procedures. In other words the map as it stands at any point in time is definitive – it does not, however, follow that the map cannot be corrected.[38]

It is obviously of importance that the information contained in definitive maps and statements should be readily available to members of the public. For this reason county councils are required to ensure that a copy of relevant parts of the map and statements is available for public inspection, free of charge and at any reasonable time, in each district and, where practicable, in each parish.[39] The information on the definitive maps has also been incorporated onto modern Ordnance Survey maps. Footpaths and bridleways are marked in green on the, appropriately named, green covered "Pathfinder" Maps (Second Series). At a scale of 1:25,000 these maps show both rights of way and the existence and shape of fields, making them the most suitable for walking in the countryside. Rights of way are

---

[37] Wildlife and Countryside Act 1981 s.56(1); *Andover Corporation v Mundy* [1955] JPL 518.

[38] *R. v S.S.E. ex p Simms* [1990] 3 All ER 490, overruling the decision in *Rubinstein v S.S.E.* [1988] JPEL 485.

[39] Wildlife and Countryside Act 1981 s.57(5).

also shown on modern, purple-covered "Landranger" maps. The scale of these is 1:50,000, a scale which permits the walker to locate and use well-defined paths, but may make accurate path-finding difficult where the route is overgrown, ploughed over, or simply not walked often enough to be self-evident.[40]

Modification

The making of definitive maps and statements has taken a good deal of time and effort on the part of county councils. Once made, proper arrangements for keeping the information up to date are necessary if the documents are to retain their value. The plan of the 1949 Act was for the survey authorities to undertake, periodically, comprehensive re-surveys of their areas. The Wildlife and Countryside Act 1981 has altered this scheme to one under which county councils are under a duty to keep their definitive maps and statements under *continuous review*, and to make modification orders as and when necessary.[41]

Modifications to the map and statement may be necessary for a variety of reasons. For example, to include paths previously omitted; or to exclude paths previously included erroneously; to correct misrouting or misdescription of ways; to reflect orders or agreements creating new paths; or orders "stopping up", diverting, widening or extending existing paths. In relation to certain of these reasons for modification,[42] any member of the public may apply to the county council for a modification order. The member of the public must comply with the procedure laid down in the Wildlife and Countryside Act 1981 and the regulations made by statutory instrument under the Act.[43] These require, for example, that all owners and occupiers of the land affected be notified. The county council is required to investigate and consider any such application and then notify the applicant of its decision. Against a refusal to make a

---

[40] 1:25,000 is the metric equivalent of the former $2\frac{1}{4}$ inches to the mile maps; 1:50,000 the equivalent of the "inch to the mile" maps (1:63,460).

[41] Wildlife and Countryside Act 1981 s.53(2)(b).

[42] Wildlife and Countryside Act 1981 s.53(5).

[43] Wildlife and Countryside Act 1981 Sched. 14; Wildlife and Countryside (Definitive Maps and Statements) Regulations 1993 (S.I. 1993/12).

modification order the applicant may appeal to the Secretary of State. If the Secretary of State considers that a modification order should be made, he can give instructions to this effect to the county council.

Where modification of a definitive map is sought, it is necessary for the applicant to prove error by cogent evidence. However, evidence can be produced which was available in the council's archives, if it was not previously considered.[44] Given that matters in dispute may well relate to events before inclusion in a map some decades ago, local authorities have been encouraged to give ample publicity in the community to applications for modification. By this means it is hoped that, when decisions are taken, they are taken on the basis of as full and complete information and evidence as can be obtained.

In cases where the council is minded on its own initiative to make a modification order, it is required,[45] first, to consult with the appropriate district and parish councils and then to publish its intended order. Objectors may then lodge representations within six weeks, whereupon the matter must be referred to the Secretary of State who, following a local inquiry or private hearing before an inspector, will decide whether or not to confirm the order. Such an order may also be challenged in the High Court though on strictly limited grounds only, and within a period of six weeks from confirmation.[46]

Obstruction of Rights of Way

Nuisance
Members of the public using a footpath or bridleway have to accept obstructions which were there when a right of way came into being, such as trees or stiles and gates; but otherwise

---

[44] *Mayhew v S.S.E.* (1992) 65 P&CR 344; *Parkinson v S.S.E.* [1993] JPL 856.

[45] Except in cases where the modification is simply to reflect the effect of some other legal procedure in the course of which objections will have been heard.

[46] Wildlife and Countryside Act 1981 Sched. 15. For more details of this standard administrative appeal procedure, see above, p.85.

the obstruction of a right of way, such as putting a barbed wire fence across a footpath, constitutes what is called a **public nuisance.** If such a nuisance exists, any member of the public wishing to exercise his right of passage is entitled to remove the obstruction; in legal parlance to "abate" the nuisance. Furthermore, criminal proceedings may be taken against any landowner or other person causing such an obstruction.[47] In this context "obstruction" has been held to include the erection of gates across a bridleway, even though the gates were readily openable, being attached in the centre by a loose piece of twine.[48]

The law of nuisance applies not only to the physical obstruction of public rights of way, it also covers other actions which, without physically barring the way, may prevent public use of the highway. So, for example, a landowner who fires guns across a right of way, engages in clay-pigeon shooting in close proximity (with consequent risk of injury from falling clay shards), hits golf balls in such an area, or who keeps fierce animals in a field crossed by a right of way will be committing a nuisance if by doing so he puts the reasonable user of the highway in fear of injury. In this context one particular instance of such interference with the public's rights has been made a specific criminal offence. Thus, it is an offence for a farmer to keep at large a bull, exceeding ten months in age, in any field or enclosure crossed by a public right of way. An exception exists, however, where the bull is kept along with cows and heifers so long as the bull does not belong to one of the following seven specified breeds:[49] Ayrshire, British Friesian, British Holstein, Dairy Shorthorn, Guernsey, Jersey and Kerry. This is not very satisfactory from the walkers' point of view. The theory behind the legislation is that foreign breeds of beef bull are less aggressive than domestic breeds of dairy bull. Not all, however, are convinced of this and the matter remains contentious. Fears have not been alleviated by advice to farmers from the Health and Safety Executive that even where

---

[47] Highways Act 1980 s.137.
[48] *Durham* C.C. *v Scott* [1991] JPL 362, DC.
[49] Wildlife and Countryside Act 1981 s.59.

a beef bull is kept with cows or heifers there is a "safety to the public" obligation to the public, under section 3 of the Health and Safety at Work Act 1994, to erect notices so that the public may guard themselves against risk of harm.

Even where no *criminal* offence is committed a farmer may be *civilly* liable in damages if a bull with known dangerous propensities injures a person using a right of way.

Ploughing

The ploughing of fields over which exist public rights of way is a matter which has given rise to a good deal of controversy; particularly so in view of the fact that an increasing proportion of paths which formerly skirted around small fields now bisect new, larger, fields as farmers have removed hedges to enhance agricultural efficiency.[50]

The extent of this problem was revealed in a survey commissioned by the Countryside Commission which was completed in 1989. A major finding of the survey, carried out by over a thousand volunteers, was that although most of the footpath and bridleway network in England and Wales was in fact in reasonable shape, its amenity value was marred by the incidence of obstacles. The survey found that obstructions to users, such as fences, overgrowth of vegetation (*eg* crops in fields), flooding and muddiness of bridleways, and in particular the ploughing of paths, meant that people intending a two mile walk stood a two in three chance of not being able to complete their route. Those intending a five mile route had only one chance in ten of getting through.

Concern at the problem caused by the ploughing of footpaths led in 1990 to specific new legislation. The Rights of Way Act 1990 has amended and developed earlier legislation, and the present rules about ploughing may be summarised as follows.

To begin with, it is clear that if a right of way was originally dedicated subject to the right to plough, the public cannot

---

[50]   These may be appropriate cases for diversion orders: see below, p.113.

complain and must re-tramp the way afresh after each ploughing. Where dedication has been presumed by twenty years user as of right and without interruption, the reservation of a right to plough will depend on the practice during that critical period.[51] However, in cases where no such reservation of a right to plough exists, the act of ploughing will constitute a criminal offence.[52] In this connection the 1990 Act has extended the criminal law so that it is now an offence not only to plough a path without legal authority but also to "disturb the surface" of a path or bridleway so as to "render it inconvenient for the exercise of the public right of way". Proceedings in respect of these offences may be brought by highway or other specified local authorities and by individuals.[53]

To the broad scope of these offences an exception, however, exists, designed to meet genuine agricultural needs. Where a footpath or bridleway crosses agricultural land, or land which is being brought into agricultural use, then if the farmer wishes, in accordance with the rules of good husbandry, to plough or otherwise disturb (*eg* by harvesting activities) the surface of the land, and it is not reasonably convenient in so doing to avoid disturbing the surface of the right of way, he may do so provided certain conditions are complied with. The right to plough does not apply to paths around the edges of fields, only to those crossing fields; and where a path is lawfully ploughed the farmer is under a duty to make good the surface of the path, so as to make it reasonably convenient for the exercise of public rights: not later than two weeks from the time ploughing began in cases where ploughing is for sowing; and where ploughing is not for sowing, reinstatement must be within 24 hours. In either case extensions may be granted by the highway authority up to a period of not more than 28 days. This is intended to take account of difficulties presented by adverse weather conditions. Failure to make good the surface constitutes a criminal offence,[54]

---

[51] *Mercer v Woodgate* (1869) LR 5 QB 26.
[52] Highways Act 1980 s.131A.
[53] Highways Act 1980 s.134(5), as amended by Countryside and Rights of Way Act 2000 s.70.
[54] Highways Act 1980 s.134(4).

in addition to that of unlawful ploughing. County councils, as highway authorities, are under a duty to enforce these rules about ploughing and restoration.[55] Individuals may also bring prosecutions for obstructions.[56]

In addition to the power, and duty, to prosecute, the county council may, in a case where there has been disturbance of the surface of a path so as to make it inconvenient to use, or unlawful ploughing or failure to restore the surface, give fourteen days' notice to the farmer of its intention to enter onto the land itself to reinstate the path. If the farmer still fails to do the work himself within that period, the council may carry out the reinstatement and recover its reasonable expenses from the farmer.[57]

Another problem dealt with in the 1990 Act has been that of the growing of crops in fields so as to encroach, obscure and make impassable, rights of way. The Act makes it an offence for an occupier of agricultural land to allow any crop, other than grass, to encroach so as to render any footpath or bridleway inconvenient for the exercise of the public right of way. In recent years a problem has been experienced of paths becoming unpassable as tall-growing oil seed rape, planted alongside paths, becomes flattened by weather conditions and obstructs such passage. Farmers should, therefore, take care not to plant this crop, or similar, too close to the route of rights of way. Once again there is here a power, on having given notice, for the local authority to take action directly by cutting a way through the crop and then recovering its costs from the landowner.

Maintenance

Duties of Highway Authorities
Highway authorities (county councils) are by law under a duty

---

[55] Highways Act 1980 s.134(6).
[56] Highways Act 1980 s.137.
[57] Highways Act 1980 s.134(8)(9).

to maintain most highways,[58] including footpaths, in such a condition as is reasonable in view of the nature and volume of traffic that may be expected to use the way.[59] This duty is, accordingly, relatively light in the case of paths across fields or open countryside. However, even in respect of such paths, it is the duty of the highway authority to prevent or remove obstructions, be they natural or artificial, and to preserve the right of way. These duties arise from the common law and have been bolstered by statute;[60] they cover both the taking of physical action to prevent and remove obstructions, and also the taking of legal proceedings, such as the prosecution of offenders[61] or the seeking of injunctions or declarations.

In addition to the duty imposed on county councils, as highway authorities, to maintain highways, the legislation has conferred discretionary powers on district, parish and community councils to undertake maintenance of footpaths and bridleways if they so wish.[62] Where districts exercise such powers they have a right to have their expenses reimbursed by the county council. Where parishes so act their expenses may be reimbursed at the discretion of the county council (or a district council which is exercising maintenance powers).

---

[58] Highways Act 1980 s.41. Strictly speaking this duty relates only to "highways maintainable at public expense"; highway authorities having powers, rather than a duty, of maintenance of privately maintainable ways. See *eg* s.57. The distinction between highways maintainable at public expense and other highways is a complex one, beyond the scope of this book. See further, Highways Act 1980 ss.37 and 38.

[59] In *R. v High Halden (Inhabitants)* (1859) 1 F&F 678 it was held that the duty was to maintain the highway so as to be reasonably passable at all seasons of the year. The duty includes the maintenance of footbridges.

[60] *Bagshaw v Buxton Local Board of Health* (1875) 1 Ch D 220; Highways Act 1980 s.130 (statutory *duty* on highway authorities to assert and protect the rights of the public to the use and enjoyment of any highway; *powers* given to district councils to do the same).

[61] *eg* under Highways Act 1980 s.137 (wilful obstruction) or s.134(5), (5A) (unlawful ploughing). Note also the offence under the National Parks and Access to the Countryside Act 1949 of erecting a sign or notice containing false or misleading information likely to deter public use of a right of way.

[62] Highways Act 1980 ss.42, 43 and 50.

Furthermore, district councils have power to assert and protect public rights in respect of any public right of way in their area,[63] and parish and community councils have power to make representations to county councils about rights of way which have been stopped up or obstructed.[64] If these representations prove to be well-founded, the county council comes under a duty to take proper proceedings. The making of such representations can be a very useful form of local activity by parish and community councils. It is a worthwhile practice to include in such representations a request that the county council should inform the parish council of the action it intends to take, and to report on progress being made in the matter.

Powers of Individuals
So far we have concentrated our attention on the duties and powers of *local authorities* in relation to the protection of rights of way. However, such authorities have many other responsibilities and calls upon their funds, and so cannot be relied upon always to survey fully the state of paths and to act with vigour where need arises. The Countryside Commission estimated that in 1986/7 some £14m was spent on rights of way maintenance (about £100 per mile). It recommended that this figure be increased by fifty per cent. It also calculated that, judged by reference to footpath usage, this still provided an amenity much more cheaply per use (10p) than did provision of swimming pools or country parks. These might be five or ten times as expensive to provide per individual user. By 1996, the Commission was pleased to be able to announce, local authority expenditure on maintenance had almost doubled, to some £25 million.

What action may be taken by *private individuals* in relation to rights of way which are obstructed or are in poor repair? As long ago as 1630,[65] it was declared by the courts that any of the King's subjects passing along a highway and finding an obstruction might take steps to unblock the path by removing

---

[63] Highways Act 1980 s.130(2).
[64] Highways Act 1980 s.130(6).
[65] *James v Hayward* (1630) Cro Car 184.

the obstruction. A word of caution is necessary, however, in relation to this self-help remedy. An obstruction may only be removed if it is preventing use of the path; if it can be walked around whilst remaining on the right of way, such clearance of the way is not authorised. Moreover, in a case in 1932,[66] Maugham J stressed that the common law permitted only the taking of the minimum action necessary to make the way passable. Thus, for example, when a locked gate is found across a path it would be lawful, where possible, to remove the lock; it would probably be to exceed self-help powers to remove the gate itself. Individuals who exceed their common law powers may be sued for damages for trespass, and may face prosecution for criminal damage.[67]

Apart from this self-help remedy, there is also a useful procedure under the Highways Act[68] by which an individual may enforce the duty of the highway authority to maintain the highway. The procedure involves serving a notice on the highway authority. If the highway authority fails to reply, or replies denying that the way is a highway, or denies that it is a publicly maintainable highway, the individual can take proceedings in the Crown Court for an order that the way be put into proper repair. The court will grant the order if it finds that the way is indeed a highway maintainable at public expense and is out of repair. If the highway authority admits its obligation to maintain the way in question, any dispute about the extent of maintenance required by law will be determined in the Magistrates' Court.

There is an important limitation to this procedure. It can only be used to enforce the duty of the authority to maintain and repair highways; it does not extend to enforcement of the duty to keep ways free from obstruction. Thus in a case in 1975,[69] it was held that the procedure was not apt to enforce the duty to remove a wire fence, or effluent from a cesspit which was obstructing public use of paths; it was appropriate, however, in

---

[66] *Seaton v Slama* (1932) 31 LGR 41.
[67] Criminal Damage Act 1971.
[68] Highways Act 1980 s.56.
[69] *Hereford and Worcester* C.C. *v Newman* [1975] 1 WLR 901.

relation to paths which have vegetation growing from their surfaces making them impassable. In the latter instance the vegetation growth meant that the surface of the right of way was in disrepair. In this connection a distinction must also be drawn between growth of shrubs or trees *beside* a right of way and growth from the surface of the way itself. The former may obstruct passage along a way; but only the latter involves disrepair requiring maintenance, and so enforceable by the procedure described above.

The Countryside and Rights of Way Act 2004 has introduced into the Highways Act 1980 new powers for enforcing the highway authority's duty to remove obstructions. Any person may serve a notice on the highway authority to remove an obstruction on a public right of way. If the obstruction is not removed within two months, an application may be made to the Magistrates' Court for an order.[70]

Gates and Stiles

The maintenance of gates and stiles which lawfully exist across footpaths or bridleways is a matter of some importance. The basic rule[71] is that they are required to be maintained in a safe and usable condition by the owner of the land.[72] However, the owner can recover a quarter of his costs in so doing from the highway authority, and the authority may pay more than this if it wishes. In default of maintenance by the owner of the land, the highway authority (or in some cases the district council) may, having given fourteen days' notice, undertake the work itself and charge some or all of its costs to the owner, as it thinks fit. The rule, referred to above, about recovery of expenses from the highway authority applies only in the absence of agreement to the contrary. Thus, where a highway authority has granted permission[73] for the erection of a stile or gate which would otherwise have constituted an unlawful obstruction,

---

[70]   Countryside and Rights of Way Act 2000 s.63 which inserts ss.130A-D into the Highways Act 1980.

[71]   Since the Countryside Act 1968.

[72]   Highways Act 1980 s.146.

[73]   Highways Act 1980 s.147.

that grant of permission will also make clear on whom the cost of maintenance shall fall.

Waymarking

Since 1968 there has been an obligation on highway authorities to erect and maintain direction posts at all points where a public footpath or bridleway leaves a metalled road, except where the agreement of the parish council is obtained to the effect that signposting in particular places is not necessary.[74] They are also empowered, though not obliged, to erect such waymarks generally as they consider necessary. Such waymarking may, with the consent of the highway authority, be undertaken by parish or community councils. In this connection the Countryside Commission (now the Countryside Agency) issued advice about waymarking, suggesting the use of a special sign, yellow for footpaths and blue for bridleways. Further, since the Wildlife and Countryside Act 1981, local authorities (counties and districts) have been authorised to appoint wardens to "advise and assist the public in connection with the use of" footpaths, bridleways, etc. in their areas.[75]

The Countryside Commission has drawn attention to the unsatisfactory state of waymarking of paths. Its survey in 1989, referred to earlier, disclosed real difficulty in determining where many paths intersected with roads, and the Commission advised of the need for some 280,000 more signs to be put in place. By 1996 the position appeared to have improved somewhat. Whilst nearly 60% of paths linking with roads still needed signposts, only about a quarter of such paths were not, in fact, reasonably clearly visible as regards their route.

Diversion and Stopping Up

According to the traditional common law, "once a highway, always a highway"; in other words a public right of way once established exists forever, and is not forfeited owing to any lack

---

74 Countryside Act 1968 s.27.
75 Wildlife and Countryside Act 1981 s.62.

of public use.[76] At common law the only way in which a right of way might be lost is by physical extinction. Thus when a right of way is washed away by erosion of the sea or a river the way is lost: there is no common law right in such circumstances to deviate along adjoining land.[77]

The position at common law is, however, modified in some respects by certain legislative provisions. There are numerous Acts of Parliament which provide for the "stopping up" (*ie* extinguishment) or the diversion of public rights of way.

The earliest of these statutory provisions was in the Highways Act 1835; now replaced by the Highways Act 1980, section 116. Under this provision the highway authority, perhaps on the request of a landowner, may apply to a Magistrates' Court for an order that the way be stopped up as being unnecessary, or that the way should be diverted to a new route on the ground that the new route is either nearer or more commodious to the public. The "new" route in the latter case will be inspected by the magistrates before approval. The consent of the local district and parish councils must be obtained before any order under this section may be made. In other words, such councils can *veto* the closure or diversion under this procedure. In order to assist the magistrates in reaching a fully informed decision, it is provided that any "aggrieved" objector to the stopping up or diversion may appear before the court and has a right to be heard.[78]

In practice, however, this is a rather elaborate and expensive procedure. To appear as an "objector" before a Magistrates' Court is a more awesome experience than to appear before a local public inquiry. A Department of the Environment Circular (1/83)[79] therefore recommended that this procedure be used only in cases involving closure or diversion of public roads carrying vehicular rights. Moreover, note that where the

---

[76] See *eg Turner v Ringwood Highway Board* (1870) LR 9 Eq 418.
[77] *R. v Bamber* (1843) 5 QB 279. Contrast the right to deviate around a merely *obstructed* path.
[78] Highways Act 1980 s.116(7).
[79] See now DOE Circular 2/93.

procedure is used to seek diversion to a new route, the new route must be "nearer or *more* commodious": a route which is a mere equivalent substitute will not suffice. The courts have also given a restrictive interpretation to the word "unnecessary", so that any actual usage is likely to defeat an application on this ground.[80]

In relation to **footpaths** and **bridleways**, the procedures laid down in sections 118 and 119 of the 1980 Act are to be preferred. These consist of the making by the local county or district council of a "public path extinguishment order" or a "public path diversion order". Notice of the making of such orders must be placed in the local press; and a copy of the notice and a copy of the orders must be served on parish or community councils. The grounds upon which such orders may be made[81] are substantially similar to those outlined above in connection with section 116. If objections are lodged to any such order, the Secretary of State will, before deciding whether or not to confirm the order (with or without modification) appoint an inspector who will hold a local public inquiry, afford objectors a private hearing, or order that the matter be considered on the basis of written representations.[82] Where a parish or community council has objected, a full public inquiry is usually held.

In addition to these *general* powers of stopping up and diversion, there are also powers conferred by other Acts of Parliament which are important in particular contexts. Thus, under the Town and Country Planning Act 1990[83] powers are given to local planning authorities to make extinguishment and diversion orders in order to enable development, for which planning permission has been granted, to be carried out. The procedure is similar to that outlined above in relation to orders made

---

80   *Ramblers' Association v Kent* C.C. [1991] JPL 530.
81   "Not needed for public use" (s.118: extinguishment); "will not be substantially less convenient to the public" (s.119: diversion).
82   Highways Act 1980 Sched. 6. See further on this standard administrative procedure, above, pp.83-85.
83   ss.247 and 257.

under sections 118 and 119 of the Highways Act 1980. It should be noted, however, that the power is not exercisable *after* development has been carried out in order to deal with inconvenient public rights of way.[84] Other examples of statutes authorising the stopping up or diversion of public rights of way include the Acquisition of Land Act 1981,[85] the Open Cast Coal Act 1958,[86] the Land Powers Defence Act 1958[87] and the Civil Aviation Act 1981. In each of these, and many other, cases the standard administrative procedure of "order subject to ministerial confirmation", with the possibility of a local public inquiry, must be followed.

Long Distance Routes: National Trails

Over the last quarter of a century there have been established a number of long distance routes (in 1989 renamed "national trails"), consisting of a series of linked rights of way. Where necessary the gaps between pre-existing rights of way have been bridged by the making of dedication agreements with landowners or, in cases where such agreement has not been forthcoming, by the making of public path creation orders.

Legal provision for such routes to be established dates from the National Parks and Access to the Countryside Act 1949.[88] The Countryside Agency (formerly the Countryside Commission) initiates proposals for consideration and approval by the Secretary of State. The proposals show any need for new paths to be created and the need, if any, for the provision of ferries, accommodation, meals and refreshments along the route: they also estimate capital outlay necessary and annual maintenance and running costs.

---

84   See *Ashby v S.S.E.* [1980] 1 All ER 508.
85   Orders in respect of land acquired compulsorily by public authorities, and also land acquired by agreement which could have been acquired compulsorily in default of agreement: 1981 Act s.32.
86   Orders to *suspend* public rights of way in order to allow open cast mining: 1958 Act s.15.
87   Orders in respect of land used for various defence purposes: 1958 Act s.8.
88   ss.51-55.

Once proposals are approved by the Secretary of State, the onus shifts from the Countryside Agency to the county councils through which the route passes. It is they who negotiate agreements with landowners and make any necessary orders, though these initial expenses are defrayed entirely by the Countryside Agency. Once established, three-quarters of the maintenance cost of the routes is borne by the Countryside Agency. Long distance routes are shown as such on the appropriate definitive maps, and are also clearly waymarked "on the ground" by distinctive symbols.

The earliest of the routes to be established was the Pennine Way. Opened in 1965, this route follows the spine of northern England for around 250 miles, from Edale in Derbyshire to Kirk Yetholm in the Scottish border country, passing on its way through three National Parks. The painstaking work necessary to secure complete linkage of rights of way is demonstrated by the fact that the ministerial approval for the Pennine Way was granted as far back as 1951.

Thirteen long distance trails have now been designated in England. Eleven of these are fully developed and two are in the process of being completed. The longest trail is the South West Coast Path. It is 1014 kilometres in length and runs through Somerset, Devon, Cornwall and Dorset. The most recent is the 140 kilometre Hadrian's Wall Path. This follows the Hadrian's Wall World Heritage Site from Wallsend in Tyne and Wear and finishes at the Solway Firth.

Information on the trails may be obtained from the Countryside Agency's website and leaflets are also available.[89]

RIVERS, CANALS AND THE FORESHORE

The public have rights of navigation over tidal rivers, and non-tidal rivers may be navigated where a public right of way of such nature has come into existence by long use or has been created

---

[89] www.nationaltrail.co.uk. E-mail nationaltrails@countryside.gov.uk.

by statute.[90] Such rights of navigation must, however, be exercised in accordance with any bye-laws which may have been made by the British Waterways Board, the Environment Agency (formerly the National Rivers Authority) or other statutory body.

Canals are artificial streams which were created by private individuals (such as the Duke of Bridgewater) or companies, in either case under the authority of Acts of Parliament. Most were constructed in the period between 1761 (opening of the Duke of Bridgewater's canal) and the middle of the nineteenth century, when the railways and later the roads replaced the canals as the principal arteries of commercial traffic. The canals are mostly now owned by the British Waterways Board, which is responsible for their maintenance and for the control of cruising and the commercial use of the canals. No member of the public has any rights of navigation over canals, but the BWB customarily allows such use in accordance with its bye-laws, and it may and does make charges for permitting such use. The recreational use of canals is, of course, becoming ever more popular. These inland waterways extend to about 2000 miles, though many decades of neglect has meant much silting up, disrepair of lock-gates and growth of vegetation in the canals.

Both rivers and canals are of great importance in terms of the habitats they provide for wildlife and plants, though the still-water habitat of canals is quite different from that of a flowing river. Also of value are the "feeder" reservoirs which were built at intervals beside many canals and from which the water level in the canals is topped up. A concern of environmentalists in recent years has been that work done to rivers to make them less prone to flooding has made many river banks less congenial than before to small riverside animals, the vegetation being much reduced and soft mud being replaced by stone or concrete. River engineers are, however, within limits imposed by budgets, becoming more sensitive to these matters in the planning and implementation of their river engineering projects.

---

[90]   See further, below, p.250 on fishing rights.

Canals have towpaths and these are in some cases, though usually are not, public rights of way. Nevertheless, the BWB commonly permits walkers, and also cyclists, to use these paths. The towpaths are very often in a better state of repair than the canals themselves and are of very considerable recreational value, being well defined routes which are safe to walkers and cyclists from the dangers of motorised traffic. It has been estimated that half the population of Great Britain lives within five miles of a BWB canal and that there are 1500 miles of tow-paths freely available for walkers.

The Grand Union Canal from London to Birmingham (145 miles) and the Kennet and Avon from Reading to Bath (87 miles) have both been designated as long distance paths. The towpaths of the Oxford Canal provide a continuous route between Oxford and Coventry and there are many circular routes which link up with the Oxford canal.

Information on available walks is available from the website of British Waterways Board.[91]

The foreshore, the area of our coast between high and low water marks, is the property of the Crown[92] except where it has been sold or leased by the Crown to some other person or body, such as a lord of a manor or, more typically in modern times, to a local authority. No general rights of access exist,[93] but as every seaside holidaymaker will be aware access is customarily permitted. Where the foreshore is owned or leased by the local authority, its use may be restricted by bye-laws or other limitations imposed by the local authority as owner. In any case, at places where much public use is made of the foreshore (*eg* at seaside resorts) the land immediately above high water mark is usually publicly owned. Although no legal right to wander at will exists in relation to the foreshore, it is possible in law for a public right of way to have come into

---

[91] www.britishwaterways.co.uk/site/walking%255FZ.asp.
[92] See further, below, p.195 on the Crown Estates.
[93] The public right to fish, including the right to collect bait, was considered in *Anderson v Alnwick D.C.* [1993] 3 All ER 613.

existence in the ways discussed earlier in this chapter. However, given the nature of the foreshore and the requirement that a right of way must follow a defined route, it is rare for such rights to exist.

There is a general public right of navigation over the sea, and this includes the foreshore at high tide. No owner of land adjoining the coast is, however, obliged to allow public access to the foreshore or sea by crossing his land unless a public right of way across the land exists. He may fence his land *from* the foreshore, but without the consent of the Secretary of State may not extend fences *across* the foreshore as this may interfere with the public's rights of navigation.[94]

THE COUNTRYSIDE AND RIGHTS OF WAY ACT 2000: RIGHTS OF ACCESS TO MAPPED OPEN COUNTRY AND REGISTERED COMMON LAND

The Countryside and Rights of Way Act 2000 introduces a new right of access on foot for open-air recreation to mapped open country, namely mountain, moor, heath, down and registered common land. Improved and semi-improved grassland is excluded from the definition. There is provision for the definition to be extended to include coastal land and for landowners to dedicate any land for public access.

Access land does not include excepted land (see below), nor does it include land over which there is an existing right of public access (*eg* commons within section 193 of the Law of Property Act 1925 or land subject to access agreements or orders under the National Parks and Access to the Countryside Act 1949); however, the existing right of access will continue.

The Act imposed a duty on the Countryside Agency and the Countryside Council for Wales to prepare maps showing all registered common land and open country, although they had power to exclude small areas on maps where they considered

---

94 Coastal Protection Act 1949 s.34.

their inclusion would serve no useful purpose. The Countryside Agency and Council also had a discretion to take a physical feature as the boundary of open country, even if the result was that some other land was included or some open land was excluded.

There was a procedure for publishing draft and provisional maps. Representations against the inclusion or exclusion of land could be made by anyone, within prescribed periods. There was a right of appeal by those with an interest in land against the inclusion on the provisional map of the land as registered common land or open country. If there were appeals or all the appeals were withdrawn or determined, the Countryside Agency (or Council) issued the map in conclusive form. Access maps are to be reviewed at least every 10 years.

Certain land, although it comes within the statutory definition of open land and is therefore shown on the maps, will not be available for public access. Such excepted land includes cultivated land, which is defined as "land on which the soil is being, or has at any time within the previous twelve months been, disturbed by ploughing or drilling undertaken for the purposes of planting or sowing crops or trees". "Ploughing" and "drilling" include respectively agricultural or forestry operations similar to ploughing and agricultural or forestry operations similar to drilling.

Land covered by buildings is also excluded. Buildings are defined to include any structure or erection and any part of a building as so defined, but not any fence or wall, or anything which is a means of access; and for this purpose "structure" includes any tent, caravan or other temporary or moveable structure. Land within 20 metres of a dwelling or livestock building is also excluded.

Other excepted land includes land used as a park or garden, or for the getting of minerals by surface working, or for the purpose of a railway or tramway or golf course, racecourse or aerodrome or land covered by works used for the purposes of a statutory undertaking or telecommunications system. In order to qualify as excepted land, any necessary planning consents must have been obtained. Land over which there are in force bye-laws made by the Secretary of State for Defence will also count as excepted land.

A further category of excepted land is land covered by pens in use for the temporary reception or detention of livestock.

Landowners will be able to exclude or restrict access for any reason for up to 28 days a year. However, no more than four of the excluded days in any calendar year may be a Saturday or Sunday. No Saturday in the period beginning with 1 June and ending with 11 August in any year may be excluded and no Sunday in the period beginning with 1 June and ending with 30 September in any year may be excluded. The purpose of these rules is to ensure that access is not precluded during the periods when the public are most likely to want to exercise the statutory right. The less strict rule for summer Saturdays after 11 August is in response to representations made by the shooting lobby.

Further exclusions or restrictions may be approved by the Countryside Agency for management reasons and on grounds of nature and heritage conservation, fire prevention, defence or national security, and to avoid danger to the public.

Regulations on the operation of exclusions and restrictions have been published.[95] It will be extremely important for any landowner who wants to exclude the public from access land, to study in detail these Regulations.

Where the right to access land exists, it is subject to various restrictions to control activities which are not compatible with the quiet exercise of that right. For instance vehicles, including bicycles, are not allowed, nor are water craft; horse riding is not permitted; there is a prohibition against the use of metal detectors; dogs must be kept on a short lead when near livestock and from 1 March to 31 July in every year, and they may be excluded for up to five years on grouse moors if it is

---

[95] The Access to the Countryside (Exclusions and Restrictions) (England) Regulations 2003 (S.I. 2003/2713).

necessary for the management of the land for the breeding and shooting of grouse, and up to six weeks in any calendar year for lambing.

Anyone not observing the restrictions commits a criminal offence and those who break or damage any wall fence, hedge or gate will become trespassers and will lose their right of access for 72 hours.

The statutory right of access does not increase the liability of a person interested in the land in respect of its state or things done on the land. The exercise of the statutory right overrules any restrictive covenant on use.

A landowner will commit an offence if he displays a notice containing false or misleading information likely to deter the exercise of the statutory right.

If land has no legal right of access, the Countryside Agency may make an application to the Secretary of State (or the Countryside Council for Wales on application to the National Assembly for Wales) for a creation order under section 26 of the Highways Act 1980.

There may also be a need for physical works to be carried out, such as the construction of gates or openings made in walls and hedges. Powers are given to access authorities (Highway Authorities or National Parks) to enter into agreements with landowners and occupiers to do the necessary works or, where agreement cannot be reached, to do the work themselves after giving the stipulated notice. Where the owner or occupier carries out the works, the agreement may provide for the access authority to pay or make a contribution towards the costs incurred.

Access authorities are given power to make bye-laws to preserve order, prevent damage and to secure good behaviour so that there is no undue interference with the rights of others. There is also a power to appoint wardens. Their job will be to advise and assist the public and landowners, and to secure compliance with bye-laws and the general restrictions.

Access authorities may put up notices indicating the boundaries of access and excepted land and informing the public of the general restrictions, and any particular exclusions and restrictions. The local Highway Authority or, where the land is in a National Park, the National Park Authority, is under a duty to establish a local access forum which will consist of members appointed in accordance with regulations. The views of local access forums are to be taken into account in preparing maps of open country, making bye-laws, appointing wardens and before making restrictions and exclusions which may last for more than six months. Liaison with landowner representatives on local access forums is therefore important.

ACCIDENTS IN THE COUNTRYSIDE

Accidents do unfortunately occur to even the most careful adults and children making recreational use of the countryside. They may be caused by the condition of the surface of a footpath, by the collapse of branches of trees, by attacks from bulls or other animals, or in numerous other ways. In what circumstances may a person who suffers injury be able to sue for damages the owner or occupier of the land in question; or, in the case of injuries caused by footpaths being in a dangerous condition, sue the local highway authority having responsibilities for their maintenance? A full discussion of this area of the law is beyond the scope of this book, but it may be appropriate to outline some of the general principles applicable and the factors which may be relevant to liability.

The starting point is that occupiers of land are expected to take reasonable care as regards the safety of persons whom they may reasonably expect to come onto their land. The obligation is to take reasonable care, and this is a matter to be determined in the light of the particular circumstances of each case. In making this assessment certain factors may be of special significance. Thus, where unsupervised young children are reasonably expected to come onto a person's land, his obligations as regards their safety may be greater than where adults only are expected. In particular this may be the case where there are on the land potentially dangerous things which may be allurements to children, such as ponds, or tree branches which may make tempting swings. Adults may be expected, to a degree, to look after their own safety but, if the presence of unsupervised children is foreseeable, the occupier of the land may be under a duty to check the condition of the water's edge or examine whether the branches are sound or rotten. In this connection a second factor may be relevant to liability. In deciding whether or not reasonable care has been taken in respect of those likely to be present, the courts take into account whether the injured visitor was an invited guest or was a trespasser. Understandably, the steps which should be taken to secure the safety of guests are of a higher order than those which the law requires in respect of foreseeable trespassers. In other words, returning to our earlier example, if an occupier of land invites children onto his land, he will be expected to take greater care as to their safety than if the children are unwelcome trespassers. Nevertheless, some obligation exists even in respect of trespassers. If land is in a condition which may present danger to trespassers, this may require reasonable steps to be taken to fence the land adequately to keep those trespassers out, or at least may oblige the occupier to give clear warning of the perils.

Until surprisingly recently, an occupier could exclude liability towards those who suffered injuries by the posting of prominent notices to that effect on the land itself, or by the insertion of appropriately worded clauses in any contract of admission to the property. Such notices or clauses are now, in relation to "business occupiers", governed by the terms of the Unfair Contract Terms Act 1977, which makes them ineffective to exclude liability in so far as they relate to death or bodily injury. They may, however, still be effective in relation to other kinds of harm. For example, the exclusion of liability in respect of torn or damaged clothing. Here the effectiveness of the exclusion notice or clause will depend on the court's view as to its reasonableness.

After the enactment of these provisions, some concern was expressed at doubts created as to the continued ability to exclude liability for death or personal injury in connection with the dangerous state of premises where a landowner (who might very likely make business use of his land, such as by farming it) allowed persons onto his land for recreational or educational purposes. Accordingly, the Occupiers' Liability Act 1984 now makes clear that any such liability will *not* be a business liability unless granting such persons such access falls within the business engaged in by the occupier. In other words a farmer can still allow educational or recreational access to his land subject to exclusion of liability so long as he does not make such activity a part of his business use of the land.

Recovery of damages may also be affected by the extent to which the injured person's own carelessness may have contributed to the accident. Such "contributory negligence" will lessen the amount of damages awarded against a defendant occupier by a proportion equivalent to the degree to which the plaintiff's own carelessness contributed to his accident.

The Countryside and Rights of Way Act 2000 has special provisions relating to liability on access land. A person who enters access land under the Act does not count as a visitor for the purposes of the Occupiers' Liability Act 1957. The occupier does, however, owe a duty of care, similar to that owed to trespassers, under the Occupiers' Liability Act 1984. But specifically excluded is any duty in respect of a risk resulting from a natural feature of the landscape or of any river, stream, ditch or pond, whether or not it is a natural feature. Plants, shrubs and trees, of whatever origin, are regarded as natural features of the landscape. Also excluded are risks of a person suffering injury when passing over, under or through any wall, fence or gate, except by proper use of a stile or gate. However, the occupier will owe a duty of care where the danger is due to anything done by the occupier with the intention of creating a risk or being reckless as to whether that risk was created.

The duty of care arises if an occupier *(i)* is aware of a danger or has reasonable grounds to believe that it exists; *(ii)* knows that a person is in the vicinity of the source of danger or may come near it; and *(iii)* the risk is one against which, in all the circumstances of the case, he might reasonably be expected to offer some protection. The duty is to take such care as is reasonable in all the circumstances to see that the person does not suffer injury. The occupier may discharge his duty by giving warnings of the danger or discouraging people from taking the risk.

In determining whether and, if so, what duty is owed by an occupier of land where there is a right of access under the Countryside and Rights of Way Act 2000, regard is to be had to:

(*a*) the fact that the existence of that right ought not to place an undue financial or other burden on the occupier;

(*b*) the importance of maintaining the character of the countryside, including features of historic, traditional or archaeological interest; and

(*c*) any relevant guidance given in codes of conduct or otherwise by the Countryside Agency or the Countryside Council for Wales.

Lastly, we may note the possibility of the local highway authority being liable in damages in respect of accidents occurring as a result of the condition of a publicly maintainable footpath. The surface of such paths belongs to the highway authority and liability depends on the authority having had a reasonable opportunity of being aware of the dangerous condition of the path, and of their having failed to take reasonable steps to remedy its condition within a reasonable period of time.[96]

---

[96] See *eg Hayden v Kent* C.C. [1978] 2 All ER 97.

Chapter 4

PROTECTION OF SPECIAL AREAS

INTRODUCTION

In this chapter we shall consider the law and practice of amenity and nature conservation with reference to a number of particular kinds of location. Some such areas may warrant special legal provision because of their visual beauty; others for reasons of habitat protection. And very often both motives may coincide. The areas we shall consider are diverse in their characteristics, from craggy mountain ranges to lowland wetlands, and areas as large as Dartmoor to ones as small as a village duck pond. Any list of types of land which are valuable in terms of scenic amenity, or habitat for flora or fauna, will be a long one: open mountains, moorlands, heaths, downlands, woodlands, marshes and wetlands, meadows, lakes, rivers and estuaries, coastal dunes and cliffs, and villages and buildings. The law must provide for effective conservation of each of these different environments and features if we are to continue to enjoy a rich and varied landscape, flora and fauna.

A variety of legal methods have been devised to attempt to achieve this protection. Thus, we shall examine the protection which may be afforded to an area as a consequence of designation as a National Park, an Area of Outstanding Natural Beauty (AONB), a Conservation Area, a Site of Special Scientific Interest (SSSI) or an Environmentally Sensitive Area (ESA). In connection with the discussion of SSSIs we shall need to consider the enhanced protection which certain of these may receive by virtue of the EC Habitats Directive and the significant changes made by the Countryside and Rights of Way Act 2000 (CRoW).

We shall in this chapter also consider the powers which exist to establish Country Parks, Nature Reserves and Marine Nature Reserves. Following that, we shall consider legal provisions which relate to the public enjoyment, and conservation, of other areas quite independently of any special designation or establishment under statutory powers. This will involve, principally, a discussion of laws relating to trees and woodlands; and the chapter will end with some reference to the activities of two major "private" landowners, each of whom generally manage their lands with an appreciation of the needs of conservation. We refer here to the National Trust and the Crown Estates.

Before considering each of these matters, certain points of general significance may be made. We shall see that, very commonly, conservation objectives are sought without going so far as taking the land in question into public ownership. The land is left in private hands but limitations or controls may operate as to what the owner may do on or with that land. An increasingly common legislative device to try to secure some regulation of a landowner's activities is that of the management agreement entered into, voluntarily, by the landowner and an appropriate public body (*eg* the Countryside Agency, English Nature, National Park Authority, or local authority). Such agreements may provide financial incentives to the landowner to use the land in ways which are least detrimental and most beneficial to the environment. The aim in the move towards management agreements is to avoid too much of a "Thou Shalt Not" image of conservation, and so far as possible to secure ends by voluntary means, by arriving at an agreed programme of land management.

This last aspect is particularly important. Conservation of the countryside is by no means a matter simply of leaving it alone; it is not just a question of outlawing a long list of environmentally detrimental practices. The landscape we wish to preserve, together with its plants and wildlife, is very largely an artificial one. It is the product of man's activities over the last few thousand years. Recent research dates such impact rather earlier than formerly thought. Forest clearance began as early as the Bronze Age; as were constructed at this time the earliest of our stone-wall field enclosures. To maintain the countryside as we wish it to remain, what is required is the continuation of a wide variety of agricultural practices, otherwise mixed landscape may degenerate to primaeval forest, managed woodlands become mere wildernesses, and so on. Effective conservation is therefore as much about the encouragement of practices which maintain cherished features as it is about forbidding or deterring more obviously harmful activities. It is in this respect that management agreements and the "voluntary principle" of conservation are to be commended compared with excessive reliance on prohibition alone.

We may now consider in turn each area or category of specially protected land. In relation to each we shall draw attention to deficiencies in the law's provisions or in the practical operation of principles or procedures. Some of these criticisms are substantial ones; nevertheless, it may be noted at the outset that collectively the laws we shall consider do provide at least some degree of special protection for a quite substantial proportion of the countryside of England and Wales.

NATIONAL PARKS

There are in England and Wales eleven areas which have been designated as National Parks. From north to south these are the Northumberland National Park, the Lake District, the North York Moors, the Yorkshire Dales, The Peak District, Snowdonia, the Pembrokeshire Coast, the Brecon Beacons, Exmoor and Dartmoor; together with the New Forest, designated in 2004. In addition, formal processes are under way which may lead to designation of the South Downs as a National Park sometime in 2005. The original legislation did not make provision for the designation of National Parks in Scotland. At the time of its enactment (1949) there were not, in Scotland, comparable pressures on scenic areas to those presented by the English urban areas. Over the years, however, matters have changed. In 1990 the Countryside Commission recommended legislative change and the establishment of National Parks in the Cairngorms, Loch Lomond and the Trossachs, Ben Nevis, Glencoe, the Black Mount and Wester Ross. Of these the Cairngorms and Loch Lomond and the Trossachs have now been designated.

The legal process for creation of National Park status for an area is that of "designation" as such by the Countryside Agency (formerly called the National Parks Commission, 1949-1968, and Countryside Commission, 1968-1999) followed by "confirmation" by the Secretary of State. The governing legislation, the National Parks and Access to the Countryside Act 1949, has authorised such designation and confirmation in relation to "extensive tracts of country" which have, in the opinion of the Agency, been worthy of protection by reason of their natural beauty and the opportunities they afford to the public for open air recreation.

An important point to stress is that our National Parks differ from similarly designated areas abroad, such as Yellowstone or Yosemite in the United States, in that legal ownership of the land is unaffected by designation. Certainly a proportion of the land in the National Parks is owned by public bodies, such as the Forestry Commission, or by the National Trust which, for example, owns about a quarter of the Lake District, but, equally, much is in purely private ownership. The creation of an area as a National Park may limit things which an owner may do on or with his land by way of stricter application of especially extensive planning controls;[1] it does not, however, deprive that person of ownership of the land. Our National Parks are areas which are farmed and "lived in" by some 300,000 people; and the consequent need for there to be employment to support the inhabitants of the small towns and villages gives rise, as we shall see, to certain problems. In no way are our Parks intended to be uninhabited "wilderness" areas: areas of landscape unmarked by man's activities, as is the pattern in the USA.

Origins and Development

Notwithstanding the retention of private ownership, the kinds of areas which have been designated as National Parks are those in respect of which members of the public have long assumed, though wrongly, some general right of access and common

---

[1]   See below, p.142.

enjoyment.[2] One does not forget the fact of private ownership of the "suburban semi" or even of intensively cultivated agricultural land, but one may tend to do so in relation to extensive areas of open upland, mountain and moorland. This was adverted to by the poet Wordsworth in his *Guide to the Lakes*, in which he commented that the Lakes are:

> "a sort of national property, in which every man has a right and interest who has an eye to perceive and a heart to enjoy."[3]

But Wordsworth was a poet, not a lawyer; and in due course the absence of public rights of access to, and enjoyment of, such areas became a matter of much contention. Until the start of this century, the number of visitors from the cities to these open areas was quite small. It was in the 1920s that conflict began to become apparent between rural estate owners, seeking to protect their grouse moors from disturbance, and ramblers from the cities, seeking solace from the grimness of the urban economic depression. The absence of public rights of way over vast tracts of open land, and hence its unavailability for public recreation, led to the mass trespass by several thousand on Kinder Scout in 1932, the establishment, by federation of local groups, of the Ramblers' Association in 1935, and also to a widespread feeling that the law should recognise areas such as these, though privately owned, as a part of the nation's heritage. As such, it was increasingly felt that they should be made subject to a legal regime which would allow public enjoyment, whilst, at the same time, providing necessary safeguards against despoliation.

Although there had been unsuccessful attempts by private members to introduce legislation in 1884 and 1908, it was pressure from groups such as the (then) Council for the Preservation of Rural England, and also from influential

---

[2] But see Chapter 3 as to the impending impact of CRoW as regards such access rights.

[3] Quoted in *Fifty Years of National Parks*, a valuable booklet published by the Council for National Parks, tracing the history of the work of its predecessor, the Standing Committee on National Parks.

individuals, which led to a government inquiry which recommended the creation of National Parks.[4] This Report, coinciding with economic crisis and change of government, did not give rise to any immediate action and so, in 1936, there came together a number of individuals and amenity and access groups to form a Standing Committee on National Parks. The Standing Committee campaigned for parliamentary action but, again, the period immediately prior to and during the Second World War proved not to be a time for such legislation. Nevertheless, the campaign was certainly assisted significantly by the images of rural England presented by the press to the public as the England which was being fought for. Furthermore, some members of the SCNP served in influential positions in the civil service during the war years. Even before hostilities were over, the idea of National Parks was accepted by government in principle,[5] and Reports after the war furnished detailed proposals and schemes. Most notably, the Dower Report followed closely the principal ideas of the SCNP.[6]

The essential idea behind the designation of National Parks was stated to involve selection of extensive areas of, relatively wild, beautiful countryside and there to **preserve** the characteristic landscape beauty, to **protect** wildlife, buildings and places of architectural and historic interest, and to **provide** access and facilities for open-air public enjoyment of the areas. It was assumed that established farming use would continue. At this time the idea of farming being conducted in such a way as to be of concern to conservationists had not yet dawned. Following the General Election of 1945, a committee under Sir Arthur Hobhouse[7] toured the various areas suggested by Dower for National Park status. This committee narrowed down to ten Dower's original list of twelve areas – excluding the South Downs and the Norfolk Broads. Eventual legislation came in

---

[4] The Addison Report (1931).
[5] Report of the Scott Committee on Land Utilisation in Rural Areas in 1942 (Cmd 6378), and White Paper on Control of Land Use, in 1944 (Cmd 6537).
[6] Cmd 6628 (1945). John Dower had been a founding member of SCNP.
[7] Cmd 7121 (1947).

the National Parks and Access to the Countryside Act 1949. The ten National Parks were all established in the period 1951-57, starting with designation of the Peak Park and culminating with that of the Brecon Beacons. Together the National Parks comprise 13,618 square kilometres; approximately 9% of the land area of England and Wales.

As indicated above, the purposes of National Park designation, as set out in the 1949 Act, were two-fold: to seek to preserve and enhance their natural beauty, and to promote their enjoyment by the public. Over the years much concern came to be expressed both as regards the limited scope of the former obligation and also about the clear potential for conflict in the attainment of the two objectives.

An opportunity was taken in the Environment Act 1995 to restate and redefine National Park rationales. It is now provided that the purpose of designation is:

(a) to secure and enhance the natural beauty, wildlife and cultural heritage of such areas; and also

(b) to promote opportunities for the understanding and enjoyment by the public of the special qualities of these areas.

The second of these matters gave rise to some controversy during the Act's passage through Parliament. Although none would deny the value and importance of National Parks for recreational purposes, there has been a good deal of concern about the use of these areas for relatively noisy activities, of a kind not contemplated by the proponents of the original legislation: power boats and jet-skis; micro-light aircraft; off-road vehicles – even, according to Lord Norrie, "towed inflatable crocodiles"!

An amendment, inserting the word "quiet" before "enjoyment" was inserted by the House of Lords, only to be deleted by the Commons. The view of the government appeared to be that a legislative embargo on all non-quiet recreational activity would be to go too far and, indeed, be potentially detrimental to the interests of the Parks. Nevertheless, the government was at some pains to acknowledge that as a general principle it is quiet enjoyment, respecting the tranquillity and peace of the landscape, which should be promoted.

As regards the potential for conflict between the two limbs, it is important to note also the duty of Park Authorities to seek to "foster the economic and social well-being of local communities" within the Parks. Further, it is expressly provided that, if there appears to be a conflict between the attainment of each of the principal two purposes (conservation and enjoyment), the park authorities "shall attach greater weight" to the former.[8] This introduces into legislative form a principle which reflects government policy of long standing (the so-called "Sandford" principle). It should be noted, however, that government takes the view that conflict is in many instances avoidable by means of negotiation or mediation. In this way a stark choice between "conservation" and "public enjoyment" should rarely arise. To this end, and more generally than just in relation to the National Parks, the Countryside Agency and the UK Sports Council have collaborated to work out how their contrasting concerns may be accommodated. The present position seems to satisfy nobody. Countryside amenity groups continually complain of intrusive sporting activities. At the same time, sporting organisations (eg water skiing) complain of increasing difficulties faced by their members in enjoying such recreation. A partial solution in relation to some sports may involve purpose-built amenities close to urban areas (eg water sports facilities).

The Norfolk Broads

The failure in the period after 1949 to have designated the Norfolk Broads as a National Park was a matter of continuing controversy. The Broads are shallow lakes which were created as recently as medieval times by the flooding of peat workings – very much a man-made area of "natural" beauty. The forty or so Broads are connected by waterways and constitute a valuable

---

8   1949 Act s.11A (added by 1995 Act s.62).

recreational area of some 50,000 acres of open water and nearly 100 miles of navigable channels. They are also of immense importance as habitat for birds and wetland plants. In 1949 the National Parks Commission, and in 1976 its successor the Countryside Commission, attempted to secure National Park status for the area. The desire for the Broads to be a National Park was for two principal motivating reasons: a wish that there should be a National Park so favourably sited to serve the densely populated south-east of England, as the Peak Park and the Lake District serve the industrial north of England; and, perhaps more importantly, to give to a single Park Authority wide powers to promote and to protect the area.

The chief problems facing the plants, birds and animals of this area are familiar ones: pollution of waterways as the numbers and proportion of motor vessels as compared with sailing boats has increased; erosion of banks as more, and more turbulent, craft use the broads; the drainage of wetlands to convert land from pasture to arable; and fertiliser run-off from agricultural land. The need for a single authority to plan and regulate the "amenity" and "conservation" future for this area increasingly became acknowledged.

Some degree of co-ordination of action on the part of the numerous district and county councils was achieved by their establishment in 1978 of a joint planning committee, thus permitting a more strategic approach to planning across the Broads region. This did not, however, suffice fully to tackle the area's needs, in particular in relation to issues of navigation and water pollution. The various local authorities in due course promoted a private bill in Parliament to establish a Broads Authority with wider and greater powers than those of the joint committee. This bill foundered in the autumn of 1985, but prompted a government bill which in due course became the Norfolk and Suffolk Broads Act 1988. This established, as of April 1989, a new Broads Authority. The legislation has created for the Broads a legal framework very much akin to that which we shall describe for National Parks. It was, however, felt by government to be appropriate to establish a special regime for the Broads rather than simply to confer National Park status because of the particular features of the area; a region of rivers, lakes and wetland rather different from the other Parks.

The Broads Authority consists of members appointed by each of the constituent district and county councils, members appointed by the Countryside Agency and English Nature, members appointed by the Great Yarmouth Port Authority, by the Environment Agency (formerly the National Rivers Authority), and by the Secretary of State for the Environment, Food and Rural Affairs.[9] In addition to becoming the sole district planning authority for the Broads area, its more general functions are to manage the Broads for the purpose of conserving and enhancing natural beauty, promoting public enjoyment, and protecting the interests of navigation. In discharging these functions the Authority is required, amongst other things, to have regard to the needs of agriculture and forestry and the economic and social interests of those who live and work in the area. As we have noted in connection with the National Parks, the aim is that the Broads shall be managed and protected as thriving and "working" areas of landscape. The intention is not that these areas be set aside as protected museum pieces.

The Broads Authority was required, as one of its first tasks, to prepare a "Broads Plan" setting out its policies for the achievement of its various statutory objectives. The plan was published, initially in draft, and was followed by a consultative process. In addition, the Authority has been required to prepare a map showing the areas within the Broads whose natural beauty it considers it to be particularly important to conserve. Both this map and the Plan are kept under review, and updated every five years.

In order to assist its protection of the Broads area, the Authority has power under the 1988 Act to make orders in respect of

---

[9]   Of the eight members currently appointed by the Secretary of State, at least three are from boating interests and two are from landowning and farming interests.

particular areas of grazing marsh, fen marsh, reed bed or broad-leaved woodland; and, in respect of any of these specified areas, to specify certain operations which appear to the Authority likely to affect the area's character or appearances. Where this power is exercised, an obligation arises on persons generally not to undertake any such operations on the land in question without having first given written notice to the authority and then –

— having received the **written consent** of the Authority; or

— having **waited for three months** following the giving of written notice, and still not have received a decision from the Authority giving or refusing consent; or

— having **waited for twelve months** from the giving of written notice, in cases where the Authority has refused consent.

Anyone acting in breach of these provisions commits a criminal offence. It will be noticed that these provisions, in themselves, do not authorise the permanent prohibition of any activity. Rather, they provide for the designation of particular activities, in specifically defined areas, and provide that those activities shall be delayed for a three or twelve month period during which time discussions can take place with the owner of the land. Such discussions may lead to a modification to the planned operation being agreed, or to a voluntary or statutory management agreement being entered into, to the satisfaction of the Authority. Where discussions are less fruitful, time should remain during which the Authority, along with other interested bodies (English Nature will have been informed) can consider taking action under other legislation; such as, for example, seeking the compulsory purchase of the land and its creation as a nature reserve.[10]

As regards navigation, the Act requires the Authority to establish a special Navigation Committee, consisting not only

---

[10] Compare the effects of designation of an area as an SSSI (below, p.162).

of members of the Authority itself but also of members with navigation interests who are not also members of the Authority. The functions of the Authority in connection with navigation are very broadly stated as being to maintain the navigation area to such standard as it thinks fit, and also to improve and develop the area for navigation as it thinks fit.

In connection with the various functions described above, the Authority has wide bye-law making powers, and also has powers to do anything necessary or expedient for the purpose of carrying out its general functions.

The establishment of this new Authority has done much to create, in effect, an additional National Park. Considered alongside the enhanced activity of the former National Rivers Authority (now the Environment Agency), the prospects for the Broads, as very significant areas of habitat and recreational value, seem better assured than hitherto.

National Parks Administration: Local or National Interests?

Returning to our discussion of the establishment of the National Parks, there was created at national level a National Parks Commission. This was, however, a rather different creature from that envisaged by the various reports mentioned above. These had recommended a powerful central body which would exercise *executive* functions in the management of National Parks. This it would do through local committees consisting of an equal number of members appointed by the National Parks Commission and by the local authorities in whose areas a Park was situated. The expenses of these committees in developing the amenities of the National Parks for the benefit of the population of the country generally would be borne by the central exchequer.

In fact, the 1949 Act introduced significantly different arrangements. A National Parks Commission was established, but as an "advisory" rather than an "executive" body, and management functions were bestowed on the local authorities in the Park areas rather than on the committees proposed. In a way this was quite logical. Given the very extensive town and country planning responsibilities which local authorities had only recently been accorded under the Town and Country Planning Act 1947, it seemed to the government only natural to assume confidence in local authorities to administer the National Parks. There were, however, worries from the start about this scheme. Essentially, the fears were that local authorities would be likely to be unduly influenced by local considerations, rather than regard the Parks as *national* resources; and that they would be unwilling to spend the sums of money necessary to realise the full amenity potential of the Parks, central funds bearing much but significantly not all of such expenditure.

These early concerns seem not to have been unfounded. Expenditure on the National Parks was, particularly in the early years, significantly less than the various Reports had recommended; and on many occasions local authorities found themselves in a dilemma, torn between their "local" concerns for the industrial and economic well-being of their areas and their broader "national" concerns for the protection of the unspoilt beauty of the Parks as recreational areas for the benefit, mostly, of "outsiders".

Boards and Committees

The detailed administrative arrangements under the 1949 Act were altered slightly at the time of the local government reorganisation of 1974. The position then became as follows. In the Peak Park the planning and management functions were in the hands of a **joint board** (the Peak Park Joint Planning Board); and in the Lake District the former joint board became, on local government reorganisation, the Lake District Special Planning Board. In contrast, the remaining eight National Parks had National Park **Committees** or, where the National Park straddled county boundaries, **Joint Committees.** The distinction between the boards in the Peak and Lake Districts and the local authority committees found elsewhere was of some significance. A board may "precept" for its expenses on the several district councils within a National Park. In other words it has power to ensure that it receives the funds it desires for its activities. The position of a committee is rather different. It submits claims in respect of its proposed expenditure to the finance committee of the local authority or authorities of which it is a committee or joint committee. The finance committee will then consider the proposed budget in the light of other calls on local authority funds and of expenditure constraints generally. It may well, therefore, choose not to allow the claim in full. Given these differing arrangements as to finance, it was not surprising that it was in relation to the Peak Park and the Lake District National Park that the activities of the Park Authorities appeared most evident.

The Environment Act 1995 introduced important changes as regards National Park administration. In essence the Act provided for the establishment during 1996, for *all* National Parks, of bodies akin to the former Peak Park and Lake District Authorities. These new National Park Authorities would, in the view of the government, be able to provide for each of the Parks the advantages of greater clarity of purpose and individual commitment to National Park objectives, together with greater freedom to manage their own affairs than was possible on the part of the former National Park Committees.

Apart from planning and specific National Park management powers, other local government functions in the Parks are undertaken by the ordinary county, district and parish councils.

We may turn now to the legal consequences which follow from designation of an area as a National Park and the establishment of a National Park Authority. The effects are, broadly, two-fold. There are certain differences to note as regards the operation of planning controls; and the park authority may exercise certain statutory powers to promote the amenity of the Park. We shall consider each of these matters in turn.

Planning

In the National Parks, the Park Authorities exercise most of the planning functions normally exercised by county and district councils. In other words development plan matters, the control of minerals, and also the day-to-day operation of development control (through planning permission and enforcement decisions) are functions of a single body with responsibilities covering the whole area of the Park.[11]

As regards the *substance* of planning control, the main special provisions in relation to National Parks arise from the fact that special provisions of the General Permitted Development Order apply to these areas,[12] thereby *reducing* the categories of development which are exempt from the requirement of obtaining planning permission.

As well as these special legal rules the actual, day-to-day, exercise of planning controls is marked by a policy of development constraint in these areas, as described earlier in Chapter 2.[13] This policy is described in the following way in the relevant Planning Policy Guidance document:[14] applications for major development should be subjected to "the most rigorous examination" and should only be granted approval "if demonstrated to be in the public interest". Such examination will involve consideration of a number of factors, including, *(i)* the need for the development in national terms and the impact of permitting or refusing it on the local economy; *(ii)* the cost and scope for development elsewhere or meeting the national need in some other way; and *(iii)* any detrimental effect on the environment and landscape and the extent to which that should be moderated. In addition, PPG7 states that the National Park Authority "may reasonably expect a prospective developer to address the issue of the impact of the proposal [by implementing an environmental assessment] ... and place more explicit emphasis on the consideration of alternative options"; and also should require that any such "construction or restoration should be carried out to high environmental standards".

---

[11] Tree preservation matters remain, however, with the district councils.
[12] For the General Permitted Development Order, see above, p.45.
[13] See above, p.72.
[14] PPG7, *Countryside.*

Management

The management of the National Parks is the responsibility of the Park Authorities. The Local Government Act 1972 imposed on the Authorities an obligation to prepare, and to review every five years, a "management plan" setting out their policies for the management of the Park and the exercise of their functions in relation to the area. Plans are produced in consultation with both the Countryside Agency (or the Countryside Council in Wales), English Heritage, and the district (or unitary) councils within the Parks. These arrangements are continued under the Environment Act 1995.[15]

The Wildlife and Countryside Act 1981 requires the preparation, by the planning authority within each National Park, of maps showing areas of mountain, moor, heath, woodland, down, cliff and foreshore whose natural beauty it is thought particularly important to preserve. Such maps are required to be prepared in accordance with guidelines as to criteria for assessing "importance" issued by the Countryside Agency, and are required to be reviewed every five years.[16] This arrangement continues as an obligation of the new Park Authorities under the terms of the 1995 Act.[17]

The National Park Authorities have a number of specific legal powers, in addition to those possessed by local authorities generally and discussed elsewhere in this book, which they may exercise in order to achieve the aims and objectives of the Parks. They may, for example, provide accommodation, refreshments, camping sites and car parks. However, since such activities may be costly and the authorities have not been over-generously funded, progress in such matters has been rather slow. An important power dating from the 1949 Act and which has been extensively used is the power to appoint Wardens,[18] who give

---

[15] 1995 Act s.66.
[16] 1981 Act s.43 as amended by the Wildlife and Countryside (Amendment) Act 1985 s.3.
[17] 1995 Act s.69(3).
[18] The Wildlife and Countryside Act 1981 has since conferred powers to appoint wardens on local authorities *generally*.

advice to users of the Parks which is often of importance in terms of safety, and they keep a wary eye open for infringements of the law or the Country Code or other threats to the ecology of the Park. The Park Authorities have not, perhaps, been able to play the part envisaged by the advisory committees of the 1940s in exploiting to the full the recreational potential of the Parks. Nevertheless, in addition to specific legal powers the National Park Authorities also pursue their general objectives by means of consultation with public bodies and landowners, giving advice on matters upon which they have developed special expertise, and giving publicity and disseminating information to the public about the Parks.

Appraisal

With what degree of success have the Park Authorities achieved their basic objectives of preserving the unspoilt natural beauty, and of promoting public enjoyment, of the designated areas? In terms of planning control over relatively minor private development in National Parks, the record has been reasonably impressive. More difficulty has been experienced in preventing intrusions by public sector bodies, and in relation to the more major development proposals of private industry. For example, the Central Electricity Generating Board succeeded in building a nuclear power station in the Snowdonia Park; oil refineries and an oil terminal have been constructed on Milford Haven on the boundary of the Pembrokeshire Coast Park; military use has been made of areas owned by the Ministry of Defence within the Dartmoor and Northumbria Parks; and, especially in the Peak District, large-scale quarrying of hillsides has been permitted. In some cases, central government has been itself responsible for controversial development in National Parks: the route chosen by the Department of Transport for the Okehampton by-pass provides an example of this. On the other hand, numerous proposals which would have had adverse effects on the landscape have not been allowed; and some of those which have been allowed have been subjected to strict conditions as regards siting and landscaping. The Llyn Celyn reservoir in Snowdonia, the development within closely defined limits of Milford Haven, and the underground pumping of water from Ullswater and Windermere are examples of this. For the future, it is likely that demand for limestone from quarries within the Parks will increase, as large quantities of this material are required to operate flue-gas-desulphurisation at electricity generating stations. Action to alleviate the problem of "acid rain" may therefore itself have deleterious effects on landscape.

A problem which planning controls have been unable to counter has been the effect on the natural beauty of the National Parks resulting from changes of agricultural use and from forestry.[19] Particular concern has been focused on the loss of heather moorland on Exmoor and on the North York Moors as a result of ploughing for more intensive agriculture or for afforestation. In this connection a provision of the Wildlife and Countryside Act 1981 should be noted. Under section 42, the Secretary of State may designate particular moorland or heath areas within any National Park for special protection. Following such designation it becomes an offence to plough or otherwise convert to agricultural use such land if the land has not been agricultural land within the previous twenty years. It is also an offence to carry on on such land any other agricultural or forestry operation specified in the ministerial order and which is likely to affect the character and appearance of the area. No offence is committed, however, in either case if the consent of the county council has been obtained; or if after three months' notice has been given the request has neither been granted nor refused; or if the action takes place over twelve months after giving notice even if consent has been refused. The idea of the scheme is thus not to forbid such actions, but to subject them to a period of delay during which discussions and negotiations may take place between the local authority, bodies such as English Nature and the Countryside Agency, and the landowner.

---

[19] The general exemption of such matters from planning controls was explained in Chapter 2, p.52, but note the discussion there of recently introduced environmental impact assessment obligations in relation to certain changes of use of *uncultivated* and *semi-natural* land.

The landowner may be persuaded to enter into a statutory management agreement, binding on the landowner and also his successors in title,[20] or it may be appropriate in some cases to protect a valuable area by making it a Site of Special Scientific Interest[21] or a Nature Reserve. In the latter case, powers of compulsory purchase are available, if necessary.[22]

AREAS OF OUTSTANDING NATURAL BEAUTY

In considering the events which led to the establishment of the National Parks, reference was made to the influential Dower and Hobhouse Reports. These proposed also that alongside the National Parks, which would be positively managed to secure the aims of landscape protection and public enjoyment, there should be designated other areas of particular landscape beauty. These other areas would generally be smaller in size than the National Parks, and would not be under the superintendence of any special managing authority in the way envisaged for the Parks; but the fact of such designation would constitute clear official recognition of the importance of preserving the attractiveness of the areas.

Procedure

The National Parks and Access to the Countryside Act 1949 implemented these basic recommendations. It gave to the National Parks Commission, now the Countryside Agency (or, in Wales, the Countryside Council), power to designate areas as Areas of Outstanding Natural Beauty (ANOB),[23] and, to date, some forty-one areas have been afforded this status. Together these areas represent around 21,000 square kilometres: about thirteen per cent of the land area of England and Wales. Designation takes place after consultation with local authorities, advertisement in the *London Gazette* (an

---

20 For example, with the local authority under s.39 of the 1981 Act.
21 This will enable English Nature to offer a management agreement: Countryside Act 1968 s.15.
22 National Parks and Access to the Countryside Act 1949 s.17. Nature Reserves and SSSIs are further considered later in this chapter.
23 National Parks and Access to the Countryside Act 1949 s.87.

HMSO publication containing official notices) and in local newspapers, and consideration of any representations, in favour or against, made by interested persons. Individual landowners are not, however, directly notified. Designation orders made by the Countryside Agency do not come into effect unless and until confirmed by the Secretary of State. Where representations have been made against any such designation, the Secretary of State may choose to convene a local public inquiry before arriving at his decision. An example of this occurred in 1985 in respect of the (then) Countryside Commission's proposed designation of a large area of land in the northern Pennines near Hadrian's Wall as an AONB. The proposal was, in due course, confirmed.

Size

There is nothing in the legislation imposing any upper or lower limit to the size of an area which may be designated as an AONB, and indeed they do vary enormously in size – the Scilly Isles being only 16 square kilometres compared with the 1730 square kilometres of the North Wessex Downs. However, it may be said that they are mostly smaller than the National Parks, but larger than the Country Parks which we shall consider shortly. Some criticism has been levelled at the substantial size of certain of the designated areas. If large areas are designated there is a risk that those wishing to act to the detriment of landscape may argue that not all of a very substantial area should merit equal and full protection. The Cotswolds, the North Wessex Downs, and the North Pennines AONBs, covering areas of 2038, 1730 and 1983 square kilometres respectively, are each larger than most of the National Parks.[24] The problem, of course, is that if a large area is indeed an area of outstanding natural beauty it deserves protection as a whole; and to divide it up into "pockets" of especially outstanding beauty may be damaging to the other areas of only outstanding beauty!

---

[24]   Pembrokeshire Coast Park (684 sq km), Exmoor (692 sq km), Dartmoor (953 sq km), Northumberland (1049 sq km), Brecon Beacons (1344 sq km), Peak District (1438 sq km), North York Moors (1432 sq km).

Unlike the National Parks, which were all created between 1951 and 1957, designation of AONBs has continued steadily throughout the period since the confirmation of the first such area, the Gower Peninsula, in 1956. Early designations included the Quantock Hills, the Lleyn Peninsula and the Northumberland Coast; recent additions to the list of AONBs have included the High Weald, Cranborne Chase and the West Wiltshire Downs, the Clwydian Hills in Wales, the North Pennines, and the Howardian Hills. It may also be noted that most of the stretches of coastline which the Countryside Agency has declared to be "heritage coasts" (not a statutory designation) fall within AONBs.

Legal Consequences

What are the legal consequences of confirmation of a designated area as an AONB? In terms of direct legal protection the answer is "surprisingly little". The 1949 Act confers general powers on local authorities to preserve and enhance the natural beauty of such areas;[25] but central government grant in aid of such matters is less generous than in connection with the National Parks, and accordingly local authorities have not been active in this respect. The 1949 Act also authorises local authorities to appoint wardens for AONBs[26] in order to enforce local authority bye-laws and to advise and assist the public. Finally, the 1949 Act requires that the Countryside Agency be consulted in relation to development plan[27] proposals affecting an AONB. However, there is no such obligation to consult the Agency about actual development proposals; though *if* consulted, the Agency is willing to give its advice. Moreover, the Agency may act positively as an "objector" to development proposals: as, for example, was the case in its opposition to a Highways Agency dual-carriageway proposal in the Blackdown Hills AONB in Somerset and Devon. The (then) Countryside Commission objected to the proposed new road through the AONB (between Ilminster and Honiton), arguing that the Highways Agency's

---

25   National Parks and Access to the Countryside Act 1949 s.11.
26   1949 Act s.92 (applicable to National Parks also).
27   As to which see above, p.68.

objectives might equally well have been obtained by improvements to the route between Ilminster and Taunton.[28]

The intention behind the AONB provisions of the 1949 Act was that designation would signal to local planning authorities the importance of applying strict development control policies to the area in order to preserve its natural beauty. In this connection a difference of emphasis between National Parks and AONBs is discernible. In considering the National Parks, it was noted that both the protection of landscape (including, now, wildlife and cultural heritage) and the promotion of recreational use are statutory objectives. As regards AONBs, the emphasis has been on protection rather than recreation; thus, for example, central government grant aid towards local authority expenditure treats more favourably projects to enhance landscape than those for recreational purposes. This may avoid certain of the special dilemmas referred to in connection with the National Parks, but the more general problems associated with rural planning control certainly remain. Indeed they become problems writ large because of the particular scenic attractions of such areas. The general policy of development constraint in rural areas should apply with particular strictness in AONBs, the onus on the developer being in such places greater than elsewhere. Quite recently the planning minister has stated explicitly that the bias against development in AONBs should be regarded as being as strong as exists within National Parks. In addition to this general policy of development constraint, the special General Permitted Development Order provisions referred to in connection with National Parks also apply to AONBs, thus bringing certain, normally excluded, development within the ambit of development control. In planning law terms, AONBs should not, therefore, be regarded as a "second-tier" level of protection as compared with National Parks.

With what degree of success has this development constraint policy protected AONBs? A fair conclusion might be to say

---

28   Following recommendations by the planning inspector, the Secretary of State gave the go-ahead for the road scheme.

that although such a policy is necessary it is not, by itself, sufficient. As stressed before, agriculture and forestry are activities which are carried on largely beyond the ambit of planning controls and each can have a very significant impact on the landscape. Much of the beauty of AONBs is not a "natural beauty" at all: it is a landscape fashioned by traditional forms and practices of agriculture and forestry, and the nature of the landscape changes if those practices alter. In AONBs, perhaps more than elsewhere, sufficient public money needs to be made available to finance management agreements with landowners, designed to secure continuation of scenically desirable agriculture and provide compensation for any lost profit in not pursuing other forms.

Following a review of AONBs in 1998, and the passing of the Countryside and Rights of Way Act 2000, AONBs have undergone a process through which Conservation Boards for each area have been established. This process, completed in early 2004, has been designed to establish Boards with responsibility for the preparation of management plans, and which also possess certain other powers of management in relation to the AONB. The aim is that a more strategic approach may result compared with what was previously possible by way of joint action by the several local authorities whose areas might have comprised an AONB.

COUNTRY PARKS

Although the National Parks are of very great importance as areas for leisure and recreation, it was apparent from the outset that they would not be sufficient alone to meet the needs of urban populations. The National Parks are at some distance from the densely populated south-east of England, and only the Peak Park is close to large city areas. In addition, therefore, to the National Parks there was a need to assist the day, or half-day, tripper to gain an experience of the countryside closer to his town home. With this intention, the Countryside Act 1968 conferred on county and district councils powers to establish and manage Country Parks.

Local Authority Powers

Country Parks may be established on land which the local authority owns; or it may purchase land, either by agreement or compulsorily, for this purpose. The Act also provides for a Country Park to be established on privately owned land by agreement with the owner.[29] Having established a Country Park, the local authority must allow access free of charge, for purposes of recreation and exercise, to all members of the public whether or not locally resident.

Within a Country Park, the local authority may provide car parks, toilets, refreshment facilities and such other amenities as it thinks appropriate. Examples of such amenities sometimes provided include adventure playgrounds for children, nature trails, camping and caravaning sites, and facilities for fishing, boating and water sports on any lake or pond within the Park.[30] Although entry to a Country Park must be free of charge, reasonable charges may be made for car parking and the use of any of the amenities provided.

The Countryside Agency has power to recommend in relation to particular Parks whether the expenditure of the local authority should qualify for 75% central exchequer grant. Since the obtaining of such financial assistance is of obvious importance to local authorities, this power of recommendation has given the Countryside Agency power to exert some influence over the location and nature of such Parks.

The Country Park idea has proved to be a considerable success. A large number have been established; the majority in the first ten years following the 1968 Act when around 150 were created. Presently, a total of around 250 have been established. They have afforded an experience of the countryside to many city residents; an experience which in some areas of intensified agriculture is not always easy for the uninitiated to gain without assistance. Conversion of much pasture to arable cultivation and the common, albeit unlawful, practice of growing crops

---

29 Countryside Act 1968 s.7.
30 These latter matters are specifically authorised by s.8 of the 1968 Act.

over footpaths, or even of ploughing them up, have led to the ironic situation that the "growth in demand for outdoor recreation has been paralleled by a great decline in the suitability of much of the countryside for these purposes".[31] The Country Parks have therefore been especially valuable in the regions with least open country and most arable land. At the same time, the Country Parks have had some beneficial effects in relieving, to a degree, pressures of congestion at other traditional beauty spots and day-trip locations. And in so far as Country Parks often embrace precious habitats for flora and fauna, the Parks are commonly managed with a view to conservation as well as simply to provide leisure and recreation. Approximately a quarter of Country Parks contain SSSIs.[32]

Local authorities have shown a good deal of flair in their presentation of Country Parks. It is common to provide a wardens service and information kiosks to meet the visitors' enquiries about the area; and, often, well written information pamphlets are provided. When the site has historical associations (such as one at Bosworth in Leicestershire) or historic buildings, these matters can, if appropriately explained, enhance considerably the interest of visitors. A good example of this is in the Sherwood Forest Country Park, where the displays at the Visitors' Centre help to explain and bring to life the traditions of Robin Hood and Maid Marian. In this particular connection, the value of Country Parks in the gentle education of the young, and less young, may be of significance. Well-marked nature trails, for example, may help stimulate an interest in, and an understanding of, conservation issues; and the greater the proportion of the community with first-hand experience of the countryside, the stronger the conservationist lobby is likely to become.

On a smaller scale, but in some ways similar to Country Parks, we may mention also the power given to local authorities by the Countryside Act 1968 to establish picnic sites, and also camping

---

[31] Bryn Green, *Countryside Conservation*, p.185.
[32] See below, p.162.

sites for holiday and recreational purposes.[33] Several hundred picnic sites have been created under this power.

CONSERVATION AREAS

These areas have already been considered in the chapter on planning. Although more commonly to be found in urban areas, there are numerous villages which are, or contain, conservation areas. The protection afforded to these areas has lain in the additional publicity attaching to planning permission applications,[34] the application of special General Permitted Development Order provisions to such areas (excluding some of the usual exemptions from the need for planning permission), and the protection afforded to trees against being felled or otherwise destroyed without local authority consent.[35] Furthermore, many local authorities have followed advice from the Department of the Environment and have established special advisory committees for the conservation areas in their districts. These consist of members of the authority and also co-opted members from local amenity societies and other interested bodies.

NATURE RESERVES

The designations considered so far have had as their principal aims, variously, the protection of scenic landscape beauty and the promotion of public recreational use of the countryside. We turn now to designations designed principally to preserve the habitats of our flora and fauna, in order to maintain the very rich diversity of plant, animal and bird life which exists in our countryside. Areas designated for this reason may in some cases be of little scenic attraction and restrictions on public access may sometimes be essential to successful habitat

---

[33] 1968 Act s.10. Note, also, the Highways Act 1980 s.112 (picnic sites and public conveniences for users of main trunk roads).

[34] The past tense is used because, since the Planning and Compensation Act 1991, such "additional" publicity requirements now apply outside and beyond those special areas. See above, p.67.

[35] See below, p.182.

protection. However, where such areas are of scenic beauty and of recreational value, public access is usually permitted in so far as the land is in public ownership and the overriding protection objectives are not endangered. We shall consider in turn each of the following: National and Local Nature Reserves, Marine Nature Reserves, Sites of Special Scientific Interest, and Environmentally Sensitive Areas. We shall then consider the significance of the EU Habitats Directive (and the earlier Wild Birds Directive) as regards the degree of protection to be afforded to such "European" sites.

National and Local Reserves

The power to establish nature reserves was given by the National Parks and Access to the Countryside Act 1949. This provides that English Nature (Countryside Council for Wales) or any local authority may establish such a reserve;[36] and defines nature reserves as land managed so as to provide opportunities, under suitable conditions and control, for study and research into the flora and fauna or geological or physiographical features of an area, or simply for the purpose of preserving and protecting the flora or fauna or such features.[37] In the light of this definition it can be appreciated why nature reserves have sometimes been called "outdoor" or "living" laboratories.

The establishment of a nature reserve may be by taking ownership of the land in question, either by agreement or by the exercise of powers of compulsory purchase; or may be by leaving the land in private ownership, and entering into agreement with the private landowner concerning the management of the land. There is also in the 1949 Act a power to acquire land compulsorily for management as a nature reserve in circumstances where there has been breach of such an agreement previously entered into. Where agreements have been entered into, these may provide for payments to be made to landowners in respect of the cost of works undertaken and

---

36 1949 Act ss.17 and 21.
37 1949 Act s.15.

also to provide compensation in respect of restrictions imposed on the owner by the terms of the agreement. Reserves which English Nature considers to be of national importance may be designated by that body as National Nature Reserves. The powers of local authorities to establish, or enter into agreements for, nature reserves are exercisable wherever it appears to the authority to be expedient in the interests of the locality. Such reserves are usually called Local Nature Reserves although, if English Nature considers such a reserve to be of national importance, it may designate it a National Nature Reserve.[38] Such designation gives English Nature certain powers in respect of the reserve.

By the end of 2000, there were over 200 National Nature Reserves, extending to over 80,533 hectares, compared with over 800 Local Nature Reserves, covering 29,000 hectares. Of the National Nature Reserves only a small proportion are on land actually owned by English Nature. Most have been established by nature reserve agreements with the landowners, or by leasing land from the landowner.

Bye-laws

Following the establishment of a nature reserve by English Nature or a local authority, there should be published in the locality a formal declaration of the existence of the reserve. This will then enable English Nature or the local authority, as the case may be, to make bye-laws in relation to the reserve.[39] Such bye-laws may cover a variety of matters necessary for the protection of the reserve, such as prohibiting or restricting access by members of the public and prohibiting actions likely to disturb or endanger any living creatures. The bye-laws may not, however, interfere with the rights of entry and access of the owners and occupiers of the land. Restrictions on the activities of owners or occupiers may, however, be contained in the nature reserve agreements, backed up by powers of compulsory purchase in the event of breach.

---

[38] There is some overlap as regards the designations described in this chapter. For example, all NNRs are also designated SSSIs.

[39] 1949 Act s.20.

Non-statutory Reserves

The discussion so far has concentrated on nature reserves established and managed under statutory powers. In addition, mention must be made of the numerous non-statutory reserves under the control of private bodies. Thus, for example, the Royal Society for the Protection of Birds has in the last three to four decades increased its landholdings from about a dozen bird sanctuaries to over 150 reserves throughout the UK, extending to over 97,000 hectares. These reserves are predominantly of value for bird protection, over ninety per cent of British breeding birds having nested on RSPB reserves. Moreover, the reserves support high proportions of British populations of a number of species, such as blacktailed godwits, bitterns and red-necked phalaropes. RSPB reserves are also of importance in terms of animal and plant habitat. For example, populations of red deer, red squirrels and otters thrive at certain reserves. The reserves include a wide variety of kinds of territory – woodland, moorland, estuaries and other wetlands. The reserves are not restricted to RSPB members, but many are closed at certain times of year to avoid disturbance of the birds. Other private reserves exist on land purchased by County Trusts for Nature Conservation. There are over forty such Trusts and they operate under the umbrella of the Royal Society for Nature Conservation. The County Trusts have established over 2560 reserves extending to 80,988 hectares. Over half of these reserves are, or include, SSSIs. Another example of a private body establishing nature reserves is the Woodland Trust. This body, established in 1972, has acquired and now manages over 1000 woods of a wide variety of ages, sizes and types. Over 150 of these are ancient woodlands of especial ecological importance. The Trust spends over £2m each year on new woodland acquisition and management and over the last six years has spent almost £60m on woodland preservation. Like the RSNC it sees itself as having an important role in stepping in and buying areas at risk of harm.

The activities of these and other bodies are of considerable importance. It must be remembered, however, that purchases by such private bodies can be by agreement only, since these bodies have no powers of compulsory purchase.[40] Moreover, once the land has been acquired, the powers of these bodies are those of the ordinary landowner. They have no power to make and enforce bye-laws regulating access to, or conduct within, the reserves.

In recent years some attention has been drawn to what might be called *de facto* reserves. These are areas which, without being specially designated or managed as reserves, nevertheless exist as relatively congenial and safe habitats for birds, animals and plants. A good example is motorway verges.[41] These areas, which are out of bounds to the public and the grass of which is not regularly cut, provide sanctuaries for much wildlife. The bee orchid, for instance, grows beside the M20 in North Kent. The verges of other roads can also provide valuable habitats but considerable harm has in the past been done in this connection by county councils in their cutting and spraying practices. In many areas, however, the councils are now attempting to preserve verges as linear nature reserves by avoiding chemical herbicides and taking care about the time of year and the heights at which they cut. Road safety is, of course, of prime importance and overgrown verges can hamper visibility. However, it seems that along most roadsides a reasonable balance may be struck between the demands of the motorist and the maintenance of congenial habitats, provided a little thought is given to the matter.

MARINE NATURE RESERVES

A further category of statutory nature reserve has been provided for by the Wildlife and Countryside Act 1981.[42] These are Marine Nature Reserves (MNR). Such reserves may be established on land covered continuously or intermittently by tidal waters, or over parts of the sea adjacent to Great Britain

---

[40] They may be given favourable non-competitive tender treatment on some sales by the Forestry Commission. See above, p.25.

[41] Other examples include country churchyards, the less well tended areas of golf courses, and the areas beside railway lines.

[42] 1981 Act s.36 and Sched. 12.

and within territorial waters. The procedure for the establishment of such a reserve is for English Nature (or, in Wales, the Countryside Council) to make application to the Secretary of State for an area to be so designated and for the Secretary of State to confirm designation. By way of contrast, note that *terrestrial* nature reserves are declared by local authorities or English Nature (Countryside Council) without central government involvement. As regards proposed *marine* reserves, the 1981 Act lays down an elaborate procedure for publication by the Secretary of State of draft orders and for consultation with appropriate bodies, such as local authorities. A local inquiry must be held if there is opposition to a proposal.[43] Marine Nature Reserves are managed in all instances by English Nature (Countryside Council); and the aims for the reserves are comparable to those in respect of reserves on land – to preserve and protect marine flora and fauna and geological and physiographical features of special interest, and to enable the study of, and research into, such flora, fauna or physical features within the reserve.

Bye-laws

The 1981 Act provides for English Nature (Countryside Council) to make bye-laws, with the consent of the Secretary of State, for the protection of any Marine Nature Reserve.[44] The proposed bye-laws must be published as part of the Secretary of State's draft designation order, so that consultation and objection can relate not just to the desirability of a reserve at the particular location but also can extend to the proposed regime for management of the reserve. Such bye-laws may provide, amongst other things, for the prohibition or restriction of entry to persons or vessels; may prohibit the killing, taking,

---

[43] The policy has been for no MNR to be declared without there being a consensus of opinion in the proposal's favour. This reflects the more public arena in which MNRs are located (*viz* seashore and coastal waters). NNRs are areas where land has been purchased for that purpose, or agreement reached with its owners.

[44] 1981 Act s.37. See, for example, the Wildlife and Countryside (Byelaws for Marine Nature Reserves) Regulations 1986 (S.I. 1986/143).

destruction, molestation or disturbance of animals[45] or plants in the reserve; may prohibit the doing of anything which will interfere with the sea bed; and may prohibit the deposit of rubbish. These wide bye-law-making powers are, however, subject to some significant limitations. The Act provides that the bye-laws shall not prohibit or restrict the exercise of any right of passage by a vessel other than a "pleasure boat" and prohibition of rights of passage of pleasure boats must not be total but must be related to particular parts of the reserve at particular times of year.[46] Furthermore, it is provided that nothing in the bye-laws shall make unlawful the discharge of any substance from a vessel;[47] and nor shall the bye-laws interfere with the statutory functions of such bodies as local authorities, the Environment Agency, or any other persons.[48] Bye-laws for the conservation of fisheries are, it should be noted, made not by English Nature (Countryside Council) but by local fisheries committees constituted under the Sea Fisheries Regulation Act 1966. These must also be published with the draft designation order so that local fishermen may know how their activities are to be restricted.

Appraisal

The marine environment may, at least until quite recently, have been a "Cinderella" area as regards conservation. Much harm has been done by such practices and activities as the discharge of sewage into the sea (a practice which distorts the natural marine environment), scallop fishing which is damaging to the seabed and its life, bait-digging[49] which can starve wading birds of lugworms (as well as producing eyesores on the landscape), and dredging operations.

Progress in the designation of Marine Nature Reserves has, however, been slow. The former NCC intended the Scilly Isles

---

[45] This expression would in this context include fish and birds.
[46] 1981 Act s.37(3).
[47] See, however, below p.300 on dumping at sea.
[48] 1981 Act s.36(6).
[49] For the right to dig for bait see *Anderson v Alnwick D.C.* [1993] 3 All ER 613.

to be the first such reserve, but this plan foundered upon fierce opposition by local fishermen. The first actual designation came in 1986 and was of Lundy, a small island off the coast of Devon. Situated amongst the warm currents of the Gulf Stream this area contains an abundance of coral, including the sunset star coral. Following Lundy, the NCC secured the designation in 1990 of Skomer and the Marloes Peninsula on the Welsh coast where large populations of seabirds, such as Manx sheerwaters, razorbills and kittiwakes depend on clear sea waters for food, and more recently Strangford Lough for its extensive mud flats and associated wildlife. Other areas which the nature conservation organisations would like designated include the Menai Straits where deep tidal rapids support specialist survivors in turbulent waters, and Loch Sween in Scotland where there are colonies of massive sponges.

The disappointing progress in designation of Marine Nature Reserves, together with the limits to the scope of bye-laws even where such a Reserve has been designated, has given rise to calls for reform as regards mechanisms for the protection of the living and physical marine environment. The matter is further exacerbated by the fact that, whereas most terrestrial nature reserves (all *national* reserves) also have protection as SSSIs, this latter protection has not been considered available beyond the territorial limits of local authority jurisdiction (*ie* the low-water mark of median tides). Thus, although the inter-tidal zone benefits from some SSSIs, there is no such protection afforded in respect of subtidal areas.

For a while the government toyed with the idea of informal and voluntary marine consultation areas – areas of broader geographical size than envisaged for MNRs – in respect of which all those contemplating potentially damaging activities would be required to engage in consultation with the nature conservation bodies. In due course (by 1993) this idea was abandoned. Attention, instead, has since focused on the need for "coastal zone management". This expression is significant. The coastal zone has suffered in that it has for too long been an area represented more by a divide of jurisdictions than by the existence of any principal environmental or conservation responsibility. What has come to be regarded as essential is for there to be devised appropriate arrangements to secure co-ordination and collaboration amongst the variety of coastal zone regulatory and managerial authorities, if possible on the basis of a "plan" for the area. Some have wanted mandatory arrangements. However, the government seems to favour reliance upon enhanced voluntary co-operation between authorities.

SITES OF SPECIAL SCIENTIFIC INTEREST

Following the enactment of the Countryside and Rights of Way Act 2000, the law relating to SSSIs has undergone a significant strengthening.

Original Scheme

Designation of SSSIs, along with the National Parks, AONBs and the Nature Reserves, dates back to the important National Parks and Access to the Countryside Act 1949. The original scheme was as follows: where the Nature Conservancy Council (NCC) was of the opinion that any area of land was of special interest by reason of its flora or fauna, or by reason of its geographical or physiographical features, it was obliged to notify the fact to the local planning authority. The planning authority was then under a duty,[50] when considering an application for planning permission for development in, or in the vicinity of, such an area, to consult with the NCC prior to coming to a decision. The planning authority was not, however, obliged to follow the advice of the NCC. Nevertheless, such advice was an important material consideration in the decision to be reached on planning merits. Furthermore, the more than just local importance attached to SSSIs rendered planning applications appropriate in some cases for ministerial "call-in".[51] The 1949 Act was passed at a time when the actions of farmers and foresters were not foreseen as being a threat to the

---

[50] Note the language of "duty": *R. v NCC ex p London Brick Property Ltd.* [1995] ELM 95.
[51] See above, p.67.

environment; and since most of their activities are, as we noted in Chapter 2,[52] outside the scope of planning controls, the system of notification of sites to the planning authority was in this context of little value.

A number of changes were made by the Wildlife and Countryside Act 1981 to seek to secure a greater degree of protection for sites. Under the revised system, English Nature (Countryside Council) was obliged not only to notify the local authorities of sites, but had to notify the Secretary of State and also the owners and occupiers. In addition, it was required that the notification should specify the flora or fauna or geological or physiographical features which made the site one of special interest, and it also had to specify any operations which appeared to English Nature to be likely to damage that flora or fauna or those features.

Those new notification requirements applied not only to SSSIs designated after the implementation of the 1981 Act, but also to all of those that had been designated before. Hence, a good deal of work had to be done in reviewing the features of pre-existing sites.

As originally enacted, the 1981 Act included a provision giving owners and occupiers a right to make representations and objections, and obliged the NCC to consider any such representations and objections. The scheme was, however, flawed in that the notices to owners and occupiers inviting comment had to be issued prior to the notification, and hence the commencement, of a site as an SSSI. Since not less than three months' opportunity to comment had to be given, the result was to give owners and occupiers at least three months' advance warning during which they could act in relation to the site as they pleased before the constraints introduced by the 1981 Act would come into operation. In other words, the procedure constituted official notice that if owners wished to plough or drain land, or do other prejudicial acts, they should do so immediately! This problem was met by the Wildlife and

___

[52] See above, p.52.

Countryside (Amendment) Act 1985[53] which amended the 1981 Act so that the statutory requirement to hear the views of owners and occupiers arose upon, rather than prior to, notification of a site as an SSSI. Again, at least three months' opportunity to comment had to be given; and within nine months of the original notification of the site, and having considered representations, English Nature (Countryside Council) had to either confirm or withdraw the notification. If it failed to do either of those things within the nine-month period, the consequence was that the original notification ceased to have effect.

The consequence of the notification under the modified 1981 Act was that, upon service of the notice, the owner or occupier would commit an offence if he carried out, or caused or permitted to be carried out, on land notified as an SSSI, any operation specified in that notification unless certain conditions were complied with. These conditions were that written notice of the proposed operations had to have been given to English Nature (Countryside Council) and that *either* their written consent was obtained, *or* that the operations carried out were in accordance with a management agreement previously drawn up with that body,[54] *or* that four months had elapsed since such written notice was given.[55] For such operations to be carried out, without reasonable excuse, except in accordance with one of these three conditions constituted a criminal offence carrying a curiously low maximum fine of £2500. It should be noted also that it was only notified operations which were subject to penalty *(cf* other damaging activities). Lists of such activities tended, however, to be quite extensive. The Act specifically provided that it should be a reasonable excuse if the operations in question were ones for which planning permission had been obtained. Therefore, the system continued to provide no protection in relation, for

---

[53] s.2.
[54] Under NPACA 1949 s.16 or the Countryside Act 1968 s.15.
[55] The 1981 Act originally specified *three* months. This was extended to four months by the Wildlife and Countryside (Amendment) Act 1985 s.2(6).

example, to activities permitted by the planning authority (possibly long before the designation and before the ecological significance of the site was appreciated). It was also a reasonable excuse if the operation was an "emergency operation", particulars of which were notified to English Nature (Countryside Council) as soon as practicable.

For the most part the 1981 Act relied on the voluntary restraint of owners and occupiers[56] rather than on clear statutory prohibition. The principle was that sites would be safe provided that owners and occupiers were made aware, by the notification procedures, of the scientific importance of their land, knew what kinds of actions were likely to be harmful to a site, and were offered reasonable sums under management agreements[57] in compensation for voluntarily accepting that they should not act so as to damage the site. The "protection" afforded has been summed up as follows: "... the regime is toothless, for it demands no more from an owner or occupier of an SSSI than a little patience. ... The Act does no more in the great majority of cases than give the Council a breathing space within which to apply moral pressure."[58]

Whether or not this voluntary approach would prove adequate was much contested during the passage of the 1981 legislation, and remained a controversial matter. In particular, the policy of "buying off" owners and occupiers by offering generous compensatory sums, under management agreements, was contentious. Although it was felt by some to be likely to be a successful policy, provided adequate sums could be made available to support such agreements, the principles behind the policy were controversial. Contrasts were drawn with the position of persons seeking to do things with, or on, their land which would be profitable but for which planning permission was necessary, for example building and operating a factory. If such permission was refused by the local planning authority,

---

[56] Note that it was only *owners* and *occupiers* of an SSSI who could commit the offence: *Southern Water Authority v NCC* [1992] 3 All ER 481.
[57] Under Countryside Act 1968 s.15.
[58] *Per* Lord Mustill in the *Southern Water Authority* case (above).

this would prevent the owner from making this more profitable use of his land. Nevertheless, there was no question of any compensation being given to him, notwithstanding that his freedom of action had been curtailed in the interests of the general public good. Why, it was asked, should those who, outside the scope of planning controls, wished to destroy or damage SSSIs be in a more favoured position?

Another criticism was that the system was open to abuse. A compensatory grant might have been sought by a person who never had any genuine intention to do things which would be harmful to a site, but who knew that such sums might be offered to him if he pretended that he intended to do those things and then was willing to agree not to do so!

Present System

As mentioned above, the Countryside and Rights of Way Act 2000 (CRoW) has fundamentally changed the framework relating to SSSIs. The single section 28 has been replaced by new sections 28-28R, which address a number of the criticisms mentioned above. Additionally, whilst there was previously a layer of European legislation strengthening the protection afforded to SSSIs,[59] it can be said that the new provisions introduced by CRoW so strengthen the protection of all SSSIs in England and Wales that this new regime may be more simply applied than that "mish mash" of overlapping national and European regulation. Whilst that which follows will apply only to new SSSI designations, English Nature (Countryside Council) is obliged to review all previously designated sites by January 2006 and to enter into appropriate management plans reflecting the new protection introduced by CRoW.

The notification process remains the same but, in addition to notifying the local planning authority,[60] the Secretary of State and the owner or occupier,[61] English Nature (Countryside

---

[59] *ie* those designated under the "Birds" and the "Habitats" Directives.
[60] This will include the National Parks Authority where applicable.
[61] Where there is a change of owner or occupier, English Nature (Countryside Council) must be notified.

Council) must also publish a notice in at least one local newspaper circulating in the area in which the land is situated. The notification to the owner or occupier includes not only details of the flora and fauna or features for which the notification is being issued, but also details of operations which are likely to cause damage and statements about the management of the land for conservation and enhancement purposes. This latter element now introduces to all SSSIs a management plan structure which was previously only afforded to those sites that were both SSSIs and designated sites under the Habitats Directive.[62] English Nature (Countryside Council) has nine months[63] in which either to confirm (with or without modifications), or withdraw, the notification.[64]

As we have seen,[65] where, under the previous system, a landowner or occupier intended to undertake an operation which was not permitted by the designation, he simply had to wait four months and could then proceed. It is now the case that such operations may not be carried out without the express written consent of English Nature (Countryside Council) unless they are already covered by a management agreement, scheme or notice.[66] The consent may contain conditions or be for a limited period, or equally no consent may be given; but in each case reasons must be given in writing;[67] and there is a right of appeal to the Secretary of State.

It is this new flexible approach which is the dynamic of the new regime. No longer is there a need to issue a comprehensive list of prohibited operations, because now there is an opportunity to vary the designations to reflect the changing circumstances of the SSSI. Management agreements no longer simply list that which cannot be done, but now require positive action to be

---

[62] See below, p.177.
[63] From the date of service on the Secretary of State.
[64] As previously enacted, this period ran concurrently with the three-month period during which the landowner or occupier could raise objections.
[65] See above, p.164.
[66] Under 1949 Act s.16 or 1968 Act s.15, or under s.28J or s.28K of the 1981 Act respectively.
[67] Where consent is not granted, compensation is payable.

taken by the landowner or occupier in order to benefit from payments. If the landowner or occupier fails to fulfil his obligations under the management agreement, English Nature (Countryside Council) may serve a management notice on him demanding that he takes the requisite action and, if he is in default, the body may undertake the work and seek its reasonable costs from the landowner or occupier and, if appropriate, suspend agreed payments.

No longer can the regime afforded to SSSIs be seen as "toothless". Upon notification, certain operations must cease, unless in the case of an emergency (and even then notice by the landowner or occupier must be given expeditiously after the event). And whereas, before, the landowner or occupier could take a fiscal decision as to whether to damage the SSSI, he is now subject to an unlimited fine, if found guilty; and for any conviction involving an SSSI the court must, in assessing the quantum of the fine, take into account the benefit to the defendant of the damage caused. Additionally, or alternatively, the court can require the defendant to rectify the damage. Furthermore, and quite separately, compulsory purchase of the site may be initiated at any time.

The new arrangements also protect the SSSI from the actions of third parties, and English Nature (Countryside Council) may make bye-laws restricting access to, or activities within, an SSSI, broadly along the lines of those which may be made in relation to nature reserves. Whilst lawful operations[68] and those undertaken in an emergency (again, provided that notice is promptly given following the emergency) are permitted, in other circumstances an offence is committed if a person either intentionally or recklessly causes damage to the SSSI or intentionally or recklessly disturbs the fauna therein.

Prior to CRoW it was not uncommonly the case that it was not the landowner or occupier who was the culprit causing damage to SSSIs but instead it was a utility provider or public authority

---

[68] Such as actions following express planning permission or consent having been obtained from an authorising body.

going about its lawful business and having little, if any, regard for the impact of its operations. Under CRoW, public authorities and statutory undertakers, whilst performing their lawful activities, now have to have have regard to the damage they may cause to the SSSI directly, or through their activities to land outside the SSSI. The provisions do not have the effect of preventing the operations, but envisage that the authority or operator will, if so advised, mitigate the damage as much as possible. The authority or undertaker must inform English Nature (Countryside Council) of its intended activity and obtain an assent to undertake the works. If there is no assent forthcoming, then a further notice must be issued detailing the works to be done, the means by which the authority or undertaker has put in place any advice from English Nature (Countryside Council), how it plans to mitigate the damage done and details of restorative works. Effectively, the regime provides English Nature (Countryside Council) with an opportunity to influence the activities or, at the very least, to have notice of such activities at SSSIs. Failure of the authority or undertaker to comply with these *procedural* provisions will lead to a criminal offence being committed.

"Super-SSSIs": Nature Conservation Orders

The effect of the Countryside and Rights of Way Act 2000 has been that the slightly higher degree of protection afforded hitherto to particular sites by their designation, not simply as SSSIs under section 28 but as "super-SSSIs" under section 29 of the 1981 Act, is no longer necessary. The new regime affecting ordinary SSSIs offers equal if not greater protection than the section 29 protection.

Designation of such "super-SSSI" sites was by the Secretary of State, following consultation with English Nature (Countryside Council), and was by means of what was called a Nature Conservation Order. Only a few such super-SSSIs were ever designated. The power was exerciseable in respect of land which, because of its flora or fauna or geological or physiographical features was of "special interest"; for the purpose of securing the survival in Great Britain of any kind of animal or plant, or of complying with international obligations; or in respect of land which, because of its flora or fauna or geological or physiographical features, was of "national importance", and for the purpose of conserving any such flora or fauna or features.

The protection afforded to super-SSSIs was in many respects the same as for (then) ordinary SSSIs: the differences lay in the following matters. The level of fines which could be imposed in respect of offences committed in relation to super-SSSIs was higher than in respect of ordinary SSSIs; moreover, the offences were defined so as to include actions done by persons other than owners and occupiers. The requirement not to take action until at least three months' notice had been given to English Nature (Countryside Council) was strengthened by a provision that if that body offered to enter into a management agreement, or offered to purchase the land, the three-month period thereby became extended. This gave to the conservation agencies a more generous period of time during which to negotiate voluntary agreements with owners, or in the last resort to purchase the land compulsorily, than was the case with ordinary SSSIs. The compulsory purchase powers exercisable were those which were possessed to acquire land to establish nature reserves. However, as with ordinary SSSIs, the value of the rules depended, ultimately, on the availability of adequate manpower and funds.

Finally, one further protective feature, applicable to super SSSIs though not (then) to ordinary SSSIs, may be mentioned. The 1981 Act provided that, upon conviction for having destroyed or damaged a super-SSSI contrary to the terms of the Act, the court could, in addition to the power to impose a fine, make an order requiring the defendant to carry out, within a period specified in the order, such operations for the purpose of restoring the land to its former condition as it specified in the order. Failure on the part of the defendant to comply with such a restoration order constituted a further offence. Moreover, where restoration was not undertaken as ordered, the statutory conservation bodies were empowered to enter on to the land to carry out those operations and then recover their expenses reasonably incurred from the person in default.

It will be evident that the new regime introduced by CRoW and applicable generally to section 28 SSSIs now has comparative provisions to those found in section 29 and, as such, designation as a "super-SSSI" adds nothing to the protection of a new SSSI.

ENVIRONMENTALLY SENSITIVE AREAS

This is a category of specially protected area the origin of which lies with the United Kingdom's membership of the European Community. Community funding is available to assist with the protection of areas where wildlife and landscape are of special importance and are particularly vulnerable to changes in agricultural practice.[69] The matter is governed in United Kingdom legislation by the Agriculture Act 1986.

Designation of Areas

This Act provides that DEFRA may by order designate an area as an Environmentally Sensitive Area (ESA) if, following consultation with the Countryside Commission and English Nature (Countryside Council), it appears that it is particularly desirable to:

— conserve and enhance the natural beauty of the area; or

— conserve the flora or fauna or geological or physiographical features of the area; or

— protect buildings or other objects of archaeological, architectural or historical interest in the area.

DEFRA must also consider that the maintenance or adoption of particular agricultural methods is likely to facilitate such conservation, enhancement or protection; and must also obtain Treasury consent.

---

[69]   Under EC Regulation 797/85 Art. 19.

Agreements

Having designated an area as an ESA, DEFRA may then make agreements with owners and occupiers of land in that area by which such persons agree, in consideration of "incentive" payments to be made by the Minister, to manage their land in accordance with the provisions of the agreement. In other words, agreements will provide for cash payments to farmers who agree not to engage in environmentally detrimental practices or who agree to revert to more environmentally beneficial forms of agriculture. The order which designates an area as an ESA may specify provisions which must be incorporated into all such agreements within that area. These provisions may, for example, relate to the particular requirements as to agricultural practices, methods, operations, or the installation or use of equipment, the period or minimum duration during which such agreements must last, the consequences of breach of an agreement's requirements, and the rates or maximum rates of payments to be made. It may be noted that much flexibility is left as to the particular terms of agreements as between different ESAs, but that within an ESA the intention of the Act is for agreements to be in fairly standard form as between different landowners and the ministry.

Unless an agreement provides to the contrary, the terms are binding on successors in title to the person who originally made the agreement. When agreements have been made, DEFRA is required to keep under review the effect on the area of performance of the obligations under the agreement, and to publish from time to time such information about those effects as it considers appropriate.

The Areas

Early in 1986 the then Countryside Commission and the NCC made recommendations as to appropriate areas for such designation, and also presented their views about "management guidelines" and grant levels. From an original list of 46 areas for consideration, the two bodies settled on 14 areas of England and Wales which they proposed should be designated as ESAs. These areas were of considerable variety, illustrating clearly the numerous different ways in which modern farming techniques and practices may be harmful to landscapes and habitats. In August 1986, MAFF designated five of the areas recommended, and schemes in respect of these areas came into operation early in 1987. The original five areas designated were:

The Norfolk Broads – where an earlier experimental scheme in respect of the Halversgate Marshes had already been operating, offering farmers £50 an acre to continue traditional grazing practices rather than draining and ploughing their land for arable cultivation.

Pennine Dales – where protection of the traditional stone-walled hay meadows has been needed against more intensive methods of livestock farming involving draining and reseeding pastures and cutting the grass for silage.

Somerset Levels – where the grazing marshes were threatened by the prospect of continued drainage and ploughing for arable.

South Downs (Eastern half) – where much of the chalk grazing downland had been ploughed for arable cultivation.

West Penwith (Cornwall) – where management guidelines have taken account of the need to protect the prehistoric archaeological interest of this area from being harmed by the "improvement" of the dairy farmland.

Since 1987 the process of designation has continued. At present there have been designated within England some 22 such areas, extending to over 10% of agricultural land.[70]

The scheme appears to be popular both with farmers and with conservationists.[71] Some 7980 farmers had, by 1997, joined the scheme. This represents a very satisfactory take-up rate,

---

[70] There are six ESAs in Wales. The 28 areas cover more than 1.5 million hectares.
[71] Although there is criticism that Biodiversity Action Plans are not mandatory requirements of ESA payments.

the only area where there appeared to be reluctance to join the scheme being the Test Valley. On joining the scheme a farmer enters into a ten year agreement under which he will receive an annual payment at the rate per hectare prescribed for the area, in return for following the prescribed farming practices which have been set down for that area. The ESA has a number of different tiers of entry[72] each requiring different levels of agricultural practice. The practices may have positive and negative aspects. For example, the farmer may have to refrain from draining his land and agree to fertiliser restrictions; he may also have to maintain hedges, barns and ponds.

ARCHAEOLOGICAL AREAS

Protection of areas of archaeological importance is provided for by the Ancient Monuments and Archaeological Areas Act 1979. This Act authorises the designation, as an Area of Archaeological Importance (AAI), of any area which appears to the Secretary of State, or a county or district council, to merit the protection of the Act.[73]

Such designation orders have been made in respect of the historic centres of five towns (Canterbury, Chester, Exeter, Hereford and York) but not in respect of any archaeologically rich areas of countryside.

Once an area has been so designated, it becomes an offence for any person, including the owner of the land, to carry out certain kinds of operations on the land unless he has served a notice relating to those operations on the appropriate authority at least six weeks previously.[74] The appropriate authority is normally the district council although, if it is a local authority itself which proposes to perform the operations, the operations notice is served on the Secretary of State. The kinds of operations to which the notice requirements apply are ones which disturb the ground, flooding operations and tipping operations.

---

[72] Approximately 80% of farmers have entered at one of the lower tiers.
[73] 1979 Act s.33.
[74] 1979 Act s.35(1).

These provisions are designed to give advance warning of potentially damaging operations. What steps may be taken on receipt of such information? The Act provides for the appointment of persons competent to undertake archaeological investigations as "investigating authorities".[75] When an operations notice has been served, the investigating authority acquires the right to enter onto the land in question, at any reasonable time, to inspect the site in order to record any matters of archaeological or historical interest, to determine whether any excavations would be desirable, or to observe the operations being carried out so as to be able to examine and record any items of historical or archaeological interest discovered during those operations.[76] When the investigating authority considers that excavation is desirable, it may acquire power to do so provided that it serves an excavation notice on the "developer" within four weeks of the service of the operations notice. The period allowed for excavation is, generally, six months starting from the date of service of the operations notice. During this period of excavation the operations described in the operations notice must not be carried out.

In addition to this protection afforded to areas of archaeological importance, the 1979 Act also provides for the protection of particular "ancient monuments" by means of a process of "scheduling". Most proposals for scheduling emerge from the work of English Heritage. Monuments protected in this way, amounting to more than 13,000, take a wide variety of forms, ranging in age from the constructions of Britain's very earliest inhabitants to the military defences erected during World War II. Some are easily recognisable (*eg* the stone ruins of medieval castles); others exist only as earthworks or appear to the untrained eye as merely an unevenness across a ploughed field. These latter kinds of feature are particularly vulnerable to damage by modern agricultural practices and equipment. The only statutory requirement is that any monument to be scheduled must be of "national importance". In fact attention

---

75   1979 Act s.34.
76   1979 Act s.38(1).

focuses on factors such as age, rarity, condition, vulnerability and documentation. That there is no duty to schedule was affirmed in relation to the underground remains of the Rose Theatre in London. The Secretary of State, being satisfied of English Heritage's approval of safeguards integrated into the development of the site, was held to have acted in the lawful exercise of his discretion not to schedule the monument.[77]

The 1979 Act, consolidating and strengthening the terms of earlier legislation, provides that any such scheduled monument shall not be demolished, destroyed, damaged, removed, repaired, altered, added to, flooded or covered up without first the Secretary of State having granted consent.[78] Breach of this obligation constitutes a criminal offence. In certain quite limited circumstances an entitlement to compensation may follow a refusal of such consent.[79] In addition, payments may be sought from English Heritage (formerly the Historic Buildings and Monuments Commission) in return for entering into management agreements.[80] Such agreements are usually for a five year period and will compensate the landowner for agreeing to take action to protect the site (eg by the erection of fencing) or for agreeing to cultivate the area in particular ways (usually avoiding deep ploughing) which help protect the site.

Finally, it may be noted that none of the provisions of the 1979 Act confer on the public any rights of access to monuments or sites.

LIMESTONE PAVEMENTS

The Wildlife and Countryside Act 1981 makes special provision, in section 34, for the protection of limestone pavements. These are defined as "areas of limestone which lie wholly or partly exposed on the surface of the ground and have been fissured by natural erosion". In relation to such locations the

---

[77] See R. v S.S.E. ex p Rose Theatre Trust Co. [1990] JPL 360.
[78] Either upon application, or within general consent under the Ancient Monuments Class Consents Order 1994 (S.I. 1994/1831).
[79] 1979 Act s.7(1).
[80] See 1979 Act ss.17 and 24.

Act provides that, where English Nature (Countryside Council) or the Countryside Agency consider that any land comprising a limestone pavement is of special interest by reason of its flora, fauna or geological or physiographical features, it shall be under a duty to notify that fact to the local county planning authority. The planning authority will then be in a position to take this into account in considering applications for planning permission for mineral extraction.

The section then proceeds to authorise the Secretary of State or the county planning authority to make limestone pavement orders. Such orders may be made when it appears that the character or appearance of a limestone pavement would be likely to be adversely affected by the removal of the limestone or by its disturbance in any way. The effect of such an order is to make it a criminal offence for any person to remove or disturb limestone on a limestone pavement to which such an order applies, unless there is a reasonable excuse for such action. It is, further, expressly provided that it shall constitute a reasonable excuse if the actions were authorised by a grant of planning permission. This covers mineral extraction which has been approved under planning controls. However, since agricultural actions affecting such areas are subject to deemed permission rather than granted permission, it seems that the general agricultural exemption from planning control does not take agricultural damage beyond the scope of this protection. Accordingly, removal of limestone by a landowner to use as lime for fertiliser will be an offence where a pavement order has been made.

SPECIAL PROTECTION AREAS AND SPECIAL AREAS FOR CONSERVATION: THE WILD BIRDS AND HABITATS DIRECTIVES

Over the past two or three decades, species protection and habitats protection have become matters in respect of which nations have begun to agree certain obligations at international level. In some instances, this has reflected the sheer necessity of concerted and co-ordinated international action if a particular problem is to be tackled effectively. For example, if migrating species are to be adequately protected, it is necessary for there to be appropriate conservation rules and policies operating in all the countries visited by those species. An important international treaty in this context is the Ramsar *Convention on Wetlands of International Importance especially as Waterfowl Habitat* (1971). Similarly, action at international level has been considered the most likely effective way to secure protection, even for non-migrating species, where the survival problem is related to the adverse impact of international trade in such species – live or dead, whole or in parts. This is the basis of the Washington *Convention on International Trade in Endangered Species* (1972).

More recently, the underlying rationale of international protection has broadened somewhat. The Rio Summit of 1992 gave strong support to the importance, for nations collectively, of their seeking to preserve and enhance bio-diversity. The aim of securement of a continued high degree (both globally and more locally) of bio-diversity is very closely linked to that other fundamental policy ideal given impetus at Rio: the idea of the need to organise ourselves in ways which make sustainable (and not wasting) use of environmental capital.

In addition to agreements such as those just mentioned, there are others which have a specific focus on Europe. Here we might mention, as significant examples, the Bern *Convention on the Conservation of European Wildlife and Natural Habitats*, and the Bonn *Convention on the Conservation of Migratory Species of Wild Animals*. These various agreements have had some considerable impact on law and policy within the United Kingdom. Their provisions were important stimuli towards the enactment of the species protection rules to be found in the Wildlife and Countryside Act 1981 (discussed in Chapter 6 below), our domestic legislation on the importation and export of endangered species, and also the decisions which have been taken as regards designation and protection of particular sites as SSSIs. For example, we have sought to secure protection for those wetland sites which we have designated under the Ramsar convention as "Ramsar Sites" by use of the SSSI designation.

Significant as these agreements and instruments have been, it is appropriate that we should devote principal attention here to two measures deriving from the European Community: the directive of 1979 on the Conservation of Wild Birds (79/409) and the directive of 1992 on the the Conservation of Natural Habitats and of Wild Flora and Fauna (92/43).

Moreover, it is with the 1992 directive that our discussion should begin. The principal aim of the Habitats Directive is to "promote the maintenance of bio-diversity" by means of the establishment across the Community of a coherent network of special areas of conservation, collectively known as Natura 2000.

The network will comprise sites falling within three categories: *(i)* those of certain *natural habitat types* listed in Annex I to the directive; *(ii)* those which provide habitat for *certain species* listed in Annex II; *(iii)* those sites which have been designated as *special protection areas* (SPAs) for the purposes of the Wild Birds Directive. In this way, it may be noted that the habitat protection provisions of the Birds Directive are secured "under the wing" of the 1992 directive's provisions.

The directive contains quite elaborate provisions as regards the process for ascertainment of, and eventual designation of, appropriate sites to comprise the Natura 2000 network. There are four categories of designation of Special Areas of Conservation (SACs) in England.[81]

(a) sites nominated by the Member State and formally designated by the Minister for the Environment, Food and Rural Affairs;

(b) sites nominated by the Member State, approved by the European Commission as sites of Community importance, and formally designated by the Minister;

(c) sites which the European Commission considers to be

---

[81] (d) does not apply to Wales and Scotland. The devolved bodies likewise have not submitted candidate sites.

Special Areas because they host *priority species* or provide *priority habitat*;

(d) sites which the government has submitted as candidates for inclusion arising from the Joint Nature Conservation Committee review in 1995.

Whilst the European Commission gave an early indication that not all candidate sites submitted by Member States would eventually be listed for designation, the government treats all such candidates provisionally as having SAC status.

The protection afforded by the directive to SACs (and also to SPAs under the Wild Birds Directive) comprises:

(i) an obligation to take appropriate steps to avoid the deterioration of such listed sites or significant disturbance of species for whose protection sites have been designated;

(ii) an obligation to subject to "appropriate assessment" any plan or project which, alone or in combination with others, is likely to have a significant effect on such a site. Following assessment of the plan or project's implications for the site, the national authorities shall permit the plan or project only if they have established that it will not adversely effect the integrity of the site.

This second obligation appears to afford a high degree of protection. It is, however, immediately followed by an exception. It is provided that, where a project will damage the conservation interest of a site, it may nevertheless be permitted provided *(i)* there are no alternative solutions, and *(ii)* it is necessary for the project to be undertaken for "imperative reasons of overriding public interest", including reasons of a "social or economic nature". In such event, the Member State must give notification to the European Commission and must also take compensatory measures intended to preserve the overall coherence of the Natura 2000 network. An example of such an operation concerned the Cardiff Bay development where habitat was lost as a result of construction of the barrage and other land near Newport was compulsorily purchased to create a new compensatory wetland scheme.

This exception provides some flexibility for Member States, albeit within reasonably closely defined limits. It should be noted, however, that in relation to sites designated in respect of *priority* species or habitats, the circumstances in which a plan or project may be permitted to proceed are somewhat more limited. In addition to the requirement that there are no alternative solutions, the grounds must relate to *(i)* "human health or public safety"; *(ii)* "environmental improvements of primary importance"; or *(iii)* other reasons of "public interest" accepted as such by the decision-maker in full awareness of the opinion of the European Commission on the matter.

In order to seek to implement these obligations, the United Kingdom has made the Conservation (Natural Habitats etc) Regulations 1994.[82] These Regulations are complex but are founded upon the basis that SACs (called by the Regulations "European Sites") should be protected by provisions substantially similar to those we have earlier described under the heading "SSSIs".

It will be remembered that, under the ordinary "pre-CRoW" SSSI arrangements, the prohibition on prejudicial activities was essentially only a temporary one, pending the negotiation of a management agreement (or ultimately, cash permitting, the compulsory purchase of the land in question). In either of the latter situations the protection afforded was noted to be only as great as the depth of the pockets of the conservation agencies! In relation to European sites, the protection afforded has always been a little stronger. Certainly, the paragraphs of the Regulations dealing with the protection afforded to European sites begin in familiar vein, seeming only to delay projected activities rather than imposing outright prohibitions. The difference comes in the situation where the national conservation agency has decided *not* to consent to the operations planned and considers there to be a risk that those operations

---

[82]   S.I. 1994/2716.

will still be carried out. The agency is then required to give notice to the Secretary of State, who may proceed to make a Special Nature Conservation Order. Such an order involves a stronger course of action than was possible under "ordinary SSSI" nature conservation order procedure. Following the making of a Special Nature Conservation Order, it is an offence to engage in operations there listed except where *(i)* notice has been given to the appropriate conservation body and the consent of that body has been obtained; or *(ii)* the actions fall within the terms of a management agreement which may have been negotiated. These provisions which have benefited EU protected sites seem rather less remarkable now that newly designated SSSI sites are similarly protected.

In addition, in relation to EU-protected sites, in cases where a plan or operation which might damage such a site is subject to the requirement of planning permission, the 1994 Regulations imposed for the first time a *legal* (rather than just political) restraint on the capacity of decision-makers to override conservation objectives on the basis that they are considered to be outweighed by "other material considerations". Furthermore, the Regulations prevent plans or projects which may have such adverse effect from coming within the ambit of permitted development rights under the General Permitted Development Order (so requiring express applications for planning consent). Moreover, where consent for development has earlier been obtained but not yet implemented (or fully implemented), and where such operations may affect a European site, an obligation has been imposed upon planning authorities to review the consent given earlier and to modify or revoke it where appropriate (with obligations to provide compensation).

TREES AND WOODLANDS

Introduction

The areas so far considered in this chapter have received protection by a process of designation, thus bringing into operation certain legal safeguards and conferring powers and duties on public authorities with respect to those areas. We turn now to consider the protection afforded to certain kinds of land quite apart from any special designation. We begin with trees and woodlands, and will then consider the activities of the National Trust, Crown Estate Commissioners, and certain other landowners, each of whom own much land of prime importance in terms both of recreation and the protection of habitats, and manage their lands with conservation in mind.

The importance of trees and woodlands to the conservation of our countryside can hardly be over-stated. Quite apart from the visual attractions of individual trees and areas of woodland in the landscape, trees are vital for the maintenance of a diverse natural world. Trees help purify the atmosphere, they prevent soil erosion and the leeching of soil nutrients, and provide habitats for birds, small mammals and a wide variety of flora.

It is a matter of considerable concern that the world's trees are under serious threat. Dangers arising from clearance of tropical rain forest to provide what, because of climate and soil changes, may only be short-term cultivatable land are beyond the scope of this book. However, even confining ourselves to this country, the extent of deforestation has been so great that Britain has less trees per acre than almost any country in Europe, having only about 10% forest and woodland cover. Furthermore, there has been disquiet in recent years about the nature of the tree cover to be found in Britain. Commercial considerations have resulted in a very high proportion of plantings this century being coniferous, and the extent of traditional, ancient, broadleaved, deciduous woodland has declined to total now only about 700,000 acres. The statements need, however, to be put into context. The figure of 10% forest cover should be contrasted with only about 5% at the time of the First World War. Also, changes to subsidy arrangements have meant that in recent times a larger area of broadleaved woodland has been planted than conifers.

The disadvantages of coniferous woodlands are two-fold. First, they provide much less in the way of wildlife and plant habitat than do many forms of broadleaved woodland; and, secondly, there has been a tendency for coniferous plantations to have been blanket-planted across a landscape in geometric pattern bearing little or no relation to the natural contours of hill and dale, and so spoiling the visual beauty of the countryside.

The loss in Britain of much of its woodland demonstrates very clearly the impact of man on his environment. Over most of Britain, except for the highest mountain regions and waterlogged lowland areas, woodland is the natural vegetation; sometimes referred to as the "climax" vegetation, the vegetation that would exist in particular physical conditions (soil, climate, etc.) independent of human activity. And Britain was, of course, once very much a wooded country. The form of tree cover varied somewhat according to region; with oak, ash, beech, elm, lime and poplar being the main trees of the deciduous broadleaved woodlands of England and Wales, and coniferous forest predominating in the Scottish Highlands.

Forest clearance began surprisingly early. Until relatively recently this was thought to have begun in a significant way only in post-conquest medieval times. However, recent researches have demonstrated the very marked effects of man in the Neolithic and, more particularly, the Bronze Ages (*ie* from about 3000 BC). Clearance began on the lighter soils of the limestone and sandstone uplands, leaving large forests on the heavy clay lowlands; and this process continued through the Roman, Saxon and medieval periods right through to modern times. The reasons for felling trees have varied with time and place. Originally clearance was mainly to provide grazing land and cultivatable land in the initial ages of agriculture; at later times the need for timber for shipbuilding and for house construction was of importance, as well as the burning of charcoal for iron ore smelting and generally the use of timber as fuel. From relatively early times concern has existed at the depletion of the forests. In Elizabethan times, for example, much planting of oaks took place in order that timber for shipbuilding should be in ready supply.

In this section we shall be principally concerned with the activities of the Forestry Commission, and with the powers of local planning authorities in relation to trees and woodlands.

Forestry Commission

Some reference was made earlier, in Chapter 1, to the Forestry Commission.[83] Established in 1919, its aim was to secure a degree of public control over timber resources. It was not, however, a matter of nationalising the forests. The Forestry Commission has sought to achieve its aims in two ways: on the one hand, by acquiring existing woodlands and other land upon which it has created new plantations; and, also, by securing the permanent dedication of privately owned woodlands to forestry and then to support the private owners by grants and other technical and scientific assistance. In other words it has both managed its own forests and supervised the private sector. Privately owned woodlands remain of immense importance. About half the timber felled annually is from such woodlands, and this includes most of the hardwood timber.

Statutory Objectives

From the inception of the Forestry Commission in 1919 through to, and including, the Forestry Act 1967, the statutory aims of the Commission were stated primarily in terms of the control and management of timber production on a commercial basis, without significant reference to the importance of forests for recreation, as places of scenic beauty or as rich habitats for wildlife and plants. Thus, the original aims were to develop and ensure the best use of the country's timber resources and to promote efficiency in the timber industry, to undertake research relevant to the needs of forestry, to combat forest and tree pests and diseases, to advise and assist in training in forestry and to administer controls and schemes for assisting private woodland owners. The aims also included those of advancement of knowledge and understanding of forestry and trees in the countryside, and to ensure the use of forest management systems and practices which safeguard the environment; but

---

[83] The Forestry Commission is devolved, with Commissions for England, Wales and Scotland. Each Director is a member of the GB Board of Commissions which deals with matters arising that affect the three countries jointly.

these appeared to be subsidiary objectives only. For many years concern was expressed at the failure of the Commission to allow, or to make adequate provision for, public access to its forests; an apparent lack of concern for the visual amenity of its plantations; and failure to undertake forestry in ways which promote rich habitats, for example by ensuring the continuance of broadleaved woodland and by "selection felling" rather than the ecologically more catastrophic practice of blanket felling.

A good deal has, however, now changed. Increasing demands for countryside recreation which became apparent during the 1950s and 1960s resulted in the Commission taking measures to accommodate these needs. The Commission embarked on a programme of creating forest walks, establishing visitor centres, caravan and camping sites, and letting forest cabins and disused cottages for holidays. As such, valuable steps have been taken in making available the recreational potential of Forestry Commission land to the public. But what about visual amenity? Here again the Commission has improved its planting techniques. Recent plantings, under the guidance of landscape architects, have been more sensitive in relation to topography, and have consisted of mixtures of species so as to produce variation of foliage colour and growth forms, as well as the use of screens of deciduous broadleaves such as beech and oak. The incorporation of reasonably wide forest drives within new plantations has the two-fold benefit of facilitating public access to forest interiors and also of acting as fire-breaks; increased incidence of forest fires being an unfortunate, but apparently inevitable, consequence of public enjoyment of these areas.

More recently, the Wildlife and Countryside (Amendment) Act 1985 has made quite clear the environmental as well as the commercial and recreational obligations of the Commission. Section 4 of the 1985 Act[84] modifies the general duties of the Commission so that in discharging its functions under the Forestry Acts the Commission shall, so far as is consistent with the proper discharge of those functions, endeavour to achieve

---

[84]   Amending the Forestry Act 1967.

a reasonable balance between *(a)* the development of afforestation, the management of forests and the production and supply of timber and *(b)* the conservation and enhancement of natural beauty and the conservation of flora, fauna, and geological or physiographical features of special interest.

A matter which aroused a good deal of controversy during the 1980s was the way that government grant and tax relief policies seemed inimical to nature conservation. Policies encouraged afforestation of the wrong kinds and in the wrong places. The argument over proposals to drain and plant forest over the Flow country in Caithness reached such a pitch that, as a result, the policies were considerably modified so as to seek to promote, rather than frustrate, conservation objectives. Then, in 1985, a new broadleaved woodland grant scheme was announced, and within three years the proportion of broadleaves in new private planting had increased from 9% to 17%. In 1988, the Forestry Commission replaced this with a new Woodland Grant Scheme, also offering higher rates of grant for broadleaf plantings. A significant feature of this Woodland Grant Scheme is that it has been designed to secure planting which positively enhances both the visual and the recreational potential of the countryside. Applicants for grants are required to specify their intentions in respect of such matters as landscape planning, wildlife conservation, and the protection of watercourses. Also in 1988, commercial woodlands were removed entirely from the scope of income and corporation tax reliefs. Thenceforth governmental support was to be by way of specific grant schemes incorporating environmental considerations, rather than by tax advantage. The "sensitivity" of planting decisions to grant-support has resulted in broadleaved plantings recently outstripping coniferous; leading, indeed, to some concern as regards adequacy of future supplies of home-grown softwood timber.

In these ways it has been hoped to encourage planting at the rate of some 33,000 hectares a year: the ultimate government aim being that the area of forested land in England should double. In addition, support is being given by government for the development of a dozen new Community Forests on the degraded urban fringes of areas such as Tyne and Wear, South Staffordshire and East London – these to be known as the Great North, Mercia and Thames Chase forests – and for the development of a new "national forest" in the East Midlands. This latter project will involve, over a 40 year period, the creation of a forest of some 40,000 hectares (150 square miles). It is the aim of the government to achieve this by means of substantial private and voluntary sector investment. The project is run by the National Forest Company which has so far agreed planting of almost 7419 hectares of new woodland. Periodically, it invites "sealed bid" project applications. Grants for planting are awarded to successful tenderers (private landowners, local authorities, conservation trusts). The bids are expected to include provision for public access.

Controls over the Private Sector

So far as management of the Forestry Commission's own forests is concerned, the outlook appears to be reasonably promising, with policies showing more sensitivity to the interests of conservation and amenity than has always been the case hitherto. As regards the private sector, it is necessary to consider separately the way in which control is exercised over the *planting* and *felling* of trees. As regards planting, the control operates by way of the economic necessity for commercial forestry to secure grant-support. Such grants require that appropriate environmental/conservation concerns are addressed. In certain situations, when planting may be likely to have adverse environmental consequences, it may be obligatory before a decision is taken about grant-support, to require applicants to provide an environmental impact assessment statement.[85]

As regards the felling of trees, the controls are exercised through the system of Tree Preservation Orders and Forestry Commission felling licences.

---

[85] See further, above, p.61.

Tree Preservation Orders

The first matter to be remembered is that the ordinary planning controls over the development of land do not apply to forestry. Thus, trees and woodlands may be planted or cut down without the need for planning permission. However, this statement needs qualification in certain respects.

To begin with, local authorities may protect trees by making Tree Preservation Orders. Such Orders may be made at any time by the district planning authority in respect of a single tree, a group of trees or an area of woodland where this action may help to conserve the amenity of the area. In other words it is visual appearance of the area in question which is the significant criterion. Trees are not protected by TPOs "for their own sake" or for reasons of nature or habitat protection. Trees may, however, merit protection either because of their individual beauty or because of their collective contribution to landscape.

Regulations have been made prescribing the form the Order should take; it must, for example, include a map showing the position of the tree or trees to which it applies.[86] Orders are made first in draft form and do not come into effect unless and until confirmed by the district planning authority. In situations where there is a likelihood of threat to a tree or trees between the draft stage and confirmation, the draft may be made so as to come provisionally into effect on the date specified in the draft (usually the date it was made). In such a case the provisional order will cease to have effect unless confirmed within six months. Orders made must be available for public inspection, and copies must be sent to owners and occupiers of the land in question. Within 28 days objection may be made to a TPO and any such objections must be considered by the district planning authority in deciding whether or not to confirm its order.[87]

Once a TPO is in force, it becomes an offence for any person

---

[86] Town and Country Planning (Trees) Regulations 1999 (S.I. 1999/1892).
[87] 1999 Regulations reg. 3.

to cut down,[88] uproot or wilfully destroy any tree so covered; or wilfully to damage, top or lop such a tree in such a manner as to be likely to destroy it[89] without the consent of the district planning authority. An exemption exists, however, in respect of trees which are dying or dead or have become dangerous, or where such action is necessary to prevent or to abate a nuisance;[90] moreover, the provisions do not apply to action by certain public authorities. It is no defence to a criminal prosecution to plead ignorance of the fact of the TPO, or belief that consent has been obtained: the offence is one of "strict liability".[91] In addition, where any tree or trees are removed, uprooted or destroyed in breach of a TPO, the owner is under a duty to plant a replacement or replacements of appropriate size and species. The TPO will then apply to the replacement tree or trees. Applications for consents in relation to trees subject to TPOs are made to district planning authorities. Consent, if given, may be either conditional or unconditional; a common condition to a consent requires the replacement of a tree by one or more new plantings in the vicinity. Against refusal of consent, or against conditions imposed, there is a right of appeal to the Secretary of State. In certain cases, compensation is payable to any person suffering loss through refusal, or only conditional grant, of consent.[92]

The environment White Paper of autumn 1990 promised a streamlining of administrative procedures associated with TPOs, and also an extension of the scope of such Orders so that they might be used to protect not just trees and woodlands but also hedgerows. The disappearance of hedgerows in post-war

---

88 Although not expressly stated in the Regulations, the Secretary of State regards the cutting of roots as potentially damaging. See *Tree Preservation Orders: A Guide to the Law and Good Practice*, HMSO.

89 For an interpretation of "destroy", see *Barnet L.B.C. v Eastern Electricity Board* [1973] 1 WLR 430.

90 Town and Country Planning Act 1990 s.198(6).

91 *Maidstone B.C. v Mortimer* [1981] JPL 112. Note that in determining the level at which to impose any fine, a court shall have regard to any financial benefit which may have accrued or be likely to accrue from the illegal act.

92 Town and Country Planning Act 1990 s.203.

years has been a matter of very considerable concern in terms both of habitat loss and landscape appearance. Some hedgerows are of very ancient origin, perhaps marking county or parish boundaries, and may deserve protection for that reason also. A report of the Countryside Commission, describing changes to the landscape of post-war Britain, has suggested that the rate of loss of hedgerows has been greater in the years since 1980 than in the earlier period, notwithstanding increased awareness of the importance of habitat retention. Hedgerows are now protected by the complex Hedgerows Regulations 1997, but these relate to the protection of "important" hedgerows in the countryside and not suburban or urban hedgerows. Important hedgerows fall into one of two categories: those that contain certain species of hedge, plant or bird; and those of an historic or archaeological significance, for instance marking manorial boundaries or ancient monuments.

Conservation Areas

Allied to the TPO protection of trees is the protection afforded to trees in a Conservation Area.[93] The legislation provides that all trees, except the smallest (under 3" d.b.h. – trunk diameter at breast height *ie* 4' 6"), in such an area shall be protected to the following degree. Action such as that forbidden by a TPO may not, on pain of criminal penalty, take place unless written warning has been given to the district planning authority, and either consent is given or six weeks elapses without a TPO being made.[94] A further exception relates to the felling, lopping or uprooting of trees less than 4" d.b.h. where this has been done to promote the growth of other trees.

Other Planning Controls

A further way in which planning authorities may have influence on trees is through their grants of planning permission. Such grants may be made subject to conditions requiring that existing trees be retained in the new development, or that trees

---

[93] See further, above, p.80.
[94] Town and Country Planning Act 1990 s.211.

be replaced, or that "additional" trees be planted. The Town and Country Planning Act 1990, section 197 imposes a clear duty on planning authorities to consider these matters, and the need for TPOs, when granting planning permission. In these ways planning authorities can play some part in the maintenance of trees and woodlands, and also may minimise scenic damage, for example where industrial building is permitted in rural areas, by insisting on adequate tree screening.

Felling Licences

The felling of privately owned trees and woodlands is controlled not only by local planning authorities, in the ways mentioned above, but also by the need to obtain a Forestry Commission felling licence in certain cases. The Forestry Act 1967 prohibits the felling of any tree without licence[95] except in the case of trees of not more than 8 centimetres d.b.h., fruit trees or trees in an orchard, garden, churchyard or public open space. The requirement of obtaining a licence also does not apply to trees to be felled under an approved plan of operation such as a Forestry Commission Woodland Grant Scheme.[96] Nor does it apply to trees which are dead, dangerous, causing a nuisance, or badly effected by Dutch Elm disease. There is also a general permission to fell trees to obtain relatively small amounts of timber for primarily non-commercial purposes.[97]

In determining whether to grant a felling licence, the Forestry Commission takes into account interests of amenity, landscape and nature conservation. Somewhat complex arrangements exist for liaison in decision-making in cases where a TPO exists in respect of a tree or trees for which a felling licence is sought.

The Forestry Act 1986 has strengthened these legal provisions by empowering the Forestry Commission to require replanting by a person convicted of having unlawfully felled trees. Against such a "restocking notice" an appeal lies to the Minister.

---

[95] 1967 Act s.9(2).
[96] 1967 Act s.14.
[97] 1967 Act s.9(3).

Notices will require not only replanting but also maintenance of the trees in accordance with the rules and practices of good forestry for a period not exceeding ten years.

THE NATIONAL TRUST

The National Trust[98] is a voluntary body, founded in 1895, with the principal object of acting as a corporation for the holding of land of natural beauty and sites and houses of historic interest for the nation's continued use and enjoyment. In the early years its acquisitions were mostly areas of high landscape value. Since the Second World War it has concentrated its attention equally on the preservation of buildings of historical or architectural interest. The Trust is now the owner of some 248,000 hectares of land, about half of which consists of tenanted farms and to which the public are not afforded free access in the same way as to the Trust's open country landholdings. However, the Trust works in close co-operation with its tenants to improve public access, and any restrictions on access to its open land are usually justified in terms of protection of young plantations and the need to keep the public away from certain nature reserves, especially during the breeding season. The Trust is currently reviewing the scope for the designation of *new* rights of way across its properties. The Trust encourages its tenant farmers to be conservation-minded in their agricultural practices but does not always have legal powers to enforce its will.

Approximately one-eighth of the total coastline[99] of England, Wales and Northern Ireland is owned by the Trust, in many cases along with the immediate hinterland. Much of this coastline was purchased out of funds raised from the Enterprise Neptune Campaign dating from 1965 and relaunched in 1985.

---

[98] The full name is the National Trust for Places of Historic Interest or Natural Beauty. Membership has increased rapidly in the post-war period. There were 35,000 members in 1935, 100,000 in 1961, the one million mark was reached in 1981, the two million mark in 1991 and there are now over three million.

[99] Almost 600 miles.

In addition to this, the Trust owns over 200 historic buildings, 49 industrial monuments and mills, all or most of 22 villages, and more splendid gardens than any other single owner in the world. In addition to land and buildings owned by the National Trust, it also holds the benefit of restrictive covenants over a further 83,000 acres. Here the land remains in "private" ownership subject to restrictions, which the Trust can enforce, on the owner's and his successors' use of the land. In this way an owner of land may preserve its future amenity without parting with its ownership.

Inalienability

Under the National Trust Act 1907 land held in freehold by the National Trust may be declared by the Trust to be "inalienable", which means that the Trust thereafter cannot sell or otherwise dispose of the land except under the authority of an Act of Parliament specifically passed to authorise that transaction. This statutory inalienability is obviously of significance in encouraging benefactors to give property to the Trust during their lifetimes or to leave their property to the Trust on their deaths.

Trust property, although inalienable, is not immune from compulsory acquisition by a government department, local authority or other public body having such powers. However, certain safeguards do exist in that rather more elaborate procedures apply than in cases where the compulsory purchase is of other land. Following the making of a compulsory purchase order in the ordinary way and the standard local public inquiry into objections, by a Department of the Environment inspector, the inspector's report is considered by the Secretary of State. Instead, however, of a decision by the Secretary of State to confirm being final, the matter must in the case of National Trust property be placed before a special committee of members drawn from both Houses of Parliament. The committee will itself hear evidence and argument and will submit a resolution either in favour of or opposing the order for the consideration and approval of Parliament. This procedure makes apparent the special degree of protection afforded to National Trust land. It does not, of course, prevent compulsory acquisition in a case where this is, in all the circumstances, considered appropriate.

THE CROWN ESTATES

Crown Estate land is administered by a body called the Crown Estate Commissioners under the terms of the Crown Estate Act 1961. The lands in question are the property of the Crown; as distinct from the private estates of the reigning monarch, and from land owned by government departments and agencies and administered by the Property Services Agency. Originally, profits from the Crown Estates went to the reigning monarch. However, since the time of George III, sovereigns have surrendered such profits to the central exchequer in return for Civil List payments. Crown Estate land comprises a diverse range of types – city centre properties and agricultural land, forests and foreshore. Although the Commissioners are expected to manage this portfolio of properties so as to make profits for the exchequer, this goal is not their only concern. The Commissioners are conscious of the need for policies which balance commercial considerations against the protection and enhancement of the countryside and the conservation of the Estate's older buildings. The idea is that those responsible for the Sovereign's estate should try to set high standards, for others to follow, in both rural and urban estate management. Similar considerations apply as to the management of the estates of the Duchy of Cornwall, amounting to around 52,000 hectares. The personal interest in conservation of the present incumbent of the Dukedom, HRH Prince Charles, ensures that an attempt is made to "marry" profit-orientated and environmentally sound estate management practices.

The Crown Estate Commissioners manage around 73,000 hectares of agricultural land in England and Wales, about 26,000 hectares of common land in Wales,[100] about half the foreshore around the coast and tidal waters of the United

---

[100] For "common land" and "rights of common" see below, Chapter 5.

Kingdom,[101] and the Windsor Estate, as well as having mineral and sporting rights which are of considerable value. The Commissioners encourage tree and hedgerow planting and often only allow a tenant farmer to remove a hedgerow on condition that equivalent planting takes place elsewhere on the holding. Many SSSIs are to be found on Crown Estate land, and a number of nature reserve agreements have been negotiated with the statutory conservation agencies and local authorities. The foreshore estates include some bird sanctuaries. An initiative of some importance in 1981 was the purchase of the Laxton estate in Nottinghamshire from MAFF in order to preserve the system of medieval strip farming which continues to be practised there. The Great Park at Windsor is open for public recreation, and a very large number of persons use this area for walking, riding, jogging, flying model planes and other activities. Good progress is being made in establishing a deer herd in the park, a process that started in 1979 with a nucleus of stock brought from Balmoral.

MISCELLANEOUS AREAS

We may make brief mention, finally, of a few particularly well-known areas which are governed by special legal rules. Perhaps the most unusual legal regime is to be found in respect of the 3000 acres of the Malvern Hills. These hills are under the general management of the Malvern Hills Conservators, a body corporate established under a series of statutes dating from 1884. The Conservators are partly elected by local ratepayers and partly nominated by local councils and the Church Commissioners. By statute they have a general duty to prevent encroachment or building on the hills and to preserve their natural beauty for the benefit of the public. They own 2500 acres of the hills, the remainder being in the safe hands of the National Trust. To meet their expenses they levy an annual precept on the local district council.

The royal forests of Dean and the New Forest are generally open to the public, subject to the rights of the commoners. In

---

[101] See above, p.119.

the case of the Forest of Dean these are the "free miners" and the "ship badgers" (sheep grazers). In the New Forest there is a special body of "verderers". These are appointed by the Crown and have duties which include the preservation of the rights of commoners and the administration of the annual pony sales.

Chapter 5

COMMONS

INTRODUCTION

In this chapter we shall outline the law relating to commons: land described by a Royal Commission in 1958 as "the last reserve of uncommitted land in England and Wales" and embracing a very wide variety of landscape and habitat types. "They range from the huge heather uplands of Dartmoor and the North Pennines, to the crags of Snowdonia and the Lake District; from the Chiltern hilltops and ancient woodlands like Epping, Ashdown and the New Forest to alluvial meadows near Oxford and on the Cambridgeshire Ouse. The coast of Norfolk, the sandy heaths of Surrey and Suffolk, and the suburban lungs like Wimbledon and Clapham in London and the Strays of York are all commons."[1]

Our principal concern will be with the modern law. However, in explaining the modern law, a little of the history of commons will be summarised. Quite apart from helping us to understand the present rules of law, this history is of some contemporary significance because a number of the legal developments of centuries past have left, as we shall see, enduring features on the landscape.

HISTORY

It is important to appreciate from the outset that the word "common" is used in two different, though related, senses. We speak of land as being "common land" and we also refer to "rights of common" or "commoners' rights" which are possessed in respect of common land by certain owners of property, though not the public generally.

Medieval Agriculture
The ideas of "common land" and "rights of common" date back

---

[1] *Our Common Right – the story of common land* (Open Spaces Society).

many centuries and were part and parcel of the medieval system of agriculture. At exactly what time the system to be described came into being is not clear; in any case it would have developed only gradually into a system, rather than have "come into being" at any particular moment. However, the pattern of rural organisation outlined below was certainly widespread in England and Wales throughout the centuries between the Norman Conquest and the eighteenth century, when significant changes occurred. Indeed, the fundamentals of the system most likely date back to Saxon times.

What, then, was this typical pattern of agriculture? Some differences existed between earlier and later periods in these centuries. At any rate from the Norman period, however, our attention must focus on the manor as the principal social, economic and agricultural unit. Lands would be owned by the lord of the manor, and would be worked by many of the local villagers. Some of the land was worked solely for the benefit of the manorial lord and this was known as his "demesne" land. In return for their services, the lord would allow the villagers to work other strips of land within the large open fields around the village for their own benefit. Disputes within the manor concerning these matters of agricultural organisation were determined by the manorial court; and this "court" also met periodically to deal generally with matters of local agricultural administration. In each case decisions were reached in accordance with the custom of the manor, and in due course entitlements under manorial custom became recognised also by the King's Courts as "copyhold tenure", and hence part of the common law itself. In time, therefore, it became appropriate to think of villagers as "owners" of their particular strips of land. In many parts of the countryside it is still possible to discern the old open-field patterns of ploughing, with the modern field divisions superimposed. In one village, Laxton in Nottinghamshire, the original system of open-field agriculture continues to this day.

However, not all land was suitable for, or needed for, arable open-field cultivation. Land not suitable for such use was "manorial waste" and villagers generally acquired, by custom, certain rights in respect of such "waste". Except perhaps as far back as the Saxon period, such land was not, it should be emphasised, considered to be collectively owned. It was owned, at least from Norman times, by the lord of the manor but his ownership became subject to rights in respect of that land of the tenants of the manor. Moreover, such rights of common developed also in respect of arable land when not in cultivation; for example, when left fallow, or after crops had been harvested, the tenants might have rights to graze their animals.

Nevertheless, our main concern is with the manorial waste. The kinds of land not suited to cultivation were of a variety of types: uplands, woodlands, lowland heath and scrub, undrained marshes and peat bogs. As such the term "common land" does not denote land of any particular physical description, apart from its nature of not having been readily cultivatable. As one writer has explained, "common land is found where mountain sheep range the fells, in fertile lowland valleys, rimming the coasts and on sandy heaths, along the verges of roadsides, in dingle and copse and fast in the grey grip of the great metropolis. Some are wide-flung, five-figured acreages of open country, others are tiny allotments tucked away among village gardens."[2] Just as the kinds of land which formed manorial waste were of a number of types, so the customary rights of the commoners took a variety of forms. Examples include the right to pasture animals, to cut peat or turf, and to take bracken. The common feature of these entitlements was that they involved the right to take advantage of the natural products, or "fruits", of the land in question. These common rights were of very considerable importance to villagers; they should not be thought of simply as rather quaint local customs. Villagers depended on these rights to gain fuel for their homes, fodder for their animals, and even to supplement their own diets. These rights of common were a very significant part of the rural economy. Commons may not have been cultivatable but they certainly were fruitful.

---

[2]   J. Wager, unpublished University of Cambridge thesis (1966), quoted in *Our Common Right*, see above, footnote 1.

Enclosures

This quite sophisticated system of self-sufficient local agricultural organisation continued, without fundamental change, until the middle of the eighteenth century. At around that time there began to be introduced certain advances in agricultural practice, such as the periodic shift between arable and pasture husbandry, which were not well suited to the open-field medieval system. Accordingly, landowners began to petition Parliament for permission, given by enactment of a specific Act of Parliament in each case, to enclose land with hedges, fences or walls, thereby excluding the commoners from the exercise of their rights. When this was to be done special Enclosure Commissioners were appointed to survey the land and assign particular parcels of land to all former owners of open-field strips. Such parcels were then enclosed, and it is from this period that many of our hedgerows and dry stone walls date. To provide access to and from landholdings, new rights of way were also created by the surveyors around the edges of the new fields.[3] These changes had a marked effect on the look of the landscape; changes which produced a strong outcry from some at the time. The poet, John Clare, wrote:

> "Inclosure, thou'rt a curse upon the land
> And tasteless was the wretch who thy existence planned."

The establishment of these landscape features apparently aroused similar reaction to that which today marks their destruction and deterioration.[4]

However, it seems these developments were not particularly harmful to the village economy. Such harm came a little later, when from around 1800 there began the enclosure, not only of the former open fields but also of the common land itself. Changes in agricultural techniques were making some of this land cultivatable whereas earlier it had not been, and the high

---

[3] See above, p.99.
[4] See John Dyson in *Countryside* (Countryside Commission) September-October 1995, p.5.

price obtainable for produce resulting from the Napoleonic
Wars prompted lords of manors to make full use of all available
land. The result was that many villagers who had previously
been able to provide for their needs by a combination of
working their small fields and exercising their commoners'
rights ceased to be able to continue to do so. The choice facing
these people was then a stark one: leave the countryside and go
to the mushrooming industrial cities, or become a hired farm
labourer. The magnitude of the changes can be seen from the
estimate that, whereas in 1790 some four-fifths of the
population lived in the countryside, this proportion had dropped
to one half by 1840.

Nineteenth Century Reaction

Enclosures continued through the first half of the nineteenth
century, some four thousand local private Acts of Parliament
being passed in the hundred years up to 1836, resulting in the
enclosure of millions of acres. In that year a General Inclosure
Act was passed which simplified enclosure by avoiding the
need for the full legislative procedures in respect of each
separate enclosure, laying down a less onerous procedure to be
followed instead, and establishing a permanent Inclosure
Commission.

This Act was soon replaced by the Inclosure Act 1845, which
was to similar effect; but by this time a reaction against
enclosure had already begun to be felt. The extent to which
common land was being lost began to give rise to concern. In
the late seventeenth century it was estimated that about half
the area of England and Wales was common or waste land. By
the mid-nineteenth century this area had reduced to around
2½ million acres.[5] The incidence of enclosure varied much,
however, from region to region, reflecting differences in
agricultural activity. Areas such as the East Midlands suffered
much enclosure. Northamptonshire has only thirty-six

---

[5]   Some 900,000 acres are believed now to be registered as common land
     under the provisions of the Commons Registration Act 1965. See below,
     p.206.

commons, of which thirty-two are smaller than one acre. By way of contrast, Cumbria possesses, still, vast tracts of common land (a fifth of the total national area), as also do, for example, Powys and North Yorkshire. Following growing concern in the mid nineteenth century, in 1865 the Commons Preservation Society was established.[6] This body, which was supported by a number of influential public figures, campaigned against enclosure of commons both by taking action in the courts to challenge unlawful fencing, and also by more direct action. An early example of action of the latter kind was the breaking down, in the hours before dawn one morning in 1866, of two miles of fences enclosing some 400 acres of Berkhamstead Common in Hertfordshire, which the owner Earl Brownlow had erected to convert that area to his own exclusive use. Similar direct action occurred in relation to enclosure of Epping Forest in the same year, this time resulting in successful legal proceedings being brought by the Society.

The general change in attitude can be seen also from legislation dating from this period. Since the Metropolitan Commons Act 1866 and the Commons Act 1876, the legislation has been more concerned with the *preservation* of commons than with easing the process of *enclosure*. The reasons for this shift of approach are not difficult to appreciate. From this period till the present day the desire to preserve commons has been motivated more by the wish to retain areas of open land where town residents may take air and exercise, than to protect the historical rights of commoners. In some areas, it is true, such rights remain of considerable economic importance. This is the case, for example, in relation to the right to graze sheep on commons in upland areas, on which the viability of much hill-farming depends. However, in many areas the modern importance of common land is seen in its recreational potential, together with the value of many such areas as habitats for animals, birds and plants.

---

[6]   The society is now called the Open Spaces Society and continues to do much useful work. It has published a very valuable account of the law of commons, to which the authors are much indebted: see P. Clayden, *Our Common Land* (5th ed. 2003).

RIGHTS OF COMMON

A considerable number of different rights of common may exist at the present day for the benefit of those owning land formerly part of the manor, and which ones apply in relation to any individual common depends on the history and practice in respect of that common. However, there are six general categories which encompass most rights, and of these the common of pasture is the most widespread and important. The six categories may be described as follows:

Common of Pasture: This is the right to graze a defined number of animals on common land. The right will be to graze particular kinds of animals, which may be, for example, horses, oxen, cattle, sheep, goats or geese. As mentioned earlier, these rights are still of very considerable economic importance in areas of hill-farming.

Estovers: This includes rights to take small branches of trees for certain purposes, such as for fuel, for fencing or for building; and to take bracken or furze for bedding and litter for animals. The practices of "coppicing" and "pollarding" trees ensured that woodlands provided a high but sustainable yield of small branches. These practices involved cutting trees low to the ground (coppicing), or above the height at which animals could chew new shoots (pollarding), so that they produced a large number of small vertical branches instead of a single trunk. In some areas there is a right, known as "housebote", to take larger pieces of timber for building.

Turbary: This right involves entitlement to cut turf or peat for fuel for the commoner's home.

Pannage: The right to take pigs to a woodland common and to allow them to feed on the acorns and beech-mast which have fallen to the ground.

Piscary: The right to take fish in reasonable numbers, for the commoner's own consumption, from waters on the common.

Common of Soil: This somewhat rare right involves the taking of stone, sand, gravel or other matter from the common for use on the commoner's own land.

THE COMMONS REGISTRATION ACT 1965

The cumulative effect of this history, and the many statutes, meant that over the years a good deal of uncertainty developed as to precisely who had what rights and over which land; and even where the *rights* were well established and well known, it often might not be clear who *owned* the common land. A Royal Commission was therefore appointed to consider the matter of common land, and one of its recommendations, in its Report in 1958, was for the establishment of a definitive register of both common land and of rights of common.[7]

This recommendation was implemented by the Commons Registration Act 1965. This required that there should be registered, in registers maintained by county councils, all land claimed to be common land and all claims to rights of common. For the purposes of the 1965 Act, common land is defined as land subject to rights of common and wasteland of a manor not subject to rights of common.

Certain areas have been exempted from the requirement: the New Forest, the Forest of Dean and other areas specified under the Act by the Secretary of State (*eg* the Stray, at Harrogate).[8] Outside these exempted areas registrations had to take place by 1970 and were initially only "provisional", thus allowing objections to be made to the registrations before they became "final". Objections had to be lodged within time periods prescribed by regulations, and at the latest by mid 1972. If no objection was lodged to a provisional registration, the registration became final. The Act provides that the consequence of final registration is that the registration is conclusive evidence of the matters registered as at the date of registration. Moreover, the converse also applies. Any rights

---

[7] Cmnd. 462.
[8] 1965 Act s.11.

which formerly existed, or any former common land, ceased to exist, or be such, if not registered by 1970.

Registers are publicly available documents, kept by county councils, metropolitan districts and London Boroughs. It was obviously of importance to secure as complete registration of land and rights as possible. Accordingly, the Act provided that local authorities (districts, parishes, communities) could take the initiative to make provisional registrations as well as private individuals.

Although the aims of this legislation were no doubt laudable, its detailed provisions have caused some difficulties. For example, in the short time provided for registration not all commons were in fact registered, and those not registered accordingly lost that status. Also, as no obligation existed to notify owners of land of a registration in respect of that land, some land has been registered incorrectly owing to absence of timely objection. A particular problem has arisen in respect of incorrectly registered commons (or village greens) on which a dwelling house is situated (or beside which such a dwelling is situated), and where the common or green is a part of the dwelling's garden (or "ancillary" land). Such properties have often proven difficult to sell, at any rate at full market value. To alleviate such problems, Parliament intervened in 1989 to provide, in the Common Land (Rectification of Registers) Act, that objections to inclusion of any such land on the register might be made up until July 1992. Such objections have been referred to the Commons Commissioners (see below) to inquire into the matter and, if satisfied that the registration was incorrect, and also that the dwelling house has been present since 1945, authorise the registration authority to cancel the registration.

Disputed Registrations: Commons Commissioners

The 1965 Act established a procedure to deal with disputed initial registrations. Where an objection was lodged in good time, the registration authority has been obliged to refer the matter to a Commons Commissioner for determination.

Commissioners are persons appointed by the Lord Chancellor, chosen from barristers or solicitors of at least seven years' standing. The Commissioner decides the dispute following the holding of a local public hearing into the matter. At the hearing witnesses may be called by both the person seeking registration and the objector, and documentary evidence may be put before the Commissioner. Local councils also have a right to be heard at such hearings. After the hearing the Commissioner issues his written determination as to the validity or otherwise of the disputed registration.[9] On this matter the decision of the Commissioner is final, subject only to a right of appeal to the High Court on a point of law. Many disputes were referred to Commissioners during the 1970s and, indeed, their work continues to this day. In addition to resolving disputes as to registrations, they also resolve disputes as to the *ownership* of commons and investigate the ownership of unclaimed common land.

Land Ceasing to be Common Land

Where after registration land ceases to be common land, an application may be made to deregister the land. However, this is not a means of correcting errors which were originally made: an event must have happened after registration which changes the status.

It has been held by the House of Lords[10] that, where land was originally registered as waste land of a manor, the subsequent severance of the manor does not give a right to deregister. It is possible that land which was subject to rights of common at the time of registration may be deregistered if the rights are extinguished. However, this will not prevent a right of public access (see below) if the land was registered as common land on 30 November 2000, the date when the Countryside and Rights of Way Act 2000 received Royal Assent.

---

9   See *Re West Anstey Common* [1985] 1 All ER 618: Commissioner should determine the validity of the registration and not simply consider the substance of the *particular* objection raised.

10   *Hampshire County Council v Milburn* [1990] 2 WLR 1240.

Proof of Rights

Where registration has been sought for rights of common and the rights are disputed, it has been necessary for the would-be commoner to prove his rights. This has been done in various ways. In some cases there may be in existence an express grant of rights of common by deed executed by the owner of land, or there may be an Act of Parliament which as part of a scheme of enclosure granted rights of common over certain of the land. More usually, however, no such express grant or statutory right can be shown and reliance is placed on the doctrine of "prescription". This is a doctrine by which a practice which can be shown to have been carried on "as of right" and "without interruption" over a period of years may thereby become a matter of legal right or entitlement. At common law a claim to prescriptive right could be defeated by showing that the practice had commenced later than the year 1189 (the so-called limit of legal memory).[11] This often made claims difficult to prove and so the Prescription Act 1832 was passed to make proof of prescriptive titles a little easier. The position under this Act is that, if the claimant can show 30 years' exercise of the asserted right of common before the objection being raised, the claimant will not lose simply because it can be shown that the exercise of the right commenced after 1189. The objector must show that the exercise commenced not "as of right" but by permission of the owner of the land; and if the alleged "right" has been exercised for 60 years, such permission of the owner must be proven by production of written evidence. Because the 1832 Act requires the use to continue up to the date of the action, reliance is often placed on the judge-made fiction of Lost Modern Grant. If 20 years' use without force, secrecy or permission can be established at any time, the courts will presume a grant which has been lost.[12]

---

[11] Medieval statutes had revised periodically the period of "living memory", but this practice ceased when the date arrived at 1189. In time, therefore, the idea of proof of practice "beyond living memory" or from "time immemorial" became proof beyond *legal* memory".

[12] *Angus & Co v Dalton* (1877) 3 QBD 85; *Tehidy Minerals Ltd v Norman* [1971] 2 QB 528.

Loss of Rights

An objection to a provisionally registered right of common may in some cases be founded, not on an assertion that no right of common has ever existed but, instead, on the plea that although such a right may once have existed it now no longer exists.

How, then, may a right of common be lost? There are a number of possible ways. It will happen if the common land and the property of the commoner have come into single ownership; and this is so even if the two parcels of land are later sold or passed to different owners. Equally, a commoner may give up his rights by deed – the owner of the common may seek to "buy out" the commoners of their rights. In respect of some rights of common, the permanent exhaustion of the product of the land may terminate commoners' rights. Thus, when all the peat is dug the common of turbary will end. Temporary exhaustion does not, however, do more than suspend rights. Another way is by the operation of statute; for example, by inclosure legislation, or where common land is purchased compulsorily by a public authority under the procedure of the Acquisition of Land Act 1981 (or its predecessors) or the Commons Act 1899. A degree of special protection is, however, afforded to commons against compulsory acquisition by public authorities. Typically, the legislation requires either that equally advantageous "exchange land" be given in its place, or that the compulsory purchase order be subjected to the scrutiny and approval of *Parliament* and not just the Secretary of State as is ordinarily the case. A final way in which rights of common may be lost is by abandonment. However, mere non-use is not the same as abandonment. The courts, or the Commissioners, will look for evidence of an *intention* to abandon a right of common. Thus, if a cottage is demolished and not replaced, this will be construed as abandonment of, for example, any right to cut peat for fuel to warm that cottage; but if the cottage is demolished in order to build another, the right will continue for the benefit of the new building. The mere non-exercise of a right of common does not, of itself, amount to abandonment; though, if non-use continues for a long enough period, it may be strong evidence of such.[13] Exactly what period of non-use may lead to such an inference of abandonment is impossible to state. Certainly the degree of exercise of a right which is needed to *maintain the right in existence* may be far less than that necessary to *establish* or create such a right under the doctrine of prescription.

PUBLIC ACCESS

So far we have been concerned principally with the relationship between the owners of common land and those property owners who have rights of common in respect of that common land. It is now time to broaden the discussion to consider rights of the public generally.

Common Law

At common law, members of the public did not have any rights to wander at will over, or even to walk across, common land. Commons are not "commonly owned", and rights of common extend only to the local commoners (not even all local residents) allowing them certain rights over that land. Beyond this, the owner of a common has the normal rights of an owner of land, including the right to evict trespassers from the land. However, he may not exclude the public by fencing the land as this will interfere with the exercise by commoners of their rights.[14] Also, as with any other land, it may be that public or private rights of way exist over the property.[15]

Statutory Rights Before the Countryside and Rights of Way Act 2000

Lawful access to commons by members of the public is generally dependent, therefore, on certain statutory provisions,

---

[13] See, for example, *Scrutton v Stone* (1893) 9 TLR 478 *per* Charles J: "In the present case the non-user has been so long that I think I am bound to infer an intention to renounce the right." On the other hand, in *Benn v Hardinge* (1992) 66 P&CR 246, non-use of a right of way for a period of 175 years did not amount to abandonment.

[14] Law of Property Act 1925 s.194 (see below, p.213).

[15] See above, Chapter 3.

or on the consent of the landowner being obtained. The statutory provisions are to be found in a variety of Acts of Parliament, though even collectively it was estimated that before the Countryside and Rights of Way Act 2000 they only authorised public access to about a fifth of the 1.37 million acres (the combined size of Surrey, Berkshire and Oxfordshire) of common land which today remain.

The earliest legislation, understandably, concerned those commons nearest to, and within, the densely-populated London area. The Metropolitan Commons Act 1866 accordingly provides for rights of access to commons in that area, such as Wimbledon and Tooting Bec. The Act, as also later Acts to be considered, provides for the making of bye-laws to regulate the public's use of the commons, and also makes provision for the proper management of the commons.

Outside the metropolis similar provision was soon made for a few commons under the Commons Act 1876. The procedure for applying this Act to a common is, however, complicated and onerous. A "provisional order" has to be made by the appropriate Minister and this has to be confirmed by Act of Parliament. Accordingly, not very many commons have been made the subject of this procedure, although the Clent Hills in Worcestershire do provide a well-known example.

The 1876 Act was supplemented by the rather simpler procedures of the Commons Act 1899. This empowers district councils to make schemes to provide public access to the commons within their areas. Something like two hundred schemes have been made under this Act.

Where commons have been acquired by the National Trust the land is required, by the terms of the National Trust Act 1907, to be kept as an open space for the recreation and enjoyment of the public. Also, some special local statutes make similar provision in relation to particular areas, such as, for example, the Malvern Hills Act 1884.

The most important provision, however, is to be found in the Law of Property Act 1925 section 193. Under this section, members of the public have rights of access for "air and exercise" on any of the commons falling within the following categories:

(a) metropolitan commons (*ie* those within the approximate area of the former Greater London Council);

(b) commons wholly or partly situated in an area which before the reorganisation of local government in 1974 was a borough or an urban district.

This section also applies to "rural" commons to which the Act has been applied by deed made by the lord of the manor or other person owning the land. The section also regulates conduct on such commons. It is made an offence, amongst other things, to drive vehicles, light fires or camp on any common to which the section applies.

The Countryside and Rights of Way Act 2000

This Act gives the public a right of access on foot for quiet enjoyment to registered common land and mapped open country unless it is excepted land. The right is subject to the general restrictions set out in Schedule 2 to the Act and access may be excluded under the provisions contained in Chapter II of the Act. Public access under the Countryside and Rights of Way Act 2000 has been discussed more fully in Chapter 3 of this book.

PROTECTION AND MANAGEMENT OF COMMONS

The most important statutory provision for the *protection* of commons is section 194 of the Law of Property Act 1925. Unlike section 193, considered immediately above, this applies to all commons which were subject to rights of common in 1926. It prohibits a number of actions in respect of commons unless the prior consent of the Secretary of State has been obtained. The actions in question consist of the erection of any building or fence, or the construction of any other work which prevents or impedes access to the land. In addition to the more usual acts of enclosure, this also includes such matters as constructing car parks,[16] sports pavilions and public conveniences. The Secretary of State is required, in reaching his decision, to advertise the application for public objection, and to have regard to the respective interests of the owner of the land and the inhabitants of the neighbourhood. In relation to constructions principally for the public's benefit, such as those mentioned above, the consent of the Secretary of State would normally be granted. Fencing may often be permitted to constrain livestock so long as adequate stiles are provided.

Each of the various statutes, which we have considered, providing for public access to commons, also contains provisions as to the management of the commons to which it applies. Accordingly, arrangements will differ depending on whether the Metropolitan Commons Act 1866, the Commons Act 1876, the Commons Act 1899, section 193 of the Law of Property Act 1925, or some other localised special legislation applies.[17] In some cases responsibilities are given to special bodies of Conservators (consisting of a mixture of interest groups); more commonly bye-law making powers have been given to district councils.

It may also be noted that the Open Spaces Act 1906 permits county, district and parish councils to purchase any open space for the purpose of public recreation. They can then make bye-laws regulating public use of the land. Such bye-laws may also be made, with consent of the owner of the land, even in respect of open spaces not owned by the local authority.

Management of commoners' rights is also needed. Over and under grazing may be a problem on commons. The position has been made worse by a recent House of Lords case which permits registered grazing rights to be severed from the land to which they were attached.[18] Some commons have efficient Commoners' Associations which control the numbers of animals turned out on the common. The difficulty is that there is no

---

[16] *A.G. v Southampton Corporation* (1969) 68 LGR 288.
[17] See, for example, the Dartmoor Act 1985.
[18] *Bettison v Langton* [2002] 1 AC 27.

legal power for the majority of commoners to make decisions which are binding on the minority, while in some areas there are no commoners' associations. The government is consulting on proposals to control the agricultural use and management of commons.

VILLAGE AND TOWN GREENS

These areas, which may or may not be commons,[19] are nevertheless also subject to the registration requirements of the 1965 Act. Separate registers are kept for commons and greens, and in the case of greens it is only the green and not the rights over it, asserted by the local inhabitants of a defined locality, which are the subject of registration. The expression "village or town green" is defined as meaning:

> "land which has been allotted under any Act for the exercise or recreation of the inhabitants of any locality **or** on which the inhabitants of any locality have a customary right to indulge in lawful sports and pastimes" or "if it is land on which for not less than twenty years a significant number of the inhabitants of any locality, or of any neighbourhood within a locality, have indulged in lawful sports and pastimes as of right, and either – *(a)* continue to do so, or *(b)* have ceased to do so for not more than such period as may be prescribed, or determined in accordance with prescribed provisions."[20]

These are often areas of land amounting to only a few acres. The need for the 1965 Act's provisions to apply was because, as with commons, much uncertainty existed as to ownership and rights over such areas.

---

[19]   The 1965 Act states that village and town greens are not to be considered as commons. Public access under the Countryside and Rights of Way Act 2000 is to registered commons, not to registered village greens. Village greens may be mapped as open country, in which case there will be public access under that heading.

[20]   Commons Registration Act 1965 s.22(1), (1A), as amended and inserted by the Countryside and Rights of Way Act 2000.

Today, many claims for registration of new village greens are made on the basis of long user. This is because a successful application for a village green will prevent development.

The claims are based not only on organised activities such as dancing round a maypole and practising archery but also on informal activities, for example dog walking, kite flying and blackberry picking. The House of Lords has held that, where such rights have arisen through long use, there is no requirement that the inhabitants should have a belief that they are exercising an established legal right. All that has to be shown is that the use has been without force, secrecy or permission. The toleration of the land owner does not amount to permission.[21] Although permission may be implied, encouragement to use the land has been held not to amount to such permission.[22]

A colourful example of customary rights is the case of *New Windsor Corporation v Mellor*,[23] in which the status as a green of an area of land in Windsor called Bachelors' Acre was investigated. The land had belonged to the borough for many centuries (since "time immemorial") and for at least 300 years local inhabitants could be shown to have practised archery, and later when the long-bow went out of use, to have practised firing their muskets. At times this use fell into abeyance but even during such periods evidence could be found to the effect that such customary rights were acknowledged to exist. In particular, in the early nineteenth century, a group calling themselves the Bachelors of Windsor had formed to assert the customary rights of inhabitants against any acts done to the land which would prejudice such continued use. The court held that the evidence produced demonstrated that there was sufficient evidence for the Commons Commissioners to have found that the land was indeed "land on which the inhabitants ... have a customary right to indulge in lawful sports and pastimes", and so was properly registered as a green.

---

21 *R. v Oxfordshire County Council* [2001] 1 AC 335.
22 *R. (Beresford) v Sunderland City Council* [2003] UKHL 60.
23 [1975] 3 All ER 44.

Greens, whether in a village or a town, may in some cases still be in private ownership, subject to these various rights of the local inhabitants; but more usually nowadays such areas are owned by parish or community councils, or in urban areas by district councils.[24] In cases where a Commons Commissioner is unable to discover in whom the ownership of a registered green is vested, it is provided that the green shall vest in the parish or community council (or the district council in an urban area).[25]

---

[24] Local Government Act 1894. Management powers may be exercised under the Open Spaces Act 1906.

[25] 1965 Act s.8.

Chapter 6

PROTECTION OF BIRDS, ANIMALS AND PLANTS

INTRODUCTION

The importance to our enjoyment of the countryside of a rich and varied flora and fauna need hardly be stressed. Moreover, it is an enjoyment which may be shared both by those knowledgeable about the natural world and those less aware. The pleasure to be gained from scenic countryside is, for all of us, much enhanced by bluebell woods, clusters of cowslips and primroses, wild flowers of all colours and forms growing in profusion along way-side verges, poppy fields, bird-song in woodlands, the fluttering of butterflies and the scampering of rabbits and other small animals which flee for cover as footsteps approach. This list could be continued almost endlessly, but the examples are sufficient to show that protection of flora and fauna is an important matter for all who gain pleasure from the countryside. It is not a matter of significance only to the trained botanist or zoologist: one can enjoy bird-song without being able to identify the caller (or even spot where it is singing from), and one can appreciate a diverse and plentiful array of wild flowers although able to name but few. The importance today of protection of flora and fauna is all the greater because, during the decades since the Second World War, much has been lost both in terms of variety and density.

The "simple pleasures" with which we began would have constituted such common features of the countryside for them to have been taken for granted only two generations ago. But things have changed very rapidly. The combination of numerous factors, such as the removal of hedgerows and small woodlands, the drainage of wetlands and ploughing of pasture for arable farming, the increased use of pesticides and herbicides, and the proliferation of coniferous woodland, has had very marked consequences; and this quite apart from the more notorious activities of builders and developers. Cowslips and primroses

219

are nowadays more readily seen in suburban gardens than in the wild, the poppy field is a sight rarely seen, and "living" broadleaved woodlands are now less common than dark, and eerily quiet, plantations of conifers. And if flora and fauna which were quite commonplace so little time ago are becoming more difficult to find, the harm done to rarer species can easily be imagined.

What measures are necessary to provide satisfactory protection for our birds, animals and plants? How may we seek to prevent further losses and try to restore depleted populations? In broad terms any policy for species protection must operate on two fronts. It must seek to ensure that the wide range of habitats essential to the continued existence of a diverse flora and fauna is maintained, paying particular regard to the kinds of habitat under greatest threat; and, also, it is necessary that there be adequate laws, sufficiently enforced, directly protecting individual species of birds, animals and plants from the harmful actions of hunters, collectors and others. The rarer the species, the more prized the quarry, and the more significant each loss.

We have already considered much of the law relating to habitat protection. Such laws, in some shape or form, may be traced back many years. For example, the original idea of a "forest" was a medieval legal concept: an area of woodland and open land within which the forest laws would apply. These laws protected game within the forest by preserving the forest habitat and by outlawing poaching. In modern times we think of habitat protection in order to preserve wildlife for its own sake, rather than to ensure good sport; and the areas of law most relevant are those we have considered relating to SSSIs,[1] Nature Reserves,[2] Marine Nature Reserves,[3] and Environmentally Sensitive Areas,[4] together with the general

---

[1]   As protected under the original domestic legislation (as amended), and also as "European sites" under the Conservation (Natural Habitats etc.) Regulations 1994 (S.I. 1994/2716) transposing obligations under the 1992 EC Habitats Directive. See further, above, p.162 and p.177.

[2]   See above, p.154.

[3]   See above, p.158.

[4]   See above, p.171.

conservation obligations of bodies such as the Forestry Commission,[5] the Water Companies and the Environment Agency,[6] and DEFRA[7] itself. Nor, of course, should the activities of bodies such as the National Trust, the RSPB or the numerous County Trusts for Nature Conservation be overlooked.

In this chapter our concern will be with the laws which seek more directly to protect particular species of birds, animals and plants from harm. Much of this law is contained in Part I of the Wildlife and Countryside Act 1981, though there are also, as we shall see, some important provisions contained in other Acts; for example, those which deal separately with badgers and deer. In this context we shall need also to consider the impact of the EC Habitats Directive of 1992. We shall not, however, be concerned with the laws which protect birds and animals from acts of cruelty[8] as distinct from acts which may endanger the species.

PROTECTION OF WILD BIRDS

Wild birds, their nests and their eggs, receive a degree of protection by virtue of a number of criminal offences contained in the Wildlife and Countryside Act 1981. The provisions are quite complex, owing to the need to differentiate between species as regards extent of protection, and to provide for circumstances in which actions which are generally prohibited may be permitted. A matter of some controversy in relation to this last matter is the extent to which the protection laws should restrict actions by owners and occupiers on their own land. Obviously the cause of conservation requires any such exemptions afforded to owners and occupiers to be closely drawn and carefully monitored. The issue is controversial because, where such exemptions do *not* apply, the legislation takes away the traditional common law right of an owner or

---

[5] See above, p.25.
[6] See above, p.20.
[7] See above, p.17.
[8] For a full account see J. Palmer, *Animal Law* (3rd ed. 2001), Shaw & Sons Ltd.

occupier of land to capture or kill (and thereby bring into his private ownership) any wild bird – or animal – on his land (and to act as he wishes in respect of wild plants growing there).

Basic Offences

The basic protection of birds is afforded by the creation of the following criminal offences. These relate to wild birds; and "wild bird" is defined[9] as "any bird of a kind which is ordinarily resident in or is a visitor to Great Britain in a wild state", not being one that has been bred in captivity, and not including "poultry"[10] nor, generally, any "game bird".[11] The provision about "bird in captivity" can give rise to difficult problems of proof, though developments in genetic "fingerprinting" may assist in determining the ancestry of a particular bird.

It is an offence intentionally:[12]

(i)   to kill, injure or take any wild bird;

(ii) to take, damage or destroy the nest of any wild bird while that nest is in use or is being built; or

(iii) to take or destroy[13] an egg of any wild bird.[14]

Furthermore, an offence is committed if any person has in his possession or control:

---

[9]   1981 Act s.27(1).

[10] Domestic fowls, geese, ducks, guinea-fowls, pigeons, quails and turkeys: 1981 Act s.27(1).

[11] Pheasants, partridges, grouse (or moor game), black (or heath) game and ptarmigan: 1981 Act s.27(1). Close seasons nevertheless apply under the Game Acts. Pheasants may be shot between 1 October and 1 February; partridges, between 1 September and 1 February; grouse, between 12 August and 10 December; black game, between 20 August and 10 December; ptarmigan, between 12 August and 10 December (Scotland only).

[12] It is the *acts* described which must be intentional. It is no defence that the defendant was unaware that the bird was "wild": *Kirkland v Robinson* (1987) Crim LR 643.

[13] The term "destroy" includes doing anything calculated to prevent an egg from hatching.

[14] 1981 Act s.1(1).

(i) any live or dead wild bird, or any part of or anything derived from such a bird; or

(ii) an egg of a wild bird, or any part of such an egg.[15]

The scope of these "possession and control" offences is, however, qualified so that no offence is committed where the person in possession or control can show that the bird or egg had not been killed or taken in contravention of the provisions of the 1981 Act, or of earlier legislation.[16] It is also a defence for the defendant to show that the bird or egg was sold (to him or any other person) otherwise than in contravention of the legislation.

Enhanced Protection: Schedule 1

The provisions described above are designed to protect the 500 or more species of wild birds in Britain generally. Certain species are, however, afforded a somewhat higher degree of protection. Schedule 1 to the 1981 Act lists a number of species. As originally enacted, in relation to these birds any person convicted of any of the offences described above was liable to a significantly higher maximum penalty[17] than in respect of other birds. Since 30 January 2001, however, the distinction between penalties has been removed. Instead, a person convicted of an offence may be liable to six months' imprisonment, a fine or both.[18] Despite this, Schedule 1 birds are afforded additional protection. Thus, it is an offence intentionally or recklessly:[19]

(i) to disturb any wild bird included in Schedule 1 while it is building a nest or is in, on, or near, a nest containing eggs or young; or

(ii) to disturb dependent young of such a bird.[20]

"Recklessness" was added in 2000 due to the difficulty in some cases of establishing that the defendant, whilst disturbing a

---

[15] 1981 Act s.1(2).
[16] Protection of Birds Acts 1954 to 1967.
[17] 1981 Act ss.1(4), 21(1), as amended by CRoW 2000 Sched. 12 para 10.
[18] 1981 Act s.21(1), as amended by CRoW 2000 Sched. 12 para 10.
[19] 1981 Act s.1(5), as amended by CRoW 2000 Sched. 12 para 1.
[20] 1981 Act s.1(5).

wild bird, *intended* to do so. English law recognises two forms of recklessness. In one form the subjectively reckless person would know the risk of disturbing the wild bird, be willing to take it and would deliberately take it. It would then be for the court to decide whether the risk had been in the defendant's mind at the time that the wild bird was disturbed. It is more likely that the other form – the objective test – will be applied to this section since the term "recklessly" was inserted to overcome the difficulties of establishing the defendant's subjective mental state at the time of disturbing the wild bird. In the case of "objective" recklessness, the risk must be obvious to a reasonable person. Thus, the defendant must have disturbed the wild bird and have either not considered the possibility of disturbance or considered it and gone ahead and disturbed it anyway. The risk need not have been obvious to the defendant, merely to a reasonably prudent person.

The provisions of Schedule 1 are set out immediately below. We have set out the common, rather than the Latin, scientific, names. The list of species is in two Parts. Part I lists kinds of bird subject to this special protection throughout the year; Part II, the birds which are specially protected during their close season only: which is, for these birds, the period between the start of February and the end of August.

SCHEDULE 1

BIRDS WHICH ARE PROTECTED BY SPECIAL PENALTIES

Part I

At all Times

Avocet
Bee-eater
Bittern
Bittern, Little
Bluethroat
Brambling
Bunting, Cirl
Bunting, Lapland

Bunting, Snow
Buzzard, Honey
Capercaillie (in Scotland only)
Chough
Corncrake
Crake, Spotted
Crossbills (all species)
Curlew, Stone

Divers (all species)
Dotterel
Duck, Long-tailed
Eagle, Golden
Eagle, White-tailed
Falcon, Gyr
Fieldfare
Firecrest
Garganey
Godwit, Black-tailed
Goshawk
Grebe, Black-necked
Grebe, Slavonian
Greenshank
Gull, Little
Gull, Mediterranean
Harriers (all species)
Heron, Purple
Hobby
Hoopoe
Kingfisher
Kite, Red
Merlin
Oriole, Golden
Osprey
Owl, Barn
Owl, Snowy
Peregrine
Petrel, Leach's
Phalarope, Red-necked
Plover, Kentish
Plover, Little Ringed

Quail, Common
Redstart, Black
Redwing
Rosefinch, Scarlet
Ruff
Sandpiper, Green
Sandpiper, Purple
Sandpiper, Wood
Scaup
Scoter, Common
Scoter, Velvet
Serin
Shorelark
Shrike, Red-backed
Spoonbill
Stilt, Black-winged
Stint, Temminck's
Swan, Bewick's
Swan, Whooper
Tern, Black
Tern, Little
Tern, Roseate
Tit, Bearded
Tit, Crested
Treecreeper, Short-toed
Warbler, Cetti's
Warbler, Dartford
Warbler, Marsh
Warbler, Savi's
Whimbrel
Woodlark
Wryneck

Part II
During the Close Season

Goldeneye
Goose, Greylag (in Outer Hebrides, Caithness, Sutherland and Wester Ross only)
Pintail

Game or "Sporting" Birds and Pests: Schedule 2

In addition to the birds in Schedule 1 which receive *special* protection, there is also a list of birds which receive *less* than the ordinary protection described at the outset. This list is in Schedule 2, set out below. In relation to any of the birds listed in **Part I** of Schedule 2 no offence under the 1981 Act is committed by killing or taking (or injuring in an attempt to kill) so long as the actions take place outside the close season.[21] This list comprises game and "sporting" birds. As originally enacted, **Part II** of Schedule 2 listed certain birds widely regarded by landowners as pests in respect of which "authorised persons" might do, with impunity, certain things which would otherwise be criminal offences. "Authorised persons" was defined[22] to mean variously the owner or occupier of land on which the actions took place (and persons acting with their authority), persons authorised in writing by the county or district council for the area on which the actions took place, and persons authorised in writing by English Nature (or, in Wales, the Countryside Council) or the Environment Agency, a local fisheries committee, a water company or a sewerage company. Any such "authorised persons" were not guilty of any of the offences listed at the start of this section by reason only of their having:

(i)   killed or taken a bird listed within Part II of Schedule 2, or injured such a bird in the course of attempting to kill it;

(ii) taken, damaged or destroyed the nest of such a bird; or

(iii) taken or destroyed an egg of such a bird.

It may be noted that birds within **Part II** of Schedule 2 might be "killed" at any time of the year but only by "authorised persons". Birds within **Part I** may be "killed" by *any* persons but only outside their close seasons.

---

[21] 1981 Act s.2(1). Generally the close season is from 1 February to 31 August. For the capercaillie (in England and Wales only) and woodcock it extends to 30 September. For the snipe it ends with 11 August. For wild ducks and geese below high water mark the period begins on 21 February.

[22] 1981 Act s.27(1).

SCHEDULE 2

BIRDS WHICH MAY BE KILLED OR TAKEN

Part I

Outside the Close Season

Capercaillie (in England and Wales only)	Mallard
	Moorhen
Coot	Pintail
Duck, Tufted	Plover, Golden
Gadwall	Pochard
Goldeneye	Shoveler
Goose, Canada	Snipe, Common
Goose, Greylag	Teal
Goose, Pink-footed	Wigeon
Goose, White-fronted (in England and Wales only)	Woodcock

Part II[23]

By any Authorised Persons at all Times

Crow	Magpie
Dove, Collared	Pigeon, Feral
Gull, Great Black-backed	Rook
Gull, Lesser Black-backed	Sparrow, House
Gull, Herring	Starling
Jackdaw	Woodpigeon
Jay	

During 1990, the government announced that, in order to comply with obligations under the EC Birds Directive (which contains a basic prohibition on the killing and taking of *all* birds), it intended to amend the 1981 Act so that owners and occupiers would need to seek permission by licence prior to taking action to kill such pest birds. Although the government stressed that the change was only to be one of form, and that such permission would be readily forthcoming in appropriate cases, the proposal was condemned by farmers as being unduly

---

[23] Prior to 1992. See below.

burdensome and bureaucratic. In the light of this response the government agreed to review the position. In due course, however, all the birds listed in Part II of Schedule 2 were removed from the Schedule[24] and, in order that the killing may continue, licences are obtainable from DEFRA.[25] The general licences[26] apply to all authorised persons: as such there is no need to make an individual application.

Areas of Special Protection

In addition to the general offences, and the rules giving greater or lesser protection to listed species, which we have considered, there is also provision for the creation, by the Secretary of State, of Areas of Special Protection.[27] The designation of such an Area requires the consent of all the owners and occupiers of the land, though such consent may be assumed if no such persons have raised objection within three months of notice having been given to them of the Secretary of State's intentions. If to give such notice to all owners and occupiers in the area in question is impracticable, the Secretary of State may advertise his proposals in a newspaper circulating in the area instead; and the three month period then runs from the date of advertisement. If within three months of actual notice or such advertisement any owner or occupier has objected, the Secretary of State shall not make the order designating the area as one of special protection unless, or until, any such objection has been withdrawn.

What is the consequence of such designation? The special protection arises from the fact that the order can create additional offences applicable to all or part of the area. To begin with, the offences of *disturbing* a bird building a nest or which is in, on, or near a nest containing eggs or young, and of *disturbing dependent young* can be made to apply to any wild birds to which the designation order applies rather than just to

---

[24] See S.I. 1992/3010.
[25] 1981 Act s.16. In Wales, Ministerial powers are exercisable by the National Assembly for Wales: S.I. 1999/672.
[26] See below, p.231.
[27] 1981 Act s.3.

those listed in Schedule 1. The designation order may apply to all wild birds or to particular species, at the discretion of the Secretary of State making the order. Secondly, it can be made an offence for any person to *enter into the area*, or any specified part of it, at any time or during any specified period. It is not, however, an offence to enter if this is done in accordance with provisions in the order.

Such designation is not particularly common (some 37 areas have been designated[28]) but may be useful when it is felt necessary to keep people well away from a particular location, such as one where a rare species may nest. A limitation on the powers of designation is the requirement that there be no objection from the owners and occupiers of the land in question. Perhaps to encourage such persons not to object, the Act contains a widely drafted provision which states that "the making of any order ...with respect of any area shall not affect the exercise by any person of any right vested in him, whether as owner, lessee or occupier of any land in that area or by virtue of a licence or agreement".[29] This would clearly prevent any order from effectively forbidding an owner or occupier from entering onto a part of his own land, or authorising others to do so. Beyond this the extent of the immunity given is not clear. What about an owner or occupier who wishes to organise a gymkhana beside the nest of a bird to which the order applies? If this is the exercise of a right vested in him as owner or occupier, and if those who attend are exercising rights arising from agreement with the owner or occupier that they may enter onto the land for this purpose, then no offence is committed notwithstanding the degree of disturbance that may be caused to the nesting bird or its dependent young. The aim of the Act seems to be to subject to criminal penalties those who trespass on the land without the approval of the owner or occupier; it does not seem greatly to restrict the activities of the owner, the occupier or those whom they have invited onto the land.

---

[28] Office of National Statistics.
[29] 1981 Act s.3(3).

General Exceptions to Liability

So far we have outlined a number of criminal offences designed to protect wild birds. However, in addition to these various provisions there are listed in the 1981 Act a number of *exceptions* to criminal liability which are applicable generally to the offences we have considered.[30] Thus, nothing done by instruction of the Minister of Agriculture, Fisheries and Food under the Agriculture Act 1947 section 98 will constitute an offence; nor anything done under, or in pursuance of, an order made under the Animal Health Act 1981 sections 21 or 22. These provisions allow various sorts of action to be taken to prevent and control plant and animal disease. The second general exception applies to the killing of a bird which has been so seriously disabled, otherwise than by the defendant's own unlawful act, that there is no reasonable chance of it recovering, and also the taking of a disabled bird solely for the purpose of tending it and releasing it when no longer disabled. In this connection it should be noted that it is not a good practice to release such a bird directly into the wild. The bird should be given to a licensed rehabilitation keeper, who may be contacted through the RSPB.

A third general exception is of special importance because of its potentially wide scope. It provides that a person shall not be guilty of an offence if he shows that the act which would otherwise constitute an offence was "the incidental result of a lawful operation and could not reasonably have been avoided". The point to note is that the Act does not require the court to ask whether it would have been reasonable to have avoided doing the "lawful operation" in the circumstances; it simply requires consideration of whether, in performing that lawful operation, the consequence was or was not one which could reasonably have been avoided. Thus, if to destroy a nest is the incidental, and not reasonably avoidable, result of removing a hedgerow (the "lawful operation") the defence applies. The defence would not, however, seem to extend to the situation where the purpose of removing the hedge was to destroy the

---

[30] 1981 Act s.4.

nest: in such a case the destruction would not be the "incidental result" of the lawful operation. Other "lawful operations" which may have harmful incidental consequences and yet be lawfully performed in full knowledge of those consequences include the drainage of wetlands, and the destruction of nests of field-nesting birds by ploughing and harvesting.

Lastly, the general exceptions to liability permit "authorised persons", as defined above, to do things which would otherwise constitute offences where they can show that such action was necessary in order to preserve public health, or public or air safety; to prevent the spread to disease; or to prevent serious damage to livestock, foodstuffs for livestock, crops, vegetables, fruit, growing timber or fisheries. These last "authorised person" exceptions do not, however, apply to acts done in relation to birds listed for special protection in Schedule 1.[31]

Methods of Killing and Taking Birds

Although it is not our purpose in this chapter to deal with laws concerned with cruelty, as distinct from those concerned more directly with species protection, it is appropriate to mention that the Wildlife and Countryside Act 1981 also contains provisions which prohibit, except under licence, certain *methods* of killing or taking wild birds; which prohibit, except under licence, the sale or offer for sale of certain live or dead wild birds or their eggs; and which provide for the registration of captive birds and lay down certain rules for their protection in captivity.

Certain of these provisions are as much the consequence of a desire for species protection as for the prevention of pain and suffering. Thus, a number of methods of killing or taking birds are outlawed on the grounds, it would seem, that they are indiscriminate as between species or simply that they are likely to be too effective in terms of numbers of birds. Accordingly, the setting in position of traps and snares calculated to cause bodily injury to any wild bird coming into contact with them

---

[31] See also, below, p.235 for the further general defence relating to actions done *under licence*. This applies to "animals" and "plants" as well as to "birds" and so will be considered towards the end of this chapter.

is unlawful; as is the setting in position of any poisonous, poisoned or stupefying substance.[32] Other provisions of the 1981 Act seem designed to ensure "fair play" between hunter and hunted, and to ensure that the birds have a sporting chance! In this connection we may note, for example, the prohibition of "any device for illuminating a target or any sighting device for night shooting" and the use of sound recordings as decoys.[33]

Trade and Advertisements

The provisions prohibiting the buying and selling of live or dead wild birds or their eggs, and prohibiting advertisements showing intent to buy or sell, are designed to suppress the trade in such items.[34] These are important offences because the willingness of collectors to pay high prices for the rarer birds and their eggs poses very real threats to such species. The mere existence of the offences may hinder this trade to some extent, but to be really effective there is a clear need for a degree of zeal in relation both to the detection of offences and the prosecution of those caught. In this matter the activities of the Royal Society for the Protection of Birds are of great importance.

The 1981 Act does not, however, prohibit all trade in wild birds and eggs. It draws a distinction between live birds (and their eggs) and dead birds. The prohibition in relation to trade in the former category is almost total, the only exceptions being birds, ringed and bred in captivity, which are of species listed in Part I of Schedule 3. As regards dead birds, the provisions prohibit trade except in relation to those of species listed in Parts II and III of Schedule 3. Part II lists species in which trade of dead birds is allowed at any time of year; Part III lists dead birds which may be traded, but only between September 1st and February 28th. Wider powers to trade in dead birds may, however, be acquired by becoming registered under regulations made by the Secretary of State.

---

[32] 1981 Act s.5(1)(a) – exceptions are provided in s.5(4) and (5).
[33] 1981 Act s. 5(1)(c) and (d).
[34] 1981 Act s.6.

Schedule 3

BIRDS WHICH MAY BE SOLD

Part I

Alive at all Times if Ringed and Bred in Captivity

Blackbird	Linnet
Brambling	Magpie
Bullfinch	Owl, Barn
Bunting, Reed	Redpoll
Chaffinch	Siskin
Dunnock	Starling
Goldfinch	Thrush, Song
Greenfinch	Twite
Jackdaw	Yellowhammer
Jay	

Part II

Dead at all Times

Woodpigeon

Part III

Dead from 1st September to 28th February

Capercaillie (in England and Wales only)	Pochard
	Shoveler
Coot	Snipe, Common
Duck, Tufted	Teal
Mallard	Wigeon
Pintail	Woodcock
Plover, Golden	

PROTECTION OF WILD ANIMALS

Basic Offences

The offences contained in the Wildlife and Countryside Act 1981 relating to the protection of wild animals in many ways parallel those described above in respect of birds. Thus, the basic offences are:

(i) intentionally to kill, injure or take any wild animal included in Schedule 5; and

(ii) to have in one's possession or control any live or dead wild animal included in Schedule 5, or any part of, or anything derived from, such an animal.[35]

The animals within Schedule 5 are listed at the end of this section. In relation to the "possession and control" offence, there is a proviso that the offence is not committed if the defendant can show that the animal had not been killed or taken in contravention of the provisions of the 1981 Act, or earlier legislation;[36] or that the animal had been sold to him or to any other person otherwise than in contravention of the legislation.

There are also parallels to the "nesting" offences which we noted earlier in relation to birds. Thus, it is an offence intentionally:

(i) to damage or destroy, or obstruct access to, any structure or place which any wild animal included in Schedule 5 uses for shelter or protection; or

(ii) to disturb any such animal while it is occupying a structure or place which it uses for that purpose.[37]

It should be noted, however, that this offence is not committed by anything done within a dwelling-house.[38]

---

[35] 1981 Act s. 9(1) and (2). For protection under other Acts of bats, badgers, deer and certain other animals, see below, pp.243-251.

[36] The Conservation of Wild Creatures and Wild Plants Act 1975.

[37] 1981 Act s.9(4).

[38] But see further, below, p.249 on "bats".

In addition, it is an offence intentionally or recklessly to disturb dolphins, whales or basking sharks.[39] The purpose of this offence is to protect this particular form of marine life from disturbance by, amongst others, tour operators, sea canoeists and surfers, without the need of proving intent in every case. However, enforceability is questionable given that police authorities are primarily land-bound and there is no provision within the 1981 Act for more marine-based authorities to gather evidence and prosecute criminal acts.

Exceptions to Liability

As in relation to birds, a number of general exceptions to criminal liability apply.[40] Thus, actions done under the powers in the Agriculture Act 1947 and the Animal Health Act 1981 to prevent and control disease will not be unlawful; and there are "mercy" clauses, like those described in relation to birds, permitting the killing of animals which have been seriously disabled and which have no reasonable chance of recovering, and the taking of an animal which has been disabled in order to tend it and then release it. The principle, noted before, which exempts from liability actions which are the "incidental result of a lawful operation and not reasonably avoidable" also operates; and the Act permits an "authorised person" to kill or injure a Schedule 5 wild animal if he can show his action was necessary to prevent serious damage to "livestock, crops, vegetables, fruit, growing timber or any other form of property or to fisheries". However, this last defence cannot be relied on except where a licence from the Minister of Agriculture, Fisheries and Food has been applied for, and only then until a decision on such a licence is taken. Such licences are considered, further, later in this chapter.[41]

---

[39] 1981 Act s.9(4A), inserted by CRoW 2000 Sched. 12 para 5.
[40] 1981 Act s.10.
[41] See below, p.242.

SCHEDULE 5

ANIMALS WHICH ARE PROTECTED[42]

Adder*
Allis shad*
Anemone, Ivell's Sea
Anemone, Startlet Sea
Apus
Atlantic Stream Crayfish*
Bats, Horseshoe (all species)
Bats, Typical (all species)
Beetle (Graphoderus zonatus)
Beetle (Hypebaeus flavipes)
Beetle (Paracymus aeneus)
Beetle, Lesser Silver Water
Beetle, Mire Pill*
Beetle, Rainbow Leaf
Beetle, Stag*
Beetle, Violet Click
Burbot
Butterflies:
  Adonis Blue
  Black Hairstreak
  Brown Hairstreak
  Chalkhill Blue
  Chequered Skipper
  Duke of Burgundy
  Glanville Fritillary
  Heath Fritillary
  High Brown Fritillary
  Large Blue
  Large Copper
  Large Heath
  Large Tortoiseshell
  Lulworth Skipper
  Marsh Fritillary

Mountain Ringlet
Northern Brown Argus
Pearl-bordered Fritillary
Purple Emperor
Silver Spotted Skipper
Silver-studded Blue
Small Blue
Swallowtail
White Letter Hairstreak
Wood White
Cat, Wild
Cicada, New Forest
Cricket, Field
Cricket, Mole
Damselfly, Southern
Dolphins (all species)
Dormouse
Dragonfly, Norfolk Aeshna
Frog, Common*
Goby, Couch's
Goby, Giant
Grasshopper, Wart-biter
Hatchet Shell, Northern
Hydroid, Marine
Lagoon Snail
Lagoon Snail, De Folin's
Lagoon Worm, Tentacled
Leech, Medicinal
Lizard, Sand
Lizard, Viviparous*
Marten, Pine
Mat, Trembling Sea
Moth, Barberry Carpet

---

[42]   Asterisks denote protection by certain offences only.

Moth, Black-veined
Moth, Essex Emerald
Moth, Fiery Clearwing
Moth, Fisher's Estuarine
Moth, New Forest Burnet
Moth, Reddish Buff
Moth, Sussex Emerald
Mussel, Fan*
Mussel, Freshwater Pearl
Newt, Great Crested
Newt, Palmate*
Newt, Smooth*
Otter, Common
Porpoises (all species)
Sandworm, Lagoon
Sea Fan, Pink*
Sea Slug, Lagoon
Shad, Twaite
Shark, Basking

Shrimp, Fairy
Shrimp, Lagoon Sand
Slow-worm*
Snail, Glutinous
Snail, Sandbowl
Snake, Grass*
Snake, Smooth
Spider, Fen Raft
Spider, Ladybird
Squirrel, Red
Sturgeon
Toad, Common*
Toad, Natterjack
Turtles, Marine (all species)
Vendace
Vole, Water*
Walrus
Whale (all species)
Whitefish

Methods of Killing or Taking Animals

The 1981 Act also prohibits certain *methods* of killing or taking wild animals. Some methods are prohibited in respect of *all* animals. For example, the use of any live mammal or bird as a decoy for the purpose of killing or taking any animal; also, the use of any self-locking snare which is of "such a nature and is so placed as to be calculated to cause bodily injury to any wild animal" coming into contact with it. Other methods are prohibited when their use kills, takes or endangers *certain species*. Thus, actions are prohibited which involve the use of certain items (such as traps, snares, poisons) to take or kill any animal listed within Schedule 6: or when they involve the setting in position of such items where they are "so placed and of such a nature as to be calculated to cause bodily injury" to an animal listed within Schedule 6. In relation to *other* species the use of non self-locking snares is permitted so long as they are inspected at least once every day. A principal reason behind these prohibitions would seem to be the indiscriminate nature of these methods. The Act also protects species within Schedule 6 from methods which are over-effective or unsporting. Thus, as with wild birds, the use of such methods as sound decoys, sighting devices for night-shooting, automatic or semi-automatic weapons and dazzling lights are prohibited.

The Wildlife and Countryside (Amendment) Act 1991 has modified these provisions to permit *certain* of the prohibited devices to be used where it can be shown that the item was set for the lawful killing of animals in the interests of public health, agriculture, forestry, fisheries or nature conservation and that all reasonable precautions were taken to seek to prevent animals protected by Schedule 6 being injured.

SCHEDULE 6

ANIMALS WHICH MAY NOT BE KILLED OR TAKEN BY CERTAIN METHODS

Badger
Bats, Horseshoe (all species)
Bats, Typical (all species)
Cat, Wild
Dolphin, Bottle-nosed
Dolphin, Common
Dormice (all species)
Hedgehog

Marten, Pine
Otter, Common
Polecat
Porpoise, Harbour
  (otherwise known as
  Common Porpoise)
Shrews (all species)
Squirrel, Red

PROTECTION OF WILD PLANTS

Basic Offences

The provisions of the Wildlife and Countryside Act 1981 concerned with the protection of wild plants are considerably less complex than those relating to birds and animals. Again, however, there are clear parallels between the basic offences. Thus, it is an offence intentionally:

(i) to pick, uproot or destroy any wild plant included in Schedule 8; or

(ii) uproot any wild plant not included in that Schedule, unless one is an "authorised person".[43]

The term "pick" is defined to include the gathering or plucking of any part of a plant without uprooting it. This would, therefore, include seed collection.

The plants contained in Schedule 8 are listed at the end of this section. Neither of the above offences are, however, committed when such acts are "an incidental result of a lawful operation and could not reasonably have been avoided."

The effect of the two offences, referred to above, is that owners and occupiers (*ie* "authorised persons") of land may on that land uproot any plant *not* within Schedule 8, but may not even pick, let alone uproot or destroy, any plant within Schedule 8. Persons who are *not* owners or occupiers of the land in question commit an offence in uprooting, without the owner's consent, any plants at all and may only pick plants not within Schedule 8.

In addition, there is an offence of having in one's possession any live or dead wild plant included in Schedule 8, or any part of or anything derived from such a plant. Furthermore, trade in such items is forbidden, as also is advertisement of willingness to trade.

Schedule 8

PLANTS WHICH ARE PROTECTED

Adder's-tongue, Least
Alison, Small
Anomodon, Long-leaved
Beech-lichen, New Forest
Blackwort
Bluebell (in respect of section 13(2) only)
Bolete, Royal

Broomrape, Bedstraw
Broomrape, Oxtongue
Broomrape, Thistle
Cabbage, Lundy
Calamint, Wood
Caloplaca, Snow
Catapyrenium, Tree
Catchfly, Alpine

---

[43] 1981 Act s.13.

Catillaria, Laurer's
Centaury, Slender
Cinquefoil, Rock
Cladonia, Convoluted
Cladonia, Upright Mountain
Clary, Meadow
Club-rush, Triangular
Colt's-foot, Purple
Cotoneaster, Wild
Cottongrass, Slender
Cow-wheat, Field
Crocus, Sand
Crystalwort, Lizard
Cudweed, Broad-leaved
Cudweed, Jersey
Cudweed, Red-tipped
Cut-grass
Deptford Pink (in England
  and Wales only)
Diapensia
Dock, Shore
Earwort, Marsh
Eryngo, Field
Feather-moss, Polar
Fern, Dickie's Bladder
Fern, Killarney
Flapwort, Norfolk
Fleabane, Alpine
Fleabane, Small
Frostwort, Pointed
Fungus, Hedgehog
Galingale, Brown
Gentian, Alpine
Gentian, Dune
Gentian, Early
Gentian, Fringed
Gentian, Spring
Germander, Cut-leaved
Germander, Water

Gladiolus, Wild
Goblin Lights
Goosefoot, Stinking
Grass-poly
Grimmia, Blunt-leaved
Gyalecta, Elm
Hare's-ear, Sickle-leaved
Hare's-ear, Small
Hawk's-bead, Stinking
Hawkweed, Northroe
Hawkweed, Shetland
Hawkweed, Weak-leaved
Heath, Blue
Helleborine, Red
Helleborine, Young's
Horsetail, Branched
Hound's-tongue, Green
Knawel, Perennial
Knotgrass, Sea
Lady's-slipper
Lecanactis, Churchyard
Lecanora, Tarn
Lecidea, Copper
Leek, Round-headed
Lettuce, Least
Lichen, Arctic Kidney
Lichen, Ciliate Strap
Lichen, Coralloid Rosette
Lichen, Ear-lobed Dog
Lichen, Forked Hair
Lichen, Golden Hair
Lichen, Orange Fruited Elm
Lichen, River Jelly
Lichen, Scaly Breck
Lichen, Stary Breck
Lily, Snowdon
Liverwort
Liverwort, Lindenberg's
  Leafy

Marsh-mallow, Rough
Marshwort, Creeping
Milk-parsley, Cambridge
Moss
Moss, Alpine Copper
Moss, Baltic Bog
Moss, Blue Dew
Moss, Blunt-leaved Bristle
Moss, Bright Green Cave
Moss, Cordate Beard
Moss, Cornish Path
Moss, Derbyshire Feather
Moss, Dune Thread
Moss, Flamingo
Moss, Glaucous Beard
Moss, Green Shield
Moss, Hair Silk
Moss, Knothole
Moss, Large Yellow Feather
Moss, Millimetre
Moss, Multifruited River
Moss, Nowell's Limestone
Moss, Rigid Apple
Moss, Round-leaved
   Feather
Moss, Schleicher's Thread
Moss, Triangular Pygmy
Moss, Vaucher's Feather
Mudwort, Welsh
Naiad, Holly-leaved
Naiad, Slender
Orache, Stalked
Orchid, Early Spider
Orchid, Fen
Orchid, Ghost
Orchid, Lapland Marsh
Orchid, Late Spider
Orchid, Lizard
Orchid, Military

Orchid, Monkey
Pannaria, Caledonia
Parmelia, New Forest
Parmentaria, Oil Stain
Pear, Plymouth
Penny-cress, Perfoliate
Pennyroyal
Pertusaria, Alpine Moss
Physcia, Southern Grey
Pigmyweed
Pine, Ground
Pink, Cheddar
Pink, Childling
Plantain, Floating Water
Polypore, Oak
Pseudocyphellaria, Ragged
Psora, Rusty Alpine
Puffball, Sandy Stilt
Ragwort, Fen
Ramping-fumitory, Martin's
Rampion, Spiked
Restharrow, Small
Rock-cress, Alpine
Rock-cress, Bristol
Rustworth, Western
Sandwort, Norwegian
Sandwort, Teesdale
Saxifrage, Drooping
Saxifrage, Marsh
Saxifrage, Tufted
Solenopsora, Serpentine
Solomon's-seal, Whorled
Sow-thistle, Alpine
Spearwort, Adder's-tongue
Speedwell, Fingered
Speedwell, Spiked
Spike-rush, Dwarf
Stack Fleawort, South
Starfruit

Star-of-Bethlehem, Early
Stonewort, Bearded
Stonewort, Foxtail
Strapwort
Sulphur-tresses, Alpine
Threadmoss, Long-leaved
Turpswort
Violet, Fen
Viper's-grass

Water-plantain, Ribbon
  leaved
Wood-sedge, Starved
Woodsia, Alpine
Woodsia, Oblong
Wormwood, Field
Woundwort, Downy
Woundwort, Limestone
Yellow-rattle, Greater

GENERAL PROVISIONS OF PART I OF THE 1981 ACT

In addition to the separate rules, summarised above, applicable to birds, animals, and plants, there are a number of provisions in the 1981 Act which apply generally to all three categories.

Acts Done Under Licence

To begin with, most of the offences we have considered will not be committed if the acts in question have been done under or in accordance with the terms of a licence granted by the "appropriate authority".[44] The "appropriate authority" may depending on context be DEFRA, English Nature (or, in Wales, the Countryside Council). Such licensing power may be useful, for example, when action is necessary to prevent one species becoming so numerous as to endanger others in a particular area. Licences will only be granted where there is no other satisfactory solution and licences for falconry aviculture, taxidermy and photography will only be issued on a selective basis and in respect of a small number of birds.

Proceedings and Penalties

Proceedings in respect of the offences that we have considered so far may also be brought where a person attempts to commit the offence or has in his possession anything capable of being used for committing the offence. Justices of the Peace can grant a search warrant to police officers where there are

---

[44]   1981 Act s.16.

reasonable grounds for suspecting that an offence has been committed. This grants the police a warrant to search the offender's premises for the purpose of obtaining evidence. Police officers and wildlife inspectors have powers to commit for DNA analysis blood or tissue of any specimen[45] in the offender's possession or control which is capable of establishing the identity or ancestry of the specimen. Wildlife inspectors[46] have powers to enter premises (which, in limited circumstances, includes dwellings) to establish whether there have been offences committed in relation to the sale of protected species, registration of wild birds or release of species into the wild. Previously, prosecution of some of the offences in Part I of the 1981 Act had to take place within six months of the commission of the offence. From 31 January 2000, prosecutions must be brought within six months from date on which sufficient evidence has been gathered, and within two years of the commission of the offence.

Almost all Part I offences are now subject to a fine of up to £5000 and/or a custodial sentence of not more than six months. For certain offences,[47] on conviction the defendant may be liable to imprisonment for a term of not more than two years, in addition to any fine. Significantly, if a fine is imposed, each bird, nest, egg, animal, plant or part may be treated as a separate offence.

BADGERS

These delightful creatures have a whole Act of Parliament to themselves, in addition to the protection already noted of being listed within Schedule 6 to the Wildlife and Countryside Act 1981 (prohibiting certain *methods* of killing or taking). The reason for the additional legislation was to deal with the

---

[45] A sample may not be taken from a live bird, animal or plant unless the person taking the sample is satisfied that there will be no lasting harm caused to the specimen. Where the specimen is a live bird or animal, only a veterinary surgeon may take the sample.

[46] 1981 Act s.19ZA, introduced by CRoW s.81(1), Sched. 12 para. 8.

[47] Under ss.14 and 19ZA(8).

menace of badger hunting and the practice of badger baiting. These animals, who do little harm to anyone, have been subjected to the "country pursuit" of being prised from their underground setts with badger tongs, and being baited by dogs (often after having had limbs broken) before finally being killed for their coats and bristles. This practice, sadly, still continues: a Nature Conservancy Council survey in the late 1980s suggesting some 10,000 badgers being killed each year by baiters; but at least now there are charges which may be brought as and when offenders are caught.

The Badgers Act 1973 made it an offence wilfully to kill, injure or take any badger, or to attempt to do any of those things. It was also made an offence to dig for a badger.

For some years prosecutors encountered difficulties when proceeding against persons who had been apprehended whilst digging, but without having actually taken or injured a badger, because such persons would claim to have been digging, quite lawfully, for a fox. The prosecution would fail unless it could be proved beyond reasonable doubt that this was untrue, and that those apprehended were in fact hunting for a badger. The law was, therefore, altered by the Wildlife and Countryside (Amendment) Act 1985 to make successful prosecution less difficult on the "digging", and also the "attempt" charges. Thus, it was provided that if in such a case there was evidence from which it could reasonably be concluded that the accused was attempting to kill, injure or take a badger, or was digging for a badger, he would be presumed to have been doing so unless the contrary was shown. This meant that the prosecution no longer needed to prove those things beyond reasonable doubt. So long as there was evidence from which the appropriate conclusion could reasonably be drawn, the onus shifted to the defence to disprove the statutory presumption. This did not, however, require the accused to prove beyond reasonable doubt that he was not after a badger; he simply had to satisfy the court that it was more likely than not that he was not acting with that purpose. However, the fact that foxes may often seek sanctuary in badger setts made this contention not always implausible, and so successful prosecution remained a difficult matter.

To overcome this difficulty, and also to provide further habitat protection, the Badgers Act 1991 established certain offences in relation to the interference with badgers' setts (defined as meaning "any structure or place which displays signs indicating current use by a badger"). It is an offence for any person to interfere with a badger sett in any of certain defined ways. These comprise: damaging the sett or any part of it; destroying the sett; obstructing access to or any entrance of a sett; causing a dog to enter a sett; and disturbing a badger when it is occupying a sett. It is provided that the defendant must have done one of these things intentionally or reckless as to whether any of the defined consequences ensued. No offence will be committed, however, where the acts in question are the "incidental result of a lawful operation and could not reasonably have been avoided". This does not apply, though, where the offence charged is that of "destruction" of a sett. For this reason, developers with planning permission will need to obtain a licence from MAFF or English Nature (Countryside Council), even if such destruction is an unavoidable incidental consequence of implementing a planning permission.

In the context of fox-hunting, it is expressly provided that a person shall not be guilty of obstructing an entrance to a sett where the act is done for the purpose of hunting foxes with hounds. The exemption applies only where the only action done in respect of the sett is the blocking of entrances and does not involve any digging into the top or the sides of the entrances. Moreover, the materials used must not be packed hard into the entrances. The materials used for blocking the entrances must consist only of (i) "untainted straw or hay or leaf-litter, or bracken, or loose soil", or (ii) "a bundle of sticks or faggots, or paper sacks either empty or filled with untainted straw, hay or leaf-litter, bracken or loose soil". Where materials in category (i) are used, the blocking must be on the day of the hunt or after midday on the day before; where of category (ii), the blocking must be on the day of the hunt and the sett must be unblocked again on that same day. The defendant must also have the authority of both the landowner and a recognised hunt. A further exception for the benefit of hunters is the provision that a person shall not be guilty of an offence by reason of his hounds "marking" a badger sett, provided the hounds are withdrawn as soon as reasonably practicable.

It is also an offence for any person to have in his possession or under his control any dead badger, or any part of or anything derived from a dead badger; though a person is not guilty if he can show that the badger had not been killed in contravention of the Act, or that the badger or other thing in his possession had been sold by the original offender to a purchaser who had no reason to believe the badger had been unlawfully killed. Possession or control of a live badger is, subject to limited exceptions, also an offence under the Act; as also is the offer for sale of live badgers.

These various prohibitions apply equally to owners and occupiers of the land in question as well as to others, an "authorised person" exemption in the 1973 Act having being removed by the Wildlife and Countryside Act 1981. However, a number of general exceptions to the operation of the offences apply. These are in very much the same form as the ones considered above in respect of protection of animals under the 1981 Act. Thus, one may take a badger in order to tend it when it has been disabled, or kill it if it has been so seriously disabled that to kill it would be an act of mercy. Equally no offence is committed when the killing or injury is the unavoidable incidental result of a lawful action. Badgers may also be killed if the person doing so can show that it was necessary to prevent serious damage to land, crops, poultry or any other form of property. However, such action is only permissible provided that an application has been made for a Ministry licence (to authorise such actions), and the action is necessary pending a decision upon such application. Such licences, like the ones under the 1981 Act, may be issued to allow, otherwise unlawful, actions for a variety of purposes. Such purposes include conservation of badgers, the ringing and marking of badgers, the prevention of serious damage to land, crops, etc. and to prevent the spread of disease. In this connection a controversial matter has been the licensing by the Ministry of Agriculture, Fisheries and Food of the killing of thousands of badgers by gassing, in order to prevent the spread of bovine tuberculosis amongst cattle. Some doubt has been expressed as to whether badgers are indeed guilty of causing this harm. Indeed, some would argue that the spread of the disease is actually the other way around; it is known that cows may infect badgers, but evidence is lacking of badgers returning the disease to uninfected cattle. In any case the problem is largely a localised one in the South-West of England and should not have been used, as it appears to have been, as an excuse for more widespread unlawful killing of badgers.

Further legislation was enacted in 1991 – the Badgers (Further Protection) Act. This enhanced the powers of the criminal courts in cases where a dog has been used in, or was present at the commission of an offence of taking, injuring, killing or being cruel to a badger. Following conviction of the defendant the court may, in addition or instead of any other punishment, *(i)* order the destruction of, or the disposal of, the dog; and *(ii)* order that the defendant be disqualified from having custody of a dog. When the dog in question is owned by someone other than the defendant, the owner may appeal against any such disposal or destruction order made.

By 1992 the legislation on badgers was contained in three principal Acts of Parliament and also several minor amending provisions of other Acts. Opportunity was therefore taken to consolidate the rules, described above, into a single piece of legislation: the Protection of Badgers Act 1992.

DEER

Although there is legislation dealing specifically with deer, this is designed principally to protect these animals from acts of cruelty and to preserve numbers of animals as a species of game, rather than to promote conservation as an end in itself. Nevertheless, since the provisions do provide some degree of species protection it is appropriate to consider them, albeit briefly, here.

The Deer Act 1963 made it an offence to take or wilfully kill deer of any species listed in Schedule 1 to the Act during the close season for that species. Schedule 1 lists four species, Red, Fallow, Roe and Sika Deer, and specifies the start and end of the close season for each sex of each species. It is also an offence to take or wilfully kill any deer, of whatever species, at night time; and this is regardless of whether it is the close season or not.

As with the other legislation we have considered, the Act provides a number of general exceptions to the scope of these offences. In particular, an authorised person (eg the occupier of the land) may take or kill any deer, other than at night, which is on any cultivated land, pasture or enclosed woodland if damage is being done to crops, vegetables, or growing timber and the action taken is necessary to prevent serious further damage.

Deer were further protected by the Deer Act 1980. The 1963 Act, as we saw, was concerned to protect certain categories of deer, at certain times of year, from actions done by any persons; even by the owner of the land upon which the deer were to be found. The 1980 Act, in contrast, was concerned to protect all deer at all times from the activities of poachers: that is, persons who enter onto land without the consent of the owner or occupier in search or pursuit of any deer and with the intention of taking, killing or injuring such deer. Even if entry onto the land was by consent, it was nevertheless still an offence, without the consent of the owner of the land, to take, kill, or injure any deer, to search for or pursue any deer for that purpose, or to remove any deer carcase. The Act also restricted lawful trade in venison to licensed game dealers,[48] who had to keep detailed records of the venison which came into their possession and also of the persons from whom the venison was obtained.

The rules described above were consolidated in the Deer Act 1991, the present principal legislation on this matter.

---

[48]   Licensed under the Game Act 1831 and the Game Licences Act 1860.

BATS

The Wildlife and Countryside Act 1981 affords a degree of protection to bats additional to that which is provided by the fact that all kinds of bats are listed within Schedule 5. As was noted earlier, the 1981 Act provides that its prohibition on intentionally damaging, destroying, or obstructing access to any structure or place which such a listed animal uses for shelter or protection, or disturbing such an animal occupying the structure or place, does *not* make unlawful anything done within a dwelling-house.[49] In the case of bats, however, this exception to the scope of the offence only applies fully to actions done within the *living area* of the dwelling-house. As regards other areas (*eg* the loft or an outbuilding) the exception to liability cannot be relied on unless the defendant has notified English Nature (Countryside Council) of his proposed actions, and allowed that body reasonable time to "advise him" as to whether the actions should be carried out and, if so, by what method.[50] This provision, it should be noted, does not require compliance with the advice given; it simply requires that the conservation agency be given an opportunity to give that advice before any disturbing action can lawfully take place. This requirement to notify, and be advised by, the relevant conservation agency also applies to the operation, in relation to bats, of the "incidental and not reasonably avoidable result of a lawful action" defence.[51] But, again, there is no requirement to comply with the advice given.

The operation of these provisions was shown in a case before the Magistrates at Bedale, in Yorkshire, in February 1986. A timber merchant was convicted of intentionally killing a colony of Brandt Bats when he had sprayed the roof space of a cottage in order to destroy woodworm, the spray also killing the bats. He was fined £500 and ordered to pay £200 costs. He would have avoided criminal liability if he had notified the forerunner of English Nature and given them reasonable time to give him advice.

---

[49] 1981 Act s.10(2). See above, p.234.
[50] 1981 Act s.10(5).
[51] 1981 Act s.10(3). See above, p.230.

If, however, such advice need not be complied with, what value is there in these provisions? Much is likely to depend on the sort of advice that is given. In this connection it is worth noting that bats do no harm within a roof-space, and that a high proportion of the declining bat population now live in the roof-spaces of modern houses. They have moved from their belfries to more modern homes. The decline of the bat population, which commenced in the 1940s, is thought to be a result of land drainage and pesticides reducing their insect food supply. If the bat population which remains is to survive it is, perhaps, necessary for us to be willing to share some part of our homes with these animals.

FISH

The common law has for centuries treated fish as a special form of property. Thus, fish in private waters or in non-tidal rivers or streams can be taken only by, or with the consent of, the owner of those waters (the owner or owners of the banks at either side), or by persons who have been granted or have acquired by long use a right to take the fish (a right of "piscary"). The Salmon and Freshwater Fisheries Act 1975 contains detailed rules about such matters as close seasons and the taking of immature fish. Certain methods of fishing are also proscribed (*eg* explosive or electrical devices).

By contrast, anyone may take fish in tidal waters or from the sea, subject only to bye-laws made by the statutory authorities which normally require purchase of a licence. Sea fishing is also controlled by legislation which specifies the sizes of mesh which may be used in nets. By virtue of the Fisheries (Wildlife Conservation) Act 1992 it is incumbent upon government to have regard, in the exercise of its powers, to the conservation of marine flora and fauna and to seek a reasonable balance between conservation and other concerns.

Sturgeon, much prized in former times as a source of caviar and isinglass, is a royal fish when found in coastal or estuarine waters, and as such may be taken only under licence from the Crown. The same principle applies to whales, which also have been regarded for centuries as the prerogative of the Sovereign. The matter is, however, dealt with on a legislative rather than merely prerogatival footing. The Whaling Industry (Regulation) Act 1934 prohibits the catching of all species of cetacean within British coastal waters. It also prohibits the catching of whales by British ships anywhere in the world (except under licence: none of which currently are in issue).

These common law and statutory provisions are not concerned primarily with the conservation of fish life, but they have acted as a limitation on the wholesale taking or slaughter of fish stocks. The voluntary regulation by anglers through their regular competitions has had much the same effect, although the widespread use of lead pellets as sinkers for their lines has been the cause of many swan deaths on our rivers. Legislation to outlaw the import and supply of lead pellets came into force at the beginning of 1987.

IMPORTED SPECIES

Lessons from the past demonstrate the harm which can sometimes result, for existing fauna and flora, from the introduction of new species from overseas. Of course, such importation is not always to be discouraged. After all, a good deal of the diversity of our existing flora and fauna is the result of introduction of plants and animals within historical times. Nevertheless, in some instances the results of importing new species have been unfortunate. Familiar examples include the release of mink and coypus into the wild. This action by breeders, disappointed at the unprofitability of keeping these species captive for their fur, has led to extensive populations in East Anglia; and the effect on levels of fish in rivers and on small animals has been quite serious. Another well-known illustration of the danger of importation of a new species is the damage that would result to potato crops if the Colorado Beetle became widespread. This danger is taken so seriously that the law imposes a positive duty on any person who spots such a beetle to take it to the police! The rapidity with which a species can become established, if the conditions suit, is shown by the fact that that common weed of disturbed soil, the rosebay willowherb, is not native to England but arrived when its seeds were imported with bales of wood from the Antipodes. More recently, the introduction in 1976 of the American Signal Crayfish has had an adverse impact upon the domestic White-clawed or Atlantic Stream Crayfish.

The law, therefore, takes a cautious stance towards the introduction of new species. The Wildlife and Countryside Act 1981 prohibits any person from releasing or allowing to escape into the wild any animal which:

(i)   is of a kind which is not ordinarily resident in, or is not a regular visitor to Great Britain in a wild state; or

(ii) is included in Part I of Schedule 9 (animals already in the wild but whose further release is undesirable).

It is also an offence for any person to plant, or otherwise cause to grow in the wild, any plant which is included in Part II of Schedule 9.

SCHEDULE 9

Part I
ANIMALS WHICH ARE ESTABLISHED IN THE WILD

Bass, Large-mouthed Black
Bass, Rock
Bitterling
Budgerigar
Capercaillie
Coypu (Myocastor Coypus)
Crayfish, Noble
Crayfish, Signal
Crayfish, Turkish
Deer, any hybrid one of whose parents or other lineal ancestor was a Sika Deer

With respect to the Outer Hebrides and the islands of Arran, Islay, Jura and Rum: *(a)* Deer, Cervus (all species) *(b)* Deer, any hybrid one of whose parents or other lineal ancestor was a species of Cervus Deer
Deer, Muntjac
Deer, Sika
Dormouse, Fat
Duck, Carolina Wood

Duck, Mandarin
Duck, Ruddy
Eagle, White-tailed
Flatworm, New Zealand
Frog, edible
Frog, European Tree
  (otherwise known as
  Common Tree Frog)
Frog, Marsh
Gerbil, Mongolian
Goose, Canada
Goose, Egyptian
Heron, Night
Lizard, Common Wall
Marmot, Prairie (otherwise
  known as Prairie Dog)
Mink, American
Newt, Alpine
Newt, Italian Crested
Owl, Barn
Parakeet, Ring-necked
Partridge, Chukar

Partridge, Rock
Pheasant, Golden
Pheasant, Lady Amherst's
Pheasant, Reeves'
Pheasant, Silver
Porcupine, Crested
Porcupine, Himalayan
Pumpkinseed (otherwise
  known as Sun-fish or
  Pond-perch)
Quail, Bobwhite
Rat, Black
Snake, Aesculapian
Squirrel, Grey
Terrapin, European Pond
Toad, African Clawed
Toad, Midwife
Toad, Yellow-bellied
Wallaby, Red-necked
Wels (otherwise known as
  European catfish)
Zander

Part II
PLANTS

Hogweed, Giant
Kelp, Giant (Macrocystis pyrifera)
Kelp, Giant (Macrocystis angustifolia)
Kelp, Giant (Macrocystis integrifolia)
Kelp, Giant (Macrocystis laevis)
Kelp, Japanese
Knotweed, Japanese
Seafingers, Green
Seaweed, Californian Red
Seaweed, Hooked Asparagus
Seaweed, Japanese
Seaweeds, Laver (except native species, *ie* Porphyra amethystea,
  P. Leucosticta, P. linearis, P. miniata, P. purpurea, P. umbilicalis)
Wakame

ENDANGERED SPECIES

Brief mention may be made of the controls which exist under the Endangered Species (Import and Export) Act 1976.[52] This chapter has been principally concerned with the protection of the flora and fauna of England and Wales, whereas the 1976 Act is designed to restrict international trade in animals and plants which are endangered in the world as a whole.

The 1976 Act creates a number of offences including making it an offence to export or import any mammal, bird, reptile, amphibian, fish, mollusc (whether dead or alive) listed in Schedule 1 or any dead or alive plant listed in Schedule 2. There is a similar prohibition on the import and export of things derived from endangered species, such as elephant tusks and certain furs, listed in Schedule 3.

The Secretary of State may vary the lists in the Schedules, and may also issue licences for the import or export of particular animals or plants, when he is so advised by the relevant scientific authority.

---

[52] As amended by the Wildlife and Countryside Act 1981 Sched. 10. The Act provides for implementation in the UK of obligations under the Convention on International Trade in Endangered Species (CITES). CITES also has been implemented at EC level by directly applicable EC Regulation (3626/82). See S.I.s 1985/1154 and 1155.

Chapter 7

POLLUTION

INTRODUCTION

In this chapter we shall be concerned with the law's response to the threats to the countryside which arise from a variety of different kinds of pollution. To begin with we shall examine the way in which the common law developed principles to protect landowners from the harmful or offensive activities of "unneighbourly" neighbours. These rules, principally the law of nuisance, still apply, and may still be of value to the individuals especially affected by the activities in question. However, it was evident from a fairly early time that the common law alone was inadequate to regulate and control what we would now call acts of pollution. It is not sufficient to rely on affected individuals to bring civil actions, at their own expense, in the courts. Moreover, others, interested in the protection of the environment but not themselves landowners affected by the pollution, would likely not have standing in the courts to bring such actions. What has been necessary has been legislation to impose statutory duties, the breach of which will constitute criminal offences; together with the conferment of licensing and detection and enforcement obligations, on public agencies.

It is, therefore, with the modern legislation of this kind that the bulk of this chapter will be concerned; the most significant legislation being the Environmental Protection Act 1990 and the Water Resources Act 1991. In considering the legislation we shall examine the controls exerted over a number of different forms of pollution. These will be considered under the following broad headings – atmospheric pollution, pollution of land, pollution of inland waters and the sea, and pollution by noise.

THE COMMON LAW

Private Nuisance

The common law, being from early times much concerned with the protection of property rights, developed long ago the action of **nuisance** in order to protect owners and occupiers of land from the harmful or anti-social activities of others. The remedies which may be granted to a successful plaintiff are an award of damages to compensate him for the nuisance suffered and an injunction forbidding continuation of the acts or activities constituting the nuisance. If an injunction has been obtained and the person to whom it is addressed fails to comply with its terms, proceedings for contempt of court may be brought. In such proceedings the court may impose penalties of imprisonment or a fine, or both. In exceptional cases, a court may refuse to award an injunction (so permitting the nuisance to continue) but award a sum of damages to reflect that ongoing and now permitted nuisance.

In addition to these court remedies there is the remedy of self-help. A person against whom a nuisance is being committed may, in certain circumstances, take action to abate the nuisance – that is, to stop the nuisance. This is, however, a limited power. It may, for example, authorise the taking of action to prevent fire spreading to one's land, or to stop water flooding onto one's property; but it would not permit physical force against the owner of neighbouring property to prevent continuance of his deliberate actions.

In what circumstances will the law regard a person's actions as constituting a nuisance? A number of general points may be made, and examples from decided cases provide illustrations. In the first place a distinction needs to be drawn between actions which harm the plaintiff's land itself, and actions which simply spoil the plaintiff's enjoyment of his land. Both kinds of action may constitute nuisance, but it is rather easier to show actionable nuisance in the former type of case than in the latter. Examples of the former kind have included: the percolation of noxious chemicals onto the plaintiff's land from that of the defendant;[1] damage to the plaintiff's trees and shrubs resulting from the emission of noxious vapours;[2] damage to the plaintiff's market garden crops caused by fumes from creosoted wood

---

[1]   *Maberley v Peabody and Co.* [1946] 2 All ER 192.
[2]   *Tipping v St. Helen's Smelting Co.* (1863) 4 B&S 608.

blocks belonging to the defendant;[3] the leakage of oil from the defendant's railway trucks, causing water on the plaintiff's land to become unfit for his cattle;[4] the causing of sewage to collect on the plaintiff's land;[5] and damage to the plaintiff's house caused by vibrations from machinery operated by the defendant.[6] These are all examples of successful claims in which the actions of the defendant caused some physical harm to the plaintiff's property.

It is more difficult to succeed when the nature of the claim is simply that there has been interference with the use or enjoyment which the plaintiff may wish to make of his land. Here the courts have long recognised that they should be careful not to pander to the susceptibilities of over-sensitive owners of land. A degree of "give and take" and of tolerance between neighbours is expected and, as was said in one case: "the law does not regard trifling inconveniences; everything must be looked at from a reasonable point of view."[7] In short, the courts will decide whether the plaintiff is being unreasonable in complaining, or whether he is being subjected to interferences by the defendant which it is not reasonable that he should have to suffer. In deciding this issue, account is taken of a variety of relevant circumstances.

Thus, for example, the neighbourhood where the events take place may be important. Noise which might not constitute a nuisance in an urban area may very well be regarded as such in the countryside; and pollution of the air by smoke or smells may be differently judged as between such areas. However, it would be wrong to suggest that any particular activity is more likely to be adjudged a nuisance in the countryside than in a town. This might be the case in respect of industrial or commercial activities; but smells from heaps of manure, the

---

3   *West v Bristol Tramways* [1908] 2 KB 154.
4   *Smith v Great Western Rail Co.* (1926) 42 TLR 391.
5   *Jones v Llanrwst U.D.C.* [1911] 1 Ch 393.
6   *Menx's Brewery Co. v City of London Electric Lighting Co.* [1895] 1 Ch 287.
7   *Tipping v St. Helen's Smelting Co.* (1863) 4 B&S 608 at 616.

crowing of cockerels and other similar everyday country matters are less likely to be considered nuisances in the country than if transported to an urban setting.

In addition to taking account of the neighbourhood where events occur, the times at which activities occur may be critical; as also the duration and frequency of alleged acts of nuisance. Noise made regularly at night[8] might be a nuisance, even though similar noise occurring only occasionally and always during the day-time might not be so regarded. In recent years a problem for some who live in the countryside has been the practice of some farmers of harvesting by night as well as day, and of illuminating their fields with powerful lights in order to do so. It is perhaps only the seasonal nature of such nocturnal activity which may prevent a sleep-starved neighbour from claiming nuisance.

An instructive example of the principle that in judging whether conduct amounts to a nuisance some regard must be had to the nature of the locality in question was provided quite recently in litigation following the privatisation and redevelopment of Chatham docks.[9] A local authority sought injunctions to restrict movement of the port operator's heavy goods vehicles at night. It was alleged that this traffic was causing a nuisance to the surrounding residential area. The trial judge accepted that the surrounding residential neighbourhood had, indeed, come to experience considerable noise disturbance. It was held, however, that there was in law no nuisance committed. The decision of the local planning authority, in 1983, to have granted planning permission for the naval dockyards to be developed as a commercial port, in full awareness that it would operate "around the clock", had resulted in a change in the character of the neighbourhood for the purpose of the assessment of whether actions or activities would amount to an actionable nuisance. It was not, of course, a matter of planning permission authorising the commission of a nuisance: that is not within the

---

[8] See eg *Rushmer v Polsue and Alfieri Ltd.* [1906] 1 Ch 234.
[9] *Gillingham B.C. v Medway (Chatham) Docks Co. Ltd.* [1992] 3 All ER 923.

power of a local planning authority.[10] Rather, it was a matter of the character of an area changing as a consequence of the permission granted, with the effect that the vehicular traffic levels and times were to be regarded, in such a locality, as not overstepping the boundaries of legal acceptability.

A particular example of the "over-sensitive plaintiff" is the plaintiff whose complaint is really no more than that he cannot use his land for especially sensitive activities because of the actions of the defendant. An example of this was a case where a plaintiff failed to show nuisance when the defendant Electricity Board's power lines interfered with his use of his land to relay television signals.[11] The stance of the law here is clearly that it is unreasonable to require defendants to act with such a degree of restraint that no harm is done to such especially sensitive operations; and that it is those who wish to so protect themselves who should either move to reliably "safe" areas or make appropriate agreements with their neighbours, probably involving compensation for their neighbours' agreement to restrict the use they make of their land. If the public interest genuinely requires protection for the activity in question, this may be achieved by a local planning authority in its operation of planning controls: that is, by refusing planning permission for activities which would have detrimental effects. Jodrell Bank telescope, in Cheshire, has received some degree of protection in this way.[12]

Given the significance of the various kinds of factors described above in determining whether in any particular case an actionable nuisance has been committed, it is not possible to state in categorical terms what actions affecting another person's enjoyment of his property will or will not be a nuisance. What

---

[10] See also the pig smells nuisance in *Wheeler v J. J. Saunders Ltd.* [1995] 2 All ER 697.

[11] *Bridlington Relay Ltd. v Yorkshire Electricity Board* [1965] Ch 436. See also *Hollywood Silver Fox Farm Ltd. v Emmett* [1936] 2 KB 468 and *Hunter v Canary Wharf Ltd.* [1997] 2 All ER 426: interruption of television signals by construction of tall buildings.

[12] See *Stringer v Minister of Housing and Local Government* [1970] 1 WLR 1281.

may be indicated, however, is that in appropriate circumstances any of a wide variety of kinds of activity may so affect a plaintiff's use and enjoyment of his land as to give him an action. Thus, smoke from bonfires may or may not constitute a nuisance depending on such matters as regularity of lighting, direction of wind, amount of smoke and times of day; and noise from model (or full-scale) power boats which is excessive in volume, regularity and duration, may well be a nuisance in a relatively quiet area.[13]

Enough has now been said to have given a general idea of the requirements for a successful action for nuisance. However, a number of further points should be noted. First of all, if the actions of the defendant are such as to constitute a nuisance, it is no defence for him to assert that the plaintiff "came to the nuisance": in other words, that the defendant was acting in the manner complained of even *prior* to the plaintiff buying or coming into occupation of his land.[14] An exception to this, however, is that it is possible to acquire a right to commit a nuisance by prescription. Thus, if for twenty years a defendant has so conducted himself openly and without objection from former owners or occupiers of the plaintiff's land, the plaintiff will be unable to sue. Secondly, in some circumstances, a body acting in accordance with statutory powers or duties may be able to raise the defence that it has "statutory authority" to cause the harm or interference in question. This may arise in various ways. Some statutes expressly exempt a public body from liability in nuisance in respect of the exercise of its statutory functions, though this is unusual; others expressly state that the statute shall *not* affect nuisance liability. Often no express mention of nuisance liability is made, and then the approach of the courts is to hold that the statute gives immunity only in respect of actions which are the inevitable consequence of the exercise of the statutory power or duty. So, for example, a statute which expressly authorised the *building* of an oil

---

[13] See *eg Kennaway v Thompson* [1980] 3 WLR 361.
[14] See *eg Fanshaw v London and Provincial Dairy Co. Ltd.* (1888) 4 TLR 694.

refinery in a particular area was interpreted as implicitly authorising the *operation* of that refinery, and as giving to the operators immunity from action in nuisance in respect of any harm or inconvenience to neighbouring residents which was the inevitable consequence of building and operating such a refinery. Any harm or inconvenience which could reasonably have been avoided (such as that arising from careless operation) would, however, be actionable.[15]

The rules so far considered, although inevitably imprecise, are nevertheless of some value in laying down standards of neighbourly behaviour. Actual recourse to the courts may be unusual except in the more extreme cases, and is certainly to be avoided wherever possible between persons who must continue to live in close proximity to each other. The real importance of the rules is in the advice that lawyers may give in the early stages of a dispute about allegedly detrimental behaviour. In a genuine case a solicitor's letter may well suffice to restrain the wrongdoer. In a case where the complainant is simply being over-sensitive to the everyday hazards of close-proximity communal living, the solicitor should so advise his client.

Public Nuisance and Statutory Nuisance

The civil wrong of nuisance could not be adequate on its own to secure protection of the environment from smoke, vapours, chemicals, noise and other menaces. What was needed were laws imposing *criminal* penalties rather than just *civil* liability, and for enforcement to be put into the hands of public sector agencies rather than be left to the private initiative of the individual affected. To a limited extent the common law itself achieved each of these things. This is in the law of **public nuisance**, as distinct from that of **private nuisance** which we have considered. Public nuisance is a crime at common law, although it may also give a right to damages to persons especially affected (*ie* over and above the harm suffered by

---

[15] *Allen v Gulf Oil Refining Ltd.* [1981] AC 1001.

members of the public generally); and in addition to proceedings in the criminal courts an action may be brought by the Attorney-General or by a local authority[16] to obtain an injunction to prevent continuance or repetition.

For a nuisance to be **public** rather than just **private** it must be of such a nature as to "materially affect the reasonable comfort and convenience of life of a class of Her Majesty's subjects".[17] By a "class of subjects" is meant a representative cross-section of a neighbourhood. Thus, if one's activities affect only one or a few individuals, one may be committing a private nuisance; if they affect local residents more generally, one may also be committing a public nuisance. In the latter case criminal sanctions and public authority action may ensue.

Although the common law of private and public nuisance remains of value in appropriate cases, the considerable *imprecision* of the common law of nuisance was a serious inadequacy. The concept of **statutory nuisance** has been developed to meet this problem in some contexts.

The Environmental Protection Act 1990 has, in Part III, consolidated miscellaneous earlier pieces of legislation, and there now exists a single statutory list of the main activities which are declared to constitute statutory nuisances. This list, subject to certain exceptions and limitations, includes:

— any premises in such a state as to be prejudicial to health or a nuisance;

— smoke, fumes or gases emitted from premises so as to be prejudicial to health or a nuisance;

— dust, steam, smell or other effluvia arising on industrial, trade or business premises and being prejudicial to health or a nuisance;

---

[16] Local Government Act 1972 s.222. The *Gillingham* case, above p.258, was argued as a *public* nuisance case.

[17] *A.G. v P.Y.A. Quarries Ltd. ex rel. Glamorgan County Council* [1957] 2 QB 169.

— any accumulation or deposit which is prejudicial to health or a nuisance;

— any animal kept in such a place or manner as to be prejudicial to health or a nuisance;

— noise emitted from premises (or from or caused by a vehicle, machinery or equipment in a street).

It is the duty of every district council (and London Borough) to inspect its area from time to time to detect any statutory nuisances which ought to be dealt with under the prescribed procedures. Where a complaint of a statutory nuisance is made to an authority by a person living within its area, the authority must take such steps as are reasonably practicable to investigate the complaint.

Where such a council is satisfied that a statutory nuisance exists, or is likely to occur, it is required to serve an "abatement notice". This notice may require the abatement of the nuisance, may forbid the occurrence of an anticipated nuisance, and may also forbid any recurrence of such nuisance. It may also require the execution of works, or the taking of necessary steps, to achieve these ends. The notice is served on the person responsible for the nuisance or, if he cannot be found, on the owner or occupier of the land in question. The person served may appeal against the notice to the Magistrates' Court. Failure to comply with the terms of a notice served is a criminal offence, unless reasonable excuse can be shown. In some situations it may be a defence to show that the "best practicable means" were used to prevent, or to counteract the effects of, the nuisance.

Until recently the maximum fine which could be imposed following conviction was generally regarded as too low, at any rate in cases where the offence had been committed by an industrial, trade or business concern. The 1990 Act has now increased the maximum penalty in such cases to a fine of £20,000; in other cases the maximum is £5000. Where offences continue even after conviction, further fines may be imposed in excess of this maximum.

Where an abatement notice has not been complied with the local authority may, whether or not it also commences a prosecution, take action itself to abate the nuisance and to execute the notice. Its expenses in so doing can then be recovered from the person responsible for the nuisance. In particularly serious cases, the local authority may take proceedings for contravention or non-compliance in the High Court rather than before the magistrates.

The 1990 Act has also extended the operation of a procedure which should be of value to individuals aggrieved by the existence of a statutory nuisance. Such individuals may themselves apply directly to the magistrates for an "abatement order", without involving the local authority. Prior to so doing the individual must give to the alleged "nuisance" written notice of his intention to bring such proceedings; and the notice must specify the matter complained of. Where the magistrates are satisfied that the alleged nuisance exists, or is likely to occur, they may issue an abatement order. In an appropriate case they may also impose an immediate fine. Non-compliance with any order issued is itself a criminal offence, subject to the sort of defences described earlier in respect of local authority abatement notices. Following a conviction, the magistrates may order the district council to take appropriate action to do any thing which the convicted person had been obliged to do under the terms of the order. In cases where the individual complainant successfully shows a statutory nuisance existing at the time of his complaint, the magistrates are required to order the defendant to pay to the complainant such expenses as that person has properly incurred.

These various provisions, in their particular contexts, are of much value. However, in themselves they could not be adequate to deal with all the more serious problems of environmental pollution. What has, in addition, been necessary has been legislation which would impose more or less precise standards and controls in relation to each of the more important categories of environmental pollution. It is to this legislation that we may now turn our attention.

ATMOSPHERIC POLLUTION

In this section we shall consider pollution by smoke and by chemical vapours, and will also examine some of the problems raised by "acid rain".

Smoke

Smoke consists of carbonaceous particles emitted in the process of combustion. It is this form of atmospheric pollution to which the Clean Air Acts of 1956 and 1968 were addressed, and in respect of which their provisions have proved a considerable success. The legislation was consolidated in the Clean Air Act 1993. The quantity of smoke emitted into the atmosphere is now much less than a few decades ago, with very beneficial consequences in terms of the health of residents of formerly dark and grimy industrial cities: a fair price to pay for the consequently less vivid sunsets and the enhanced black-spot fungal disease of roses.

Dark Smoke

The Clean Air Act 1956 imposed a prohibition on the emission of dark smoke from any chimney (industrial or domestic);[18] and this was extended by the Clean Air Act 1968 to cover emissions of dark smoke from any industrial or trade premises even though not from a chimney.[19] The 1968 Act accordingly has prohibited the emission of dark smoke from fires on open sites so long as they are used for industrial or trade purposes. Therefore, to produce dark smoke from a fire on a demolition site would constitute an offence under this legislation.[20]

Certain exceptions to this criminal liability are provided for. So, for example, there are defences which recognise that emission of dark smoke may be unavoidable during the lighting up of a cold furnace; that furnaces may produce dark smoke owing to some malfunction which was not reasonably

---

[18] Clean Air Act 1993 s.1(1)(2).
[19] Clean Air Act 1993 s.2(1).
[20] *Sheffield City Council v A.D.H. Demolition Ltd.*, *The Times*, June 18, 1983.

foreseeable or avoidable; or that unsuitable fuel may have to be used in circumstances where suitable fuel is unavailable. Also, no offence is committed if the emission of dark smoke lasts no longer than such periods as are specified in regulations made by the Secretary of State.[21]

Given the generality of this prohibition on "dark smoke", it is important that this term be understood. Fortunately the matter is quite simple. The 1956 Act states that dark smoke means smoke which, if compared in the appropriate manner with a chart known as a Ringelmann Chart, would appear to be as dark as or darker than Shade 2 on that chart. Ringelmann charts are pieces of card which when viewed at an appropriate distance (15 metres) appear to show a variety of shades from near black to white.

The regulation of dark smoke alone would not, however, have been sufficient to have dealt with the the problems of smoke pollution. Accordingly, the 1956 Act provided that thenceforth new furnaces of any considerable size which were installed should, so far as practicable, be smokeless; and also that such new furnaces be provided with "arrestment plant" to prevent grit and dust particles from being emitted.[22] In each case the requirements of the Act are satisfied provided that the furnace installed complies with plans submitted to, and approved by, the local authority. Moreover, the height of new chimneys is subject to special controls designed to prevent the emissions from the chimney being a nuisance or being prejudicial to health in the neighbourhood.[23] The control here is that of local authority approval of the height of a proposed chimney, together with the requirement of using the chimney in accordance with any conditions imposed. There is a right of appeal to the Minister, against refusal or conditions.

---

[21] See *eg* the Dark Smoke (Permitted Periods) Regulations 1958 (S.I. 1958/498).

[22] 1993 Act ss.4 and 6.

[23] 1993 Act s.14.

Smoke Control Areas

As regards *domestic* premises, the most important provisions of the legislation have been those relating to "smoke control areas", or in more common parlance "smokeless zones". The 1956 Act provided that a local authority may make an order declaring all or any of its area to be such.[24] At one time such orders needed ministerial confirmation, but this is no longer the case. Nor, now, is there required to be a local inquiry into objections to a proposed order, though the obligations to advertise proposals and to consider any objections lodged remain.

A smoke control area order comes into effect six months after it has been made. It then becomes an offence to emit smoke (*any* smoke, not just *dark* smoke) from the chimney of any building within the smoke control area, subject to it being a defence to show that the emission of smoke was caused only by the use of "authorised fuel". "Authorised fuels" are those declared to be such by ministerial regulations. These regulations list particular brands of solid fuel produced by particular manufacturers, and also gas.

Smoke control orders may exempt specified buildings or classes of buildings from their controls, and may exempt specified fireplaces or classes of fireplace. There is also a power given to the Secretary of State to exempt generally any particular kinds of fireplace which are capable of burning unauthorised fuel without producing a substantial quantity of smoke. Numerous such exempting orders have been made.

It may be noted that domestic bonfires are not prohibited in smokeless zones. Any such prohibition will be a matter for local authority bye-laws made under the Local Government Act 1972.

Certain provisions reinforce these smoke control rules. Thus, local authority grants are available to assist with the cost of adapting domestic fireplaces to enable them to burn authorised fuels. This subsidy has been of very great importance to the

---

[24] 1993 Act Part III.

success of smoke control zones. The cost does not fall entirely on local authorities; they themselves are subsidised in this expense by the central exchequer. Another provision of some importance is that it is an offence to sell by retail any fuel other than authorised fuel for delivery to a building in a smoke control area. Given that dealers in fuel should know the boundaries of smoke control areas and should know what fuels are authorised, this provides a degree of protection to the unwitting householder. A problem has arisen in recent years of the sale of non-smokeless coal from local shops and garages. The Environmental Protection Act 1990 contains a provision permitting the Secretary of State to make regulations banning such sales in smoke control areas. This should help further prevent the unwitting use of "illegal" fuel by members of the public.

Gaseous Emissions

Whereas control over smoke pollution is a matter for the environmental health officers of local authorities, functions in relation to, often less visible, chemical vapours and gases emitted by industry are divided between those officers and the Environment Agency.

The principal legislation on chemical vapours was for long the Alkali, etc. Works Regulation Act 1906, supplemented by the Health and Safety at Work etc. Act 1974. There was under these Acts a long list of "scheduled works" and "scheduled processes". Such works and processes were required to be registered annually with the Industrial Air Pollution Inspectorate, and were subject to inspection by that body. It was an offence for the owner or person having control over such a work or process to fail to use the "best practicable means" for preventing the emission of noxious or offensive gases or substances into the atmosphere from the premises.[25]

These air pollution control arrangements were superseded and strengthened by important new provisions of the Environmental

---

[25] 1906 Act s.2; Health and Safety at Work etc. Act 1974 ss.5 and 33.

Protection Act 1990. This Act followed the earlier approach of concentrating attention principally on those industries and processes which have the potential to cause most harm to man and the environment, but went beyond the former legislation by introducing, in respect of the most polluting of those targeted processes, a system of Integrated Pollution Control. The earlier approach had possessed a weakness in that controls which had been exercised to protect one environmental medium had, on occasion, resulted in an increase of harm to another medium, and an increase in the harm to the environment overall. For example, technology now enables industry to reduce or make harmless many of its emissions to the atmosphere. A by-product of the technology may, however, be an additional quantity of solid or liquid waste for disposal, usually either by landfill or by discharge into water. It can be the case that the disposal of the by-product of pollution control technology is more problematic than were the avoided discharges to the atmosphere.

What became apparent during the 1980s was the need for an approach to pollution control which sought not only to regulate the production processes of an industry so as to minimise the quantity of harmful solid and liquid waste and gaseous emissions to be disposed of, but which also took an overall "integrated" view of the best way of disposing of that waste and those emissions.

The 1990 Act sought by its system of Integrated Pollution Control to achieve these aims. The system was phased in as regards some 5,000 industrial installations during the 1990s. This coincided with the integration of air pollution, water pollution and waste management licensing functions in the new Environment Agency, established in 1996. That integrated Agency has, in determining IPC authorisations, had the task of securing that emissions and discharges from regulated processes shall be as low as "practically" and "economically" possible; and also that the option adopted in terms of the balance between atmospheric emissions, liquid discharges to water, and waste for disposal is that which represents the *Best Practicable Environmental Option* (BPEO).

The concept of "integrated pollution control" found favour during the 1990s in different forms in a number of European countries and in due course was adopted by the European Commission as the basis of the 1996 EU directive on Integrated Pollution Prevention and Control (IPPC). This directive shares many features of the UK system of IPC but differs in a number of important respects. Early suggestions that, owing to the broad similarities, implementation of IPPC in the UK would be straightforward have therefore been proven over-optimistic.

The principal similarities between IPC and IPPC may be summarised as follows: both take an integrated approach to the minimisation of overall pollution to the several environmental media; both are founded on securing emission/discharge levels which are as low as practically and economically achievable (in the jargon, by adoption of BAT: "Best Available Techniques"); and both are targeted at the more polluting sectors of the economy. Under IPPC, the BAT standards applied in the licensing process are informed by guidance afforded, sector by sector, by BAT Reference Documents emerging gradually from technical committees established at EU level.

The systems differ, however, in that IPPC extends somewhat more broadly as regards activities regulated than did IPC (for example, it covers intensive livestock operations); IPPC is concerned with the regulation of certain matters not covered by IPC (*eg* energy consumption, waste minimisation); and IPPC imposes a potentially very onerous obligation that, after the regulated processes cease to operate, the site on which operations have taken place must be remediated to the "base-line" standard (*ie* back to site conditions at the commencement of IPPC regulation). A further difference is that, whereas all integrated pollution control functions under IPC were vested in the Environment Agency, certain of the relatively more simple sectors under IPPC are under the control of local authorities. This local authority IPPC jurisdiction is something over and beyond the air pollution (*ie* single environmental media) control which was formerly referred to as Local Authority Air Pollution Control (under the 1990 Act) and is now referred to as Local Authority Air Pollution Prevention and Control (of Part B processes under the Pollution Prevention and Control (England and Wales) Regulations 2000).

IPPC, under the 1996 directive, is being phased in sector by sector as a replacement for IPC over a number of years. Where an operation covered by the directive is newly established, or where an existing operation is subject to a substantial change, the activities will require a permit governed by the IPPC directive (called in the UK a "Pollution Prevention and Control" authorisation) from the date of commencement of those activities. In the case of existing installations, however, these remain within IPC (assuming they are presently so regulated) until the date set for their sector to come within IPPC. IPPC will be fully operational in respect of all sectors covered by early 2007.

Acid Rain

A pollution problem with important implications for nature conservation which has come to prominence since early indications of problems in the 1970s is that of "acid rain". Whereas the imposition of obligations to emit gases only from sufficiently tall chimneys has been reasonably successful in alleviating industrial smoke-stack pollution problems for the immediate surrounding population and landscape, it has become apparent that the gases emitted from the chimneys can be carried long distances on the prevailing winds, and can produce adverse environmental effects not only far away within a single country, but may produce a situation, contrary to international law, where activities in one country may result in environmental harm in another.

The gases which contribute most to the phenomenon called acid rain are sulphur dioxide (SO_2 – produced when coal or oil is burnt) and oxides of nitrogen (NO_X – produced when a wide variety of materials are burnt). The principal sources of emission of these gases to the atmosphere are the burning of fossil fuels at power stations and other large combustion plants, and from motor vehicle exhausts. The emissions travel through the atmosphere, in some cases for hundreds of kilometres, eventually being deposited in dry or liquid sulphuric or nitric acid form. In this way, deposition often occurs beyond national borders from the source of the pollution. Only about 20% of UK sulphur emissions are deposited within the UK. At the same time, some 30% of sulphur deposition within the UK comes from overseas sources.

The effects of acid rain may be various. It may result in an increase in the acidity of rivers and lakes, thereby causing harm to fish and other aquatic life. Such effects were first observed in Scandinavia but the problem is now known to be quite widespread, occurring also closer to home in the mountains of Wales and in Scotland. Acidic gases seem also to have adverse effects on the growth and health of trees, they may cause corrosive deterioration in the stonework of buildings and in stained-glass windows, they may cause toxic releases of forms of aluminium from soils resulting in harm to plants and also to adjacent water pollution.

To assist in the assessment of the "harm" caused by such changes in the acidity of soils and lakes, a concept of "critical loads" has been developed. This seeks to assess, location by location, the quantity of pollution which may be tolerated without harmful effects occurring. This allows surveys to indicate to what extent "critical load" thresholds are being exceeded in particular areas. Over time, it becomes possible through this method to assess whether the problem of acid rain is getting greater, or whether measures to alleviate the problem are meeting with success.

The very nature of this particular pollution problem has required there to have been some concerted international action. For this reason, in 1979, the United Nations Economic Commission for Europe (UNECE) drew up a Convention on Long Range Transboundary Air Pollution (LRTAP), and this now has more than 40 signatories within Europe and North America. Ancillary to the Convention are more specific agreements, called Protocols, in relation to particular pollutants. Early Protocols for sulphur dioxide and oxides of nitrogen set simple targets for all countries: for example, for a 30% reduction of sulphur emissions by 1993, and to decrease emission levels of oxides of nitrogen to those of 1987 (by 1994). In 1994, a new "effects based" Protocol for sulphur, based on critical loads, was agreed. This defined a target for each European country based on its pollutant emissions, the costs of abatement and the contribution those emissions made to acid deposition on sensitive ecosystems across Europe. More recently, a so-called "Multi-pollutant, Multi-effect" Protocol was signed in Gothenburg in 1999. This is more sophisticated still, taking into account effects of acidity, excess nutrient nitrogen and also photochemical oxidants (low level ozone). As acidification can result from sulphur, oxides of nitrogen and ammonia, all three of these atmospheric pollutants are included in this Protocol.

At EU level, two directives in particular deal with acid gas emissions: the National Emissions Ceiling Directive (2001) and the Large Combustion Plants Directive (LCP) (dating from 1988 but significantly revised in 2001). There is some overlap between these directives but, broadly, the former requires that national emissions of four gases (including SO_2 and NO_X) shall not, at 2010, exceed certain levels. The latter imposes specific emission standards on power stations, the particular limit (and the date the obligations take effect) depending on the age of the power station. The LCP Directive does, however, permit a Member State to meet obligations as regards power station emissions by way of a National Plan (relating to overall, rather than individual, power station emissions). Under such a plan it would be possible for individual power stations to exceed limits, provided that overall national emissions remain within the aggregate envisaged by the directive. It is this approach to implementation which is being proposed by the United Kingdom.

Measurements over the last ten years show a significant drop in sulphur dioxide concentrations and deposited sulphur for all parts of Europe. However, oxides of nitrogen and ammonia emissions have proved more difficult to reduce; largely, in the former case, because of the significance to such emission levels of ever-increasing road transport. Even where levels of acid deposition may have reduced over this period, the benefits to affected areas may by no means be immediate; and, in order to achieve recovery at the most sensitive sites, it seems likely that emissions of sulphur, oxides of nitrogen and ammonia will need to be decreased further (and this will need to be accompanied by a programme of land management and site-specific remedial measures).

Stubble Burning

The practice of burning stubble on fields following harvesting of crops, particularly cereals, became widespread in the 1980s and gave rise to a good deal of public concern. This centred on a variety of matters, such as the pollution of the atmosphere resulting from the large quantities of smoke, the danger to drivers of motor vehicles on nearby roads as visibility became reduced, the damage to hedgerows and trees when fires got out of control, and the harm done to flora and fauna. Moreover, objection was also raised to the practice in terms of good husbandry; the argument here being that the traditional practice of ploughing stubble into the soil was preferable in terms of maintaining soil condition and nutrients. The justification generally put forward in favour of burning stubble was an economic one. It is cheaper in terms of labour costs to burn stubble, and then add artificial fertilisers, than to plough stubble into the soil.

The response of Government was, initially, to resist pleas that stubble burning be prohibited, and instead to seek to *regulate* the practice. A set of model bye-laws was published in 1984, and local authorities were encouraged to make bye-laws in this form. Although there was no obligation on local authorities to make such bye-laws, a very large number did so. The bye-laws did not have to be in accordance with the "model" but, since bye-laws require ministerial approval before they can come into effect, good reasons were needed to justify any departure.

Notwithstanding such bye-laws, public concern continued. As a consequence, the Environmental Protection Act 1990 introduced a power by which the Secretary of State might himself make regulations to restrict the burning of crop residues. Under this authority have been made the Crop Residues (Burning) Regulations 1993.[26] These prohibit the burning, on agricultural land, of various crop residues: cereal straw, cereal stubble and residues of oil-seed rape, field beans harvested dry and field peas harvested dry. The regulations expressly permit the burning of linseed residues. Certain exceptions to the prohibition apply; for example, in relation to disease control.

Where burning is permitted, it must be done in accordance with the requirements of Schedule 2. This, for example, prescribes that burning must not occur within specified distances from buildings, roads or hedgerows; nor may burning take place other than during the day-time; nor may it take place at weekends or Bank Holidays. Those engaged in the burning must be familiar with the regulations and the person in general control must have experience in burning crop residues. Notice of proposed burning must be given to the fire authority and to occupiers of adjacent premises. Following the burning, it is required that the ashes of cereal straw or cereal stubble be ploughed back into the soil within twenty-four hours, unless wind conditions during this period of time render such operations a potential nuisance.

In addition to these provisions, the Highways (Amendment) Act 1986 has imposed general criminal liability where the lighting of a fire causes the user of any highway consisting of or comprising a carriageway to be injured, interrupted or endangered by the smoke from the fire (or any fire caused by that fire). It is a defence to such a prosecution for the defendant to show that at the time the fire was lit he was satisfied on reasonable grounds that any such consequence was unlikely, and also that before and after the fire was lit he had done all that he reasonably could to prevent any such consequences.

---

[26] S.I. 1993/1366.

NOISE POLLUTION

Noise pollution is more a problem of the cities than it is of the countryside. Nevertheless, where noise is experienced in rural areas it may be especially offensive, spoiling the tranquillity normally to be expected. The main general legislation is Part III of the Control of Pollution Act 1974, though other Acts deal with specific problems.

Noise Nuisances

Reference was made earlier in this chapter to the concept of statutory nuisance, and the procedures associated with the tackling of such nuisances. In this context it should be remembered that "noise" may qualify as a statutory nuisance. Local authorities are therefore, by virtue of Part III of the Environmental Protection Act 1990, under a statutory obligation to inspect their areas from time to time to detect anything which ought to be dealt with as a noise nuisance.

Where such a nuisance is discovered (or, more likely, has been reported to the authority) the procedure involves the service of a noise abatement notice on the person responsible for the nuisance. This notice will prohibit or restrict the noise in question. The person served may appeal against the notice to the Magistrates' Court. In the absence of a successful appeal, it is an offence to fail to comply with the notice and proceedings may be taken, by the local authority, in the Magistrates' Court. It is, however, a defence if it can be shown by the defendant that he had used the best practicable means to prevent, or counteract the effect of, the noise. As mentioned in other contexts, this imports a rather uncertain standard into the statutory obligation. Some guidance may, however, be gained from Codes of Practice issued by the Secretary of State and to which the magistrates are required to have regard.[27] Such Codes have been issued in relation to a number of matters, such as ice-cream van chimes, model aircraft noise, noise from open construction sites and from audible intruder alarms.

---

[27] 1974 Act s.72(6).

The 1990 Act also permits proceedings before the magistrates in respect of noise nuisances to be taken by individual aggrieved persons. The procedure here is for the magistrates to make an order, any failure to comply with which renders the person to whom it is directed guilty of an offence.

Noise Abatement Zones

There has, since the 1974 Act, also been power in district councils to create "noise abatement zones";[28] a power not, in fact, very commonly used. An order creating such a zone will specify whether it applies to the whole area of the local authority or just part of it, and will specify to which buildings or class of buildings it applies. If objections are lodged to a council's proposed order, these objections must be considered by the authority prior to finally deciding whether or not to make the order.

What is the consequence of the making of an order establishing a noise abatement zone? The answer is that once such an order has come into effect, it becomes an offence for the level of noise from any building to which the order applies to increase unless the written consent of the local authority has been obtained.[29] Once the order has been made, the local authority is required to measure the levels of noise emanating from such buildings and to record this information in a "noise level register".[30] Although there is no right of appeal against the making of a noise abatement zone order, there is a right of appeal to the Secretary of State against any entry in the noise level register. There is also a right of appeal to the Secretary of State against a refusal of permission to exceed the registered noise level, or against conditions contained in a consent given.

The creation of a noise abatement zone also gives to the district council power to serve a "noise reduction notice".[31] This may be done where it appears to the local authority that the level

---

28 1974 Act s.63(1).
29 1974 Act s.65.
30 1974 Act s.64.
31 1974 Act s.66.

of noise emanating from any building to which the noise abatement order applies is not acceptable, and that reduction in that level of noise is practicable at reasonable cost and would afford a public benefit. The notice will be served on the person responsible for the noise and will indicate to what level the noise must be reduced, any steps necessary to achieve that result, and the time by which the result must be achieved. This power, therefore, permits local authorities to order reductions in noise level to below that recorded in the noise level register. There is a right of appeal against a noise reduction notice, this time to the magistrates. To contravene such an order without reasonable excuse is an offence, though in proceedings for such an offence it is a defence to show that the "best practicable means" have been used to prevent, or to counteract the effect of, the noise.

POLLUTION OF LAND

Contaminated Land

Land "contamination" is an issue which is sometimes regarded as of urban significance only. Certainly it may be that most contaminated land is to be found in the traditional industrial areas within our cities but it is also the case that activities conducted in the past in rural areas may have had serious contaminative effects. In instances where rural land is to be put to a new use which is sensitive to land contamination, it may be necessary to make inquiries into past use of the land in question (and its surrounds) and also perhaps to conduct analysis of soils.

Until quite recently there was no discrete body of English law on this important subject. However, following a lengthy process of consultation, there was enacted within the Environment Act 1995 a set of rules and procedures designed to do two principal things: to provide for the identification of contaminated sites, and to lay down rules as to where liability to remediate that land should fall.

The 1995 Act added a new Part to the Environmental Protection Act 1990: Part IIA, which came into force in 2000. The provisions of Part IIA are highly complex. However, in themselves they tell only a part of the story; the primary legislation is supplemented by detailed and highly complex policy and interpretational Guidance documents issued by the government under statutory authority.

The essential policy behind Part IIA is clear. It is that it should give effect to the "polluter pays" principle of environmental policy. As we shall see, Part IIA imposes principal liability to remediate contaminated land on the person or persons who caused the contamination. Moreover, the liability on such persons may be imposed retrospectively: there is no requirement that the act of polluting the land was unlawful at the time the polluting events occurred. The policy is that remediation liability should attach to persons by virtue of present *ownership* of a contaminated site only in circumstances where the actual polluter(s) cannot be "found".

Equally, it has been clear that the policy behind Part IIA is that the so-called "suitable for use" approach will be taken to determine whether land should be regarded as "contaminated" and the standards of remediation to be required. In other words, land will not be assessed in abstract against objective criteria and be required to be clean enough for any potential land use. Land will only be regarded as "contaminated" for the purposes of Part IIA where it is found to be causing or presenting risk of "harm" to living organisms or the ecological system, or be causing or threatening pollution of controlled water. Therefore, Part IIA applies to situations where a parcel of land is problematic *at present* and in relation to its *current use*. Where land is to be redeveloped, the remediation requirements necessary for the new proposed land-use are imposed via planning conditions under the system of development control, and the remediation costs will fall on the developer rather than the original polluter, to be factored into the economics of the overall redevelopment.

The new legal regime proceeds by way of imposing duties on local authorities to survey their areas with a view to finding sites which fall within the above concept of "contaminated".

Where such sites are found, there is an obligation to determine whether the features of the site or the contamination are such as may make it appropriate for designation as a "special" site, with the consequence that it becomes the Environment Agency rather than the local authority which will exercise powers to determine the nature and scope of remediation required. The next step is to engage in a process of statutory dialogue with potentially liable parties: a process designed to offer those parties an opportunity to be proactive in suggesting and designing remediation solutions. Should no acceptable solutions be volunteered, the enforcing authority will issue a remediation notice to the party or parties who bear remediation liabilities under Part IIA.

By way of a brief overview of liabilities under Part IIA, we may begin by distinguishing between the following:

Parties with "Primary" Liability under Part IIA of EPA: Class A Parties
Under Part IIA, liability to pay the cost of the remediation of contaminated land is cast *primarily* on the persons who "caused" or "knowingly permitted" the polluting contaminants to be present on the land in question (Class A parties).

Secondarily Liable Parties: Class B Parties
It is only where the enforcing authority (local authority or Environment Agency) is not able to find any such "Class A" person in relation to an instance of contamination that remedial liability may attach to other persons by virtue solely of their ownership or occupation of the site in question (Class B parties).

The meaning of "found" – the critical word within the legislation – is imprecise and remains to be judicially tested. The advice from government is that a "natural" person must be alive in order to be a person who can be found; and that a corporation which has been dissolved cannot be "found". However, the same advice refers also to the possibility of acting against the estate of a person who has died, or of seeking the judicial annulment of the dissolution of a company. These matters, and others, remain to be clarified.

Nevertheless, it is clear is that where a Class A party *has* been "found" in respect of an instance of land contamination no liability exists, as regards that contamination, in any Class B party. Furthermore, this remains the position notwithstanding that (i) there may be other Class A parties who cannot be found, and/or (ii) the Class A party/parties who have been found have insufficient funds to meet in full the anticipated costs of remediation.

The policy behind the Part IIA regime is to impose liability squarely on past polluters but care has also been taken to seek to achieve a just and fair allocation of remediation costs as between several polluters where (as will be commonplace) more than one primarily liable party has been found. Complex guidance on this matter has been issued by government.

Litter and Abandoned Vehicles

The defilement of the countryside by the deposit of litter and the disposal of waste materials is a matter with which it is important that the law should deal adequately. There are a variety of culprits. Picnickers discard paper and empty bottles, motorists throw cigarette packets and toffee papers from car windows, farmers leave empty containers and broken machinery in their fields, and businesses deposit unwanted by-products in unsightly heaps. Moreover, as controls tighten over the legitimate disposal of waste material, the problem of fly-tipping of such items becomes all the greater.

Litter

Provisions of the Environmental Protection Act 1990 have relatively recently extended legal controls over the problem of litter. To begin with, the Act extends the scope of the offence of "leaving litter". Under earlier legislation this offence only applied to the leaving of litter on land in the open air and to which the public had free access. The expression "open air" did however extend to covered places which were open to the air on at least one side. The 1990 Act provides that the offence may be committed in such places, but also prohibits the leaving of litter on certain land owned by local authorities, by designated statutory undertakers, by designated educational institutions, by the Crown, and on land within a "litter control area". The substance of the offence consists of the throwing down, or dropping, and then leaving of any thing whatever in such circumstances as to cause, or contribute to, the defacement by litter of any such land. No offence is committed in circumstances where the deposit and leaving of the thing in question was authorised by law, or was done with the consent of the owner or occupier of the land.

In relation to this offence the 1990 Act has introduced a new "fixed penalty" system under which authorised local authority officers who have reason to believe the offence has been committed may give to the suspect a notice offering that person the opportunity to discharge any liability to conviction for that offence by payment instead of a penalty. The penalty is currently £50, but this figure can be raised by the Secretary of State.

In addition to this litter offence, the 1990 Act imposes *duties* on various bodies to take steps to keep their property and to keep highways clear of litter, so far at least as is reasonably practicable. The bodies under this obligation are district councils in respect of highways (or the Secretary of State in respect of trunk roads), local authorities generally in respect of their own land, the Crown and certain statutory undertakers and educational institutions in respect of their land, and occupiers of property in litter control areas. In complying with these obligations, the body in question is required to have regard to the terms of a Code of Practice issued by the Secretary of State.

Mention has been made above of "litter control areas". The 1990 Act provides that such areas may be designated by district councils in respect of land falling within descriptions prescribed by the Secretary of State. Such orders may only be made in circumstances where the council considers that, unless it makes the order, the presence of litter is likely to be such as to be prejudicial to the amenity of the area. Once designated, the land becomes land in respect of which the basic litter offence will apply, becomes land which the occupier must keep reasonably clear of litter, and also becomes land in respect of which two further new procedures will apply. These are the "litter abatement notice" and the "street litter control notice".

The former is a notice served on the owner or occupier of land to which it applies (broadly the categories of land described above in connection with the litter offence and the "clearing litter" obligations) requiring that person or body to comply with the statutory clearing obligations. Failure to comply with the terms of such a notice is an offence triable in the Magistrates' Court. There are also the usual default powers under which a local authority may itself take steps to clear the litter and recover its expenses from the person or body in default of the notice.

"Street litter control notices" are a device designed to deal with the problem of activities which cause litter on adjacent highways or open land. The most significant instance of this is the litter problem associated with the sale of take-away food. The notice is served by the district council on the occupier of the premises on which the activities causing the litter take place, and will state what is required to be done by the occupier to deal with the problem. The terms of the order are at the discretion of the local authority. They must, however, comply with or fall within certain requirements specified in the 1990 Act itself or in ministerial regulations.

These various provisions do much to strengthen the law in respect of defacement by litter. Their practical effect in alleviating the problem may depend much on the resources allocated by the public bodies in question to complying with the obligations imposed directly upon them and to enforcing the compliance of others. In times of expenditure constraint, there is a clear danger that the costs involved may result in the legislation not being of great practical effect. With this danger in mind the Act contains an important provision permitting *individuals* aggrieved by the defacement by litter of any land covered by the Act to take proceedings before the magistrates.

At least five days' prior warning must be given to the person responsible for the land. If the magistrates find for the complainant, they will make a litter abatement order and will order the individual's expenses in taking the proceedings to be paid by the defendant. This should prove a valuable procedure by which citizens may prompt performance of duties on the part of the public bodies, and may enforce the obligations imposed by the Act on other persons (*eg* occupiers of premises in litter control areas).

Abandoned Vehicles

The Refuse Disposal (Amenity) Act 1978 imposes obligations on district councils in respect of abandoned vehicles. Where it appears to such a local authority that a motor vehicle has been abandoned without lawful authority on any land in the open air, the local authority is under a duty to remove the vehicle.[32] The cost of removing such a vehicle is recoverable from the "person responsible".[33] This term covers the person who abandoned the vehicle and also, if it is a different person, the vehicle's owner unless he can show that he was not aware of the abandonment. In addition to the duty to remove and dispose of abandoned vehicles, the 1978 Act also empowers local authorities, if they think fit, to remove other things which have been abandoned.[34]

Waste Disposal

Each year industry, commerce and households generate some 170-210 million tonnes of waste. Household (municipal) waste amounts to some 28 million tonnes, of which about 79% (23 million tonnes) is landfilled.

Properly managed landfill sites should involve little harm to the environment, or harm, or nuisance (smell, litter, etc.) to local inhabitants. The reality for many years was, however, a large number of poorly managed and inadequately inspected sites.

---

[32]   1978 Act s.3. Such abandonment is an offence under s.2.
[33]   1978 Act s.5.
[34]   1978 Act s.6.

The proper operation of landfill is not just a matter of tipping into a hole. It is necessary first to engineer the site in advance of filling in order to ensure reasonable containment of liquids, once filling commences to ensure an appropriate mix of materials, to ensure that liquid effluent is contained on-site and does not leak onto surrounding land or pollute adjacent watercourses, to monitor the emission and build-up of gases from the site, to seal the site on completion of tipping and to restore the surface of the site for agricultural or other amenity use.

Traditionally, landfill has been much the cheapest method of disposal of waste. The Environmental Protection Act 1990 contains a number of important provisions, the compliance with which has raised, quite considerably, the cost of landfill disposal. This has been a matter of deliberate governmental policy, intended to encourage waste minimisation, waste recycling, and other disposal methods such as incineration. This general policy was taken a step further in October 1996 by the imposition of the Landfill Tax. As from April 2004, the rates of Landfill Tax have been £2 per tonne for inert waste and £15 per tonne for other waste.

Over the years, local authorities performed a wide variety of functions in relation to waste. They were collection authorities, operated waste disposal sites, and exercised regulatory controls both under the planning legislation and under the site licensing provisions of the Control of Pollution Act 1974. The combination of these various functions in a single body was much criticised, and the 1990 Act provided that, although local authorities should retain their *regulatory* functions, local authority disposal sites were to be *operated* only by private sector companies or by new local authority waste disposal companies which would operate at arms-length from the local authority in its regulatory capacity. The new local authority companies would compete for waste disposal contracts with the private sector disposal companies, and be subject to equally strict regulatory controls.

These arrangements, introduced in the years immediately after the 1990 Act, have recently been modified by the

Environment Act 1995. In establishing the new Environment Agency, the former local authority waste regulatory functions were transferred to that new body.

Planning controls, described earlier in Chapter 2, apply to the establishment or extension of a waste disposal landfill site. Moreover, local planning authorities are required to produce strategic waste disposal plans estimating the nature and quantity of waste arisings which will need to be disposed of, and the disposal facilities needed to meet this demand. Decisions on individual planning applications to establish or enlarge a site are then be taken in the light, amongst other things, of the information in the disposal plan.

In addition to obtaining planning permission, it was necessary, as a requirement of the 1990 Act and superseding the pioneering but somewhat more rudimentary system of site licensing under the 1974 Act, for a waste management licence to be obtained. The Act provides that it is an offence to deposit, keep, treat or dispose of controlled waste (a term which covers household, industrial and commercial waste) in or on any land unless a waste management licence authorising such activity has been obtained and the activity is in accordance with the terms (conditions) of the licence. Even where a licence has been obtained and has been complied with, it is nevertheless still an offence to treat, keep, or dispose of controlled waste in any manner likely to cause pollution of the environment or harm to human health. More recently, in order to comply with the terms of the EU Landfill Directive, landfill operations have been brought within the scope of Part A of the PPC (Pollution Prevention and Control) licensing system. Waste management operations not involving landfill remain within the ambit of the 1990 Act.

A very significant development made within the 1990 Act was the change from waste *disposal* licensing to the licensing of *waste management*. The 1990 Act's provisions have applied to a broader range of activities in respect of waste (*eg* storing it; recycling it) than just disposing of it to landfill.

The 1990 Act has concerned itself not just with the technical requirements to be imposed by conditions on operators, it also concerns itself with the general suitability of the proposed operators to manage a site. Up until this time, all too many sites were managed by persons without an adequate level of technical expertise and without an appropriate level of financial resource. The 1990 Act has sought to tackle this problem by its requirement that the Environment Agency should grant licences only to applicants who are "fit and proper persons". A person will fail to meet this requirement if he (or an associate) has been convicted of certain offences, if the management of the site is not to be in the hands of a technically competent person, or if the applicant is unable to arrange adequate financial support to discharge the various obligations which may arise from the grant of such a licence. The aim is to rid the waste industry of "crooks", "cowboys" and "men of straw". Even where the applicant meets these criteria, a licence can be refused if rejection is necessary to prevent pollution of the environment, harm to human health, or serious detriment to the amenities of the locality.

The Environment Agency is required to supervise licensed waste activities to ensure that harm to the environment, to human health or to amenity does not occur. The Agency has power to take any necessary action itself to prevent any such occurrences, and its expenses in so acting may be charged to the licence holder. The liability of the licence holder continues even after the tip is full and has been closed. In other words a duty of after-care exists. It is no longer possible, as was the case before the 1990 Act, for an operator to surrender a licence unilaterally in order to evade financial responsibilities in complying with continuing licence conditions aimed at keeping the site safe to the environment and to local inhabitants. Under the 1990 Act such responsibility remains with the licensee until such time as the local authority may grant a certificate of completion. This will only be issued when an authority is satisfied that no risk of pollution or harm remains. This is likely to be the case only some considerable time after the closure of the tip. Experience shows that tips which may well have appeared quite safe for a number of years may suddenly, and inexplicably, begin emitting methane and/or leachate. The complex chemistry of reactions within landfill tips is as yet not fully understood. Once a waste authority grants a certificate of completion, it takes upon itself any further financial responsibility in respect of the site.

The 1990 Act also introduced tighter controls over the handling of waste, from the point of its creation through transportation and treatment to the point of its final disposal. A "duty of care" is imposed on all who handle the waste, and the duty applies not only to a person's own actions in respect of the waste but also involves an obligation to ensure that the person to whom the waste is passed is a suitable and competent person (and, in some instances, a duty not to *accept* waste from a person lower down the waste-chain). Failure to comply with this duty is a criminal offence. The content of the duty of care is stated in general terms in the legislation and is amplified in a Code of Practice (first issued in 1993, revised in 1996).

As explained above, the 1990 Act imposed an enhanced level of regulatory control over those engaged in landfill operations. Nevertheless, the substance of the controls imposed was largely left to the discretion of the Environment Agency. However, the EU Habitats Directive (1999) is, as its provisions take effect, imposing EU-wide rules and standards in this particular context. The aim of the directive is to prevent or reduce, as far as possible, negative effects on the environment from the landfilling of waste, by introducing stringent technical requirements for waste and landfills; and also, where possible, by diverting waste streams from landfill disposal.

Under the directive, all landfills have had to be categorised by their operators as within one of three classes:

— landfills for hazardous waste;

— landfills for non-hazardous waste;

— landfills for inert waste.

From July 2004, hazardous waste within the meaning of the directive must be assigned only to a hazardous waste landfill (of which only a small number have been designated by operators). Landfills for non-hazardous waste must be used for municipal waste and for non-hazardous waste; and landfill sites for inert waste must be used only for inert waste. In addition, the directive requires that the following wastes may not be accepted in a landfill:

> liquid waste;
> flammable waste;
> explosive or oxidising waste;
> hospital and other clinical waste which is infectious;
> used tyres, with certain exceptions.

The directive also sets challenging national targets for the reduction of biodegradable municipal waste going to landfill. By weight, the UK targets are to reduce biodegradable municipal waste going to landfill to 75% of the 1995 level by 2010; to 50% of the 1995 level by 2013; and to 35% of the 1995 level by 2020.

WATER QUALITY AND QUANTITY

The EU Water Framework Directive

It needs no explanation that legal controls over the input of pollutants into lakes, rivers and streams are necessary in order to avoid adverse effects on the water environment, associated flora and fauna and general amenity. It is also readily apparent that the release of pollutants on to land which may work their way through soils into subsurface groundwater (water in saturated underground rock strata) may have long-term, and not readily remediable, impacts on the quality of that important drinking water resource. In respect of each of these contexts of water pollution, there have been laws and regulatory controls in place for some substantial time and these are considered in the coming pages.

What has been a more neglected matter has been the related issue of water *quantity*. As pressures on water supplies have coincided with warm summers and dry winters, low river flows and depletion of groundwater resources within aquifers have become a matter of concern in recent years.

At EU level, these combined water quality and water quantity concerns are reflected in the challenging Water Framework Directive adopted in 2000. The directive requires that Member States shall implement necessary measures, with limited exceptions, to prevent any deterioration in the quality of all bodies of surface water. More positively, a target is set that Member States shall protect, enhance and restore all bodies of surface water with the aim of achieving "good surface water status" and "good groundwater status" by 2015. Given that low water levels resulting from overly-high surface water abstraction will have adverse consequences in terms of surface water quality, it is evident that the surface water "quality" obligation has "quantity" implications also. In the case of groundwater, there is explicit reference to the requirement of ensuring a balance between "abstraction" and "recharge".

The directive goes further than merely setting these demanding "quality" and "quantity" objectives. It also imposes obligations on Members States as to how they are to plan and manage the achievement of those targets. The directive requires, for example, that water resource planning be organised on the basis of river basins (something which has been a feature of UK water authority organisation since the 1970s) and requires that there be planned for each river basin a "programme of measures" designed to enable the directive's substantive obligations to be achieved. Such measures include promoting efficient and sustainable water use and controls over the abstraction of surface water and groundwater. The work of determining river basins, examining their hydrological and ecological conditions, and devising appropriate "plans" and "programmes of measures" is to be done in accordance with a timetable of dates between 2003 and 2015.

Water Abstraction

Since 1963, there has been a system of licensing control over water abstraction in England and Wales. In recent years, however, certain features of that system have become regarded as inadequate in the light of demand pressures on water resources, and in consequence the system has been significantly modified by the Water Act 2003.

The original legislation provided that certain categories of persons were, at the outset, entitled to non time-limited abstraction licences. Subsequent applicants for licences could be granted time-limited or non time-limited licences, and in more recent times the time-limited option became the rule. The Water Act 2003 now makes all new licences time-limited. An abstraction licence protects water abstraction rights and, if non time-limited, protects against variation or revocation except on the basis of payment by government of compensation.

The 2003 Act makes important changes in this respect, empowering the Secretary of State to vary or revoke non time-limited licences without triggering rights to compensation for having taken away protected water rights. It is provided that no compensation will be payable where the ground for such revocation or variation is that such action is necessary in order to protect surface water, groundwater or dependant flora or fauna from serious damage. In short, those who presently hold non time-limited licences may now find their abstraction rights varied or revoked without compensation where environmental considerations may render this necessary.

In the case of time-limited abstraction licences granted after the 2003 Act came into effect, there is also some limitation on compensation rights where the licence is varied. Where a licence is for more than 12 years' duration and the variation proposed will allow the licensee to continue to abstract more than a "minimum value" figure set at the time the licence is issued, no compensation will be payable. Those who now obtain new licences for more than 12 years will know that they have protected rights to the full abstraction licence permission for six years but that for the following years of the licence they risk being reduced to lower abstraction rights without compensation (but not below the lower level identified in the original licence).

The Water Act 2003 also reduces the protected rights of existing abstractors in one further way. A right of compensation exists for persons with protected rights to abstract in cases where the Environment Agency has granted a licence which derogates from the capacity of those existing abstractors to exercise their rights. Such right to compensation is, however, lost in cases where the abstractor claiming compensation has not in fact exercised abstraction rights for a period of seven years. Under the Water Act 2003 this seven-year period has been reduced to four years.

Pollution of Inland Waters

We shall consider this subject under three broad headings. First, we shall note a provision which creates a specific statutory nuisance in relation to polluted inland water. Then we shall consider the controls which exist over discharges into sewers; and then finally we shall outline the controls over discharges directly into rivers and streams and other inland "controlled" waters.

Statutory Nuisances

The important provision here is section 259 of the Public Health Act 1936. We have already noted elsewhere[35] the standard procedures in respect of statutory nuisances under this Act, involving the service by district councils of abatement notices on those responsible, followed by prosecution before the magistrates in the event of failure to comply with such notices. These procedures are made applicable to polluted water by section 259, which provides for the following matters to be statutory nuisances:

— any pond, pool, ditch, gutter or watercourse which is so foul or in such a state as to be prejudicial to health or a nuisance; and

— any part of a watercourse, not being a part ordinarily navigated by vessels employed in the carriage of goods by

---

[35] See above, p.261.

water, which is so choked or silted up as to obstruct or impede the flow of water and thereby to cause a nuisance, or give rise to conditions prejudicial to health.

In addition to the ordinary powers of district councils to take action in respect of statutory nuisances, there is also in this context power given to parish or community councils to deal with any such filthy or stagnant water, which is likely to be prejudicial to health, by draining, cleansing, covering or taking other preventive action. In addition to taking action itself, it may contribute to the expenses of any other person in doing such things.[36]

Discharge into Sewers[37]

The law gives to every person the right to cause the drains from his premises to be connected to a public sewer. Controls over the discharges that might be made from drains into sewers and thence, possibly after some degree of purification, into rivers and the sea began with statutes of the nineteenth century. The law is now contained in the Water Industry Act 1991, which prohibits the passing of certain dangerous matters into public sewers. The prohibition covers:

(a) matter likely to injure the sewer, or to interfere with the free flow of its contents, or to affect prejudicially the treatment and disposal of its contents;

(b) chemical refuse, waste steam, or liquid above a certain temperature which, either alone or in combination with the other contents of the sewer, is dangerous or may cause a nuisance or be prejudicial to health;

(c) petroleum spirit or carbide of calcium.[38]

This necessary, but rather generally worded provision, dating

---

36 1936 Act s.260.
37 See, generally, S.H. Bailey, *Garner's Law of Sewers and Drains* (9th ed. 2004), Shaw & Sons Ltd.
38 "Petroleum spirit" is widely defined, including for example "any product of petroleum or mixture containing petroleum".

from the Public Health Act 1936, was reinforced by legislation the following year: the Public Health (Drainage of Trade Premises) Act 1937. The scheme of the 1937 Act remains today: that prior to discharging any trade effluent into any public sewer, the person wishing to do so is required to have served a trade effluent notice on the local sewerage company and is required to comply with any conditions which that body may impose on such discharges. In addition to imposing conditions on such discharges, the authority may prohibit the discharge entirely. This applies to what is called "special category effluent".

The trade effluent notice, served on the sewerage company, is required to state the nature and composition of the effluent, the maximum quantity which it is proposed to discharge on any one day, and the highest rate at which it is proposed to discharge effluent.[39] The conditions imposed on a consent may relate to any of these matters, and also may restrict effluent discharge to particular periods of the day, may require the elimination or diminution of any specified constituent of the effluent before it enters the sewer, where otherwise its treatment would be specially difficult or expensive, and may restrict the temperature of any discharge or its acidity or alkalinity. In addition, consent may be conditional on the payment of additional charges, the installation of manholes or meters to ease the making of checks as to the nature, quantity and rates of effluent discharge, and the keeping of records and making of returns about such matters. Any such conditions imposed may be varied from time to time. There is a right of appeal to the Director General of Water Services against any refusal of consent or conditions imposed.

In determining whether to grant trade effluent consent and, if so, what conditions to impose, the sewerage company will take into account the capacity and performance of its sewage treatment works, and the obligations which it is itself required to meet as regards its own discharges from those works.

---

[39] Water Industry Act 1991 s.119.

Discharges into Inland and Coastal Waters
We are here concerned with the protection from pollution of rivers, streams, estuaries and coastal waters, and also the protection of underground water supplies. Former legislation has been recently superseded by the present principal measure, the Water Resources Act 1991. In addition to the water pollution provisions of this Act, it should be emphasised that decisions taken in relation to, for example, Integrated Pollution Prevention and Control and waste management licensing will be taken with a view, amongst other things, to the impact of operations on the aquatic environment. The link between the system of trade effluent consents for discharges into sewers and the protection of river water quality is closer still.

An important stage in modern water protection law was the establishment in 1989 of the National Rivers Authority. This body had a variety of functions, extending beyond that of water pollution control to the strategic management of water resources (an important aspect of this from an environmental point of view being the regulation under a licensing regime of abstraction of water from rivers – some rivers having suffered much in terms of habitat value because of increased levels of water extraction coinciding with recent dry years), flood defence and land drainage, salmon and freshwater fisheries and, in some areas, navigation.

The establishment of the NRA ended the former unsatisfactory situation under which the former public sector water authorities were at one and the same time engaged both in polluting activities (*eg* by discharging sewage into rivers and coastal waters) and as the bodies with the principal pollution control responsibilities. These latter functions were, in 1989, transferred to the NRA which, now as part of the Environment Agency, monitors and regulates the activities of the new privatised water and sewerage companies as well as those of other industrial and agricultural concerns.

Under the Water Resources Act 1991, the Secretary of State, on the advice of the Environment Agency, sets statutory water quality objectives in respect of coastal and inland waters, replacing the informally set objectives of the various former water authorities. The standards set will take into account the purpose or purposes for which each area of water is to be used. The Agency is then under a statutory duty to exercise its various powers to ensure that these water quality standards are met.

A prime means by which the Agency seeks to comply with this obligation is by its exercise of its discharge consent powers. It is an offence, as it was under earlier legislation, to cause or knowingly permit any poisonous, noxious or polluting matter or any solid waste matter to enter any "controlled water". The expression "controlled water" covers a three mile territorial sea, estuarine waters, rivers and streams, as well as certain reservoirs, lakes and ponds. It also applies to underground water.

The very wide terms of this offence are, however, moderated by the provision in the legislation that no offence is committed where the discharge is made under and in accordance with a discharge consent. Such consents are now granted by the Environment Agency.

In the past there was much criticism that consents imposed were insufficiently strict, and insufficiently rigorously enforced by way of prosecution of those who were found to have breached consents. The NRA, in its brief period of existence, became, in its own words, a "tougher and more effective regulator" and this approach has continued in the actions of the Environment Agency. At the same time the NRA stressed that it must also be "realistic in its approach and expectations". It warned that it is pointless to set unrealistic discharge standards, that it should take into account the time and cost involved in introducing pollution control technology to a particular plant, and that prosecution of breaches is best restricted to situations where recurring breaches have occurred, evidencing a disregard for the law or a failure to supervise discharges adequately, and situations where a single discharge is one which has given rise to severe pollution or is clearly attributable to culpable mismanagement or neglect.

It is principally by these means that the Environment Agency may seek to ensure that the standards set either nationally or by the EC in relation to water quality are met. Such standards have been much in the news in the last few years, in particular the standards relating to drinking water and to bathing waters. As regards the former, a particular concern in Britain has been the level of nitrates in our drinking water. In some areas the levels have exceeded the maximum permitted levels under the EC Drinking Water Directive. A principal source of the nitrates in water is the leaching of chemicals from agricultural land, and this has been attributed to the increased use of artificial nitrogenous fertilisers in post-war years. In order to try to tackle this problem, the Water Act 1989 made provision for the designation of Nitrate Sensitive Areas in which certain agricultural operations, such as the use of fertilisers, could, through voluntary agreements with farmers in certain areas, be brought under control. These early measures have, however, now been superseded by the mandatory requirements of the EU Nitrates Directive (1991). The UK determined to implement the directive by establishing a network of Nitrate Vulnerable Zones, within which farmers' activities in relation to nitrates would be closely regulated. Following initial consultations, some 66 NVZs, covering some 600,000 hectares (8%) of England, were designated in 1996. In due course, and following a judgment by the European Court of Justice in December 2000 which ruled that the UK had failed to designate sufficient areas to protect all surface and groundwaters, not just drinking water sources, against diffuse nitrate pollution from agriculture, the UK designated a number of further NVZs in 2002, extending the combined area of NVZs to 55% of the land area of England.

Farmers within designated Nitrate Vulnerable Zones using fertilisers or handling manures have, since December 2002, been required *(i)* to limit inorganic nitrogen fertiliser application to crop requirements, after allowing fully for residues in the soil and other sources; *(ii)* to limit organic manure applications to 210kg of total nitrogen per hectare per year on arable fields (reducing to 170kg after four years) and 250kg of total nitrogen per hectare per year on grassland; *(iii)* on sandy or shallow soils, to ensure adequate slurry storage capacity for annual closed periods during which applying of some types of manure (slurries, poultry manures, liquid-digested sewage sludge) to land is prohibited – these dates are 1 September to 1 November (grassland or autumn sown crop) or 1 August to 1 November (arable without autumn sown crop) inclusive; and (iv) to keep adequate farm records, including cropping, livestock numbers and the use of organic manures and nitrogen fertilisers.

Pollution of the Sea

Only a rather brief summary of this topic is justified in a book on the law of the countryside. However, some discussion is needed because, even if the quality of the sea and ocean environment is a little beyond our scope, we *are* concerned with the state of beaches and estuaries, and what is deposited in the sea all too often becomes washed up on land.

The legislation on this matter is largely the implementation into United Kingdom domestic law of obligations which we have agreed to in multilateral treaties with other States; and the importance of concerted international action in this matter need hardly be stressed. In addition to the discussion which follows, it may be remembered that we have already considered certain provisions now to be found in the Water Resources Act 1991 which apply to discharges into coastal waters.

Oil Pollution

A number of Acts of Parliament seek to deal with the problem of oil pollution. The Prevention of Oil Pollution Act 1971[40] creates a number of criminal offences. Most important for our purposes is that it is an offence for any oil, or mixture containing oil, to be discharged from land or a vessel into the territorial waters of the United Kingdom or its inland waters which are navigable by sea-going ships.[41] The 1971 Act also makes it an offence to discharge oil, or any mixture containing

---

40   Consolidating earlier legislation dating from 1955.
41   Prevention of Oil Pollution Act 1971 s.2.

oil, into any part of the sea (high seas and territorial waters) from a pipeline, or as a result of sea-bed exploration or exploitation operations.[42] It may be noticed that the 1971 Act does not apply to oil pollution from ships or offshore installations beyond the territorial sea limit. Such pollution is controlled by the Merchant Shipping (Prevention of Oil Pollution) Regulations 1983.[43] In addition to containing rules about oil discharge, these regulations require ships to be surveyed periodically and their construction to conform to certain requirements.

The 1971 Act conferred emergency powers on the executive to deal with large scale oil pollution to the coast or territorial waters of the United Kingdom resulting from a shipping accident. The powers are now to be found in the Merchant Shipping Act 1995. The powers apply where an accident has occurred to a ship and are available when the Secretary of State considers them to be "urgently needed" because oil from the ship is likely to cause large scale pollution of the coast or coastal water. The powers consist of authority to give directions to persons such as the owner, master or salvor. Such directions might, for example, be that a ship be towed away from a coast before being sunk. Such directions must be complied with, on pain of criminal penalty. If giving directions is likely to prove inadequate, the Secretary of State can order the taking of such governmental action as is necessary, including sinking or destroying the vessel. Persons suffering damage or expense as a result of such directions or action may in certain, quite limited, situations claim for compensation from the Secretary of State. This is when the directions or action were not reasonably necessary in the circumstances to prevent or reduce oil pollution, or were such that the good done was likely to be disproportionate compared with the damage suffered or loss incurred.

In order that prompt action may be taken to deal with oil spillages, a Marine Pollution Control Unit was established in 1979. This has available to it a number of aircraft at very short

---

[42] 1971 Act s.3.
[43] S.I. 1983/1398. See especially Regulations 12 and 13.

notice, stocks of dispersant located at some twenty places around the coast of Great Britain, and other special equipment. It has, however, been questioned whether such provision is adequate – for example, in relation to the promptness and effectiveness of the response to the *Sea Empress* incident off the coast of Pembrokeshire in early 1996. The executive powers in relation to spillages from vessels have quite recently been extended to spillages from offshore oil and gas installations (Offshore Installations (Emergency Pollution Control) Regulations 2002).[44]

In addition to these criminal offences relating to oil pollution, there is also legislation designed to ensure that compensation is available to those who suffer damage through oil pollution. Primary liability to compensate is imposed on the shipowner[45] but in appropriate circumstances claims may be made against the International Oil Pollution Compensation Fund, a sort of insurance fund established from contributions from those who import oil.

Dumping
So far we have considered the discharge of oil into the sea. The deposit of other substances is governed by Part II of the Food and Environment Protection Act 1985.[46] This subjects to licensing controls the dumping from vessels of any substances and articles into the sea or under the seabed.[47] The provisions apply to British vessels anywhere in the world, and to foreign vessels within the three mile territorial waters. The term "substances and articles" is not further elaborated in the Act and is clearly of broad scope. This has made necessary a long list of operations, involving deposit of substances or articles into the sea, which are exempt from licensing control. These include the deposit by dredgers of water overflow, and the launching of vessels into the sea! The most common activities in respect of which licences have traditionally been sought

---

44　S.I. 2002/1861.
45　Merchant Shipping Act 1995 s.153.
46　Repealing and replacing the Dumping at Sea Act 1974.
47　1985 Act s.5.

include disposal of solid waste dredgings, sewage sludge, liquid industrial waste and sludge, colliery waste and fly ash from power stations; also, licences for incineration at sea.

The licensing authority is generally DEFRA. In determining applications for licences, regard must be paid to such matters as the "need to protect the marine environment, the living resources it supports and human health", the need to "prevent interference with legitimate uses of the sea", the "practical availability of alternative methods" of dealing with such substances or articles, as well as other matters considered by the licensing authority to be relevant.[48] Licences may be granted subject to such conditions as the licensing authority considers appropriate. Such conditions might, for example, require initial dilution of a substance prior to discharge, or discharge into the wake of the dumping ship to ensure more rapid dispersal, or require the dumping ship to be moving at a minimum speed whilst dumping. In practice, the key determinant of the availability and content of permissions is the commitments which the UK may periodically agree internationally within the framework of the OSPAR Convention for the Protection of the Marine Environment of the North-East Atlantic (1998, replacing the earlier Oslo and Paris Conventions).

Against conditions imposed, or against outright refusal of a licence, there is no right of appeal as such; instead the Act provides a right to make representation to an independent committee,[49] though in practice matters are resolved more informally than by this procedure.

Dumping at sea without a licence, and failure to comply with conditions imposed on a licence, are criminal offences.[50] Remedial action may be taken by government to protect the marine environment, the living resources it supports and human health from harm which is threatened as a consequence

---

[48] 1985 Act s.8.
[49] 1985 Act s.8 and Sched. 3.
[50] 1985 Act s.9.

of dumping either without licence, or otherwise than in accordance with licence conditions. Expenses reasonably incurred in this matter may be recovered from any person convicted of such illegal dumping.[51]

---

[51] 1985 Act s.10.

Appendix A

COUNTRYSIDE CODE

The Countryside Code has been revised to reflect the introduction of new open access rights (Countryside and Rights of Way Act 2000) and changes in society over the last 20 years. Launched on 12th July 2004, this Code has been produced through a partnership between the Countryside Agency and Countryside Council for Wales. Each aspect of the Countryside Code is expanded upon in detail – see www.countrysideaccess.gov.uk/countryside_code.

COUNTRYSIDE CODE – ADVICE FOR THE PUBLIC

Be safe – plan ahead and follow any signs

Even when going out locally, it's best to get the latest information about where and when you can go; for example, your rights to go onto some areas of open land may be restricted while work is carried out, for safety reasons or during breeding seasons. Follow advice and local signs, and be prepared for the unexpected.

Leave gates and property as you find them

Please respect the working life of the countryside, as our actions can affect people's livelihoods, our heritage, and the safety and welfare of animals and ourselves.

Protect plants and animals, and take your litter home

We have a responsibility to protect our countryside now and for future generations, so make sure you don't harm animals, birds, plants or trees.

Keep dogs under close control

The countryside is a great place to exercise dogs, but it's every owner's duty to make sure their dog is not a danger or nuisance to farm animals, wildlife or other people.

Consider other people

Showing consideration and respect for other people makes the countryside a pleasant environment for everyone – at home, at work and at leisure.

COUNTRYSIDE CODE – ADVICE FOR LAND MANAGERS

People visiting the countryside provide important income for the local economy. Most like to follow a visible route, prefer using proper access points like gates, and generally want to do the right thing – but they need your help.

Know your rights, responsibilities and liabilities

- Where can people go on your land?

- What rules apply to people while they are on your land?

- What are your rights and responsibilities towards people on your land?

Make it easy for visitors to act responsibly

- How can you help people get access to your land responsibly and keep to the Countryside Code?

- What help and advice can you get?

Identify possible threats to visitors' safety

- Are there any risks to the safety of people on your land, and how can you deal with these risks?

Appendix B

ORGANISATIONS AND ADDRESSES

GOVERNMENTAL ORGANISATIONS

Broads Authority
18 Colegate, Norwich, Norfolk NR3 1BQ
Tel: 01603 610734   www.broads-authority.gov.uk

Council for National Parks
246 Lavender Hill, London SW11 1LJ
Tel: 020 7924 4077   www.cnp.org.uk

Countryside Agency
Head Office, John Dower House, Crescent Place, Cheltenham
    GL50 3RA
Tel: 01242 533222   www.countryside.gov.uk

Countryside Council for Wales
Maes-y-Ffynnon, Penrhosgarnedd, Bangor, Gwynedd LL57 2DW
Tel: 0845 1306229   www.ccw.gov.uk

Crown Estates Commission
16 Carlton House Terrace, London SW1Y 5AH
Tel: 020 7210 4377   www.crownestate.co.uk

Department for Environment, Food and Rural Affairs
Nobel House, 17 Smith Square, London SW1P 3JR
Tel: 08459 335577   www.defra.gov.uk

English Heritage
PO Box 569, Swindon SN2 2YP
Tel: 0870 333 1181   www.english-heritage.org.uk

English Nature
Northminster House, Peterborough PE1 1UA
Tel: 01733 455000   www.english-nature.org.uk

Environment Agency
Rio House, Waterside Drive, Almondsbury, Bristol BS32 4UD
Tel: 0845 933 3111   www.environment-agency.gov.uk

Forestry Commission GB & Scotland
Silvan House, 231 Corstorphine Road, Edinburgh EH12 7AT
  Tel: 0131 334 0303   www.forestry.gov.uk

Joint Nature Conservation Committee
Monkstone House, City Road, Peterborough PE1 1JY
  Tel: 01733 562626   www.jncc.gov.uk

Scottish Natural Heritage
12 Hope Terrace, Edinburgh EH9 2AS
  Tel: 0131 447 4784   www.snh.org.uk

VOLUNTARY ORGANISATIONS

British Trust for Conservation Volunteers
163 Balby Road, Doncaster, South Yorkshire DN4 0RH
  Tel: 01302 572244   www.btcv.org

Campaign for the Protection of Rural Wales
Ty Gwyn, 31 High Street, Welshpool, Powys SY21 7YD
  Tel: 01938 552525   www.cprw.org.uk

Civic Trust
Winchester House, 259-269 Old Marylebone Road, London
  NW1 5RA
  Tel: 020 7170 4299   www.civictrust.org.uk

Campaign to Protect Rural England
128 Southwark Street, London SE1 0SW
  Tel: 020 7981 2800   www.cpre.org.uk

Country Land & Business Association
16 Belgrave Square, London SW1X 8PQ
  Tel: 020 7235 0511   www.cla.org.uk

Cyclists' Touring Club
Cotterell House, 69 Meadrow, Godalming, Surrey GU7 3HS
  Tel: 0870 8730060   www.ctc.org.uk

Friends of the Earth
26-28 Underwood Street, London N1 7JQ
  Tel: 020 7490 0881   www.foe.co.uk

Game Conservancy Trust
Fordingbridge, Hampshire SP6 1EF
Tel: 01425 652381 www.gct.org.uk

Greenpeace
Canonbury Villas, London N1 2PN
Tel: 020 7865 8100 www.greenpeace.org.uk

International Tree Foundation
Sandy Lane, Crawley Down, Crawley, West Sussex RH10 4HS
Tel: 0870 774 4269 www.internationaltreefoundation.org

Landscape Institute
33 Great Portland Street, London W1W 8QG
Tel: 020 7299 4500 www.l-i.org.uk

Marine Conservation Society
Unit 3, Wolf Business Park, Alton Road, Ross-on-Wye,
Herefordshire HR9 5NB
Tel: 01989 566017 www.mcsuk.org

National Farmers' Union
164 Shaftesbury Avenue, London WC2H 8HL
Tel: 020 7331 7200 www.nfu.org.uk

National Trust
36 Queen Anne's Gate, London SW1H 9AS
Tel: 0870 609 5380 www.nationaltrust.org.uk

Open Spaces Society
25A Bell Street, Henley-on-Thames, Oxfordshire RG9 2BA
Tel: 01491 573535 www.oss.org.uk

Ramblers' Association
2nd Floor, Camelford House, 87-90 Albert Embankment,
London SE1 7TW
Tel: 020 7339 8500 www.ramblers.org.uk

Royal Society for the Prevention of Cruelty to Animals (RSPCA)
Wilberforce Way, Southwater, Horsham, West Sussex
RH13 9RS
Tel: 0870 333 5999 www.rspca.org.uk

Royal Society for the Protection of Birds
The Lodge, Sandy, Bedfordshire SG19 2DL
Tel: 01767 680551   www.rspb.org.uk

Wildlife Trusts
The Kiln, Waterside, Mather Road, Newark, Nottinghamshire
NG24 1WT
Tel: 0870 036 7711   www.wildfile.co.uk

Woodland Trust
Autumn Park, Dysart Road, Grantham, Lincolnshire NG31 6LL
Tel: 01476 581135   www.the-woodland-trust.org.uk

Worldwide Fund for Nature
Panda House, Weyside Park, Godalming, Surrey GU7 1XR
Tel: 01483 426444   www.wwf-uk.org

Youth Hostels Association
Trevelyan House, Dimple Road,Matlock, Derbyshire DE4 3YH
Tel: 01629 592600   www.yha.org.uk

TABLE OF STATUTES

TABLE OF STATUTORY INSTRUMENTS

TABLE OF CASES

ALPHABETICAL INDEX